State, Market and Salt-Tobacco Road in Modern China (1935–1949)

Benmo Jiang · Zhao Zhou · Yujing Tan ·
Haoqi Meng

State, Market and Salt-Tobacco Road in Modern China (1935–1949)

palgrave
macmillan

Benmo Jiang
Hong Kong Chronicles Institute
Hong Kong, Hong Kong

Yujing Tan
Institute for Area Studies
and International Studies
Leiden University
Leiden, The Netherlands

Zhao Zhou
College of Business
Shanghai University of Finance
and Economics
Shanghai, China

Haoqi Meng
The Insurance Institute of Guizhou
Guiyang, China

ISBN 978-981-97-7653-5 ISBN 978-981-97-7654-2 (eBook)
https://doi.org/10.1007/978-981-97-7654-2

This Book was Supported by The Yonyou Foundation (用友基金会)

This Palgrave Macmillan imprint is published by the registered company Springer Nature Singapore Pte Ltd.
The registered company address is: 152 Beach Road, #21-01/04 Gateway East, Singapore 189721, Singapore

Acknowledgments

This book would not have been possible without the support and data resources provided by several archives. We are deeply grateful to the Guizhou Provincial Archives, Guiyang Municipal Archives, Qianxi Municipal Archives, Guiding County Archives, Longli County Archives, Sansui County Archives, Weining County Archives, and Zhenyuan County Archives for granting us access to their extensive collections, which were crucial for the research and writing of this book.

We would also like to extend our thanks to Yun Jiang from Guizhou Provincial Women's Federation, Yunduan Zhang from Guizhou People's Press, Yuwei Ma from The People's Insurance Company of China, Qiandongnan Branch, and Yongli Wang from Guizhou Provincial Architectural Design & Research Institute. Your support and expertise have been invaluable.

Unit Conversion

Unit of Length
1Chinese li=500 meter

Mass Unit
1*jin*=16*liang*=500 gram
1*qian jin*≈1.4*jin*=700 gram
1*zai*(傤)=12*yin*(引)=600*bao*(包)=108000jin=54000 kilogram=54 ton

Currency Unit
1 Silver Dollar=0.72*liang*=22.5 gram (silver)
1 Silver Dollar=5 Copper Dollar=100 cent

Area Unit
1*mu*=667 square meters

Unit of Output
1 large box=10 Small box=120 Piece=1200 Pack=24000 cigarettes.

Contents

List of Maps

Chapter 2

CHAPTER 1

Introduction

Benmo Jiang and Zhao Zhou

Though many states throughout history have tried to control the production and distribution of commodities that contribute to fiscal revenue, few examples show equivalent embeddedness to salt administration in China. Unlike in Europe, where salt was no longer a principal commodity when patterns of trade developed, the salt trade in China retained its importance both in volume and as an economic activator when the Qing Dynasty ended in the early twentieth century.[1] Current studies on the salt trade of China have provided us with a comprehensive understanding of how the complex state-granted monopoly on salt worked in the Ming and Qing Dynasties. Furthermore, they have shown that from the Ming Dynasty onward the combination of changes to salt administration policies and the development of salt merchants' networks not only affected how salt was produced and distributed but also had various influences on the connections and boundaries between different localities.[2]

[1] Samuel Adrian M. Adshead, *The Modernization of the Chinese Salt Administration, 1900–1920* (Cambridge: Harvard University Press, 1970), 13–14.

[2] See Huang Guoxin 黄国信. *Qu yu jie: Qingdai Xiang Yue Gan jielin diqu shiyan zhuanmai yanjiu* 区与界:清代湘粤赣界邻地区食盐专卖研究 [Regions and Boundaries: An Analysis of Qing Salt Monopoly at the Provincial Border of Hunan, Guangdong, and Jiangxi] (Beijing: SDX Joint Publishing Company, 2006); Huang Guoxin, *Guojia yu shichang: Mingqing shiyan maoyi yanjiu* 国家与市场:明清食盐贸易研究 [State and Market: Salt Trade of Ming-Qing Period) (Beijing: Zhonghua Book Company, 2019].

B. Jiang et al., *State, Market and Salt-Tobacco Road in Modern China (1935–1949)*, https://doi.org/10.1007/978-981-97-7654-2_1

After the Qing Dynasty ended, salt was still one of the most important sources of tax revenue. Additionally, the continuous conflicts and wars of this period made salt a principal strategic material. Though the free trade of salt was promoted by some reformers and temporarily practiced,[3] the republican government, not to mention warlords, realized that it was necessary to take as much control as possible over the production and distribution of salt. When the KMT's National Government gained its legitimacy nationwide, it began to implement a controlled economy and restore a state monopoly on salt with modernized transportation and financial devices. Though it has been widely accepted that the KMT's wartime salt administration policies brought structural changes to the salt industry and had profound impacts after the anti-Japanese War ended, how these policies were implemented in particular areas, how they impacted local society, and how the established local trade networks dealt with changes to salt administration in different localities remain to be further analyzed and discussed.[4]

Guizhou, the focus of this book, is the only province south of the upper Yangtze River in China that does not produce salt. Thus, it has always relied on its neighbors to fulfill people's basic daily needs, and controlling salt distribution was an integral part of controlling local communities. By the end of the Qing Dynasty, the routes and related networks of the salt trade covered at least 70% of Guizhou's hinterland in both a spatial and social sense, and this significance continued into the Republican period (1912–1949).

Puk Wing Kin, T*he Rise and Fall of a Public Debt Market in 16th-century China: The Story of the Ming Salt Certificate* (Boston: Brill, 2016); Madeleine Zelin, T *he Merchants of Zigong: Industrial Entrepreneurship in Early Modern China* (New York: Columbia University Press, 2005); Kwan, Man Bun, *The Salt Merchants of Tianjin: State-making and Civil Society in Late Imperial China* (Honolulu: University of Hawai'i Press, 2001).

[3] Though Adshead's analysis of salt administration's modernization in China speaks highly of Richard Dane's reform during early Republican period, he also admits that the free trade of salt is the least successful part of Dane's reform. See Samuel Adrian M. Adshead, *The Modernization of the Chinese Salt Administration, 1900–1920*, 110.

[4] Tang Mingsheng 唐明胜, *Na yan gui cang: 1800–1960 nianjian zhejiang de yanzheng bianqian yu yanchang shehui* 纳盐归仓: 1800–1960 年间浙江的盐政变迁与盐场社会 [Collecting Salt into Granary, the Changes of Salt Administration and Saltern Society in Zhejiang, 1800–1960] (PhD. Diss., Shanghai: East China Normal University, 2022):138–139.

It was not until 1935 that the central government regained its control of Guizhou and began to actively intervene in the development of the local economy as a response to the crisis of war. In 1937, Wu Dingchang 吴鼎昌, who had been the head of the Ministry of Industry and was experienced in business and politics, was appointed as the governor of Guizhou and launched a series of incentives to develop the province's economy soon after taking office. Then, when the central government retreated inland, the capital was relocated to Chongqing. Thus, Sichuan, the province of this temporary capital, along with the neighboring provinces of Yunnan and Guizhou, became the most important region for the Chinese army, and policy to fully mobilize the financial and economic resources of these provinces to fulfill the needs of war became a focus of the nationalist government. For a southwestern province previously remote from political and economic centers, this presence of the central government undoubtedly affected local power structures.

Madeleine Zelin has mentioned in her analysis of Zigong's salt merchants that the revival of the province's salt industry after years of chaos under warlords was not a result of merchants regaining their leverage regarding salt administration, but a part of the general move toward state capitalism.[5] Guizhou's salt merchants faced a similar situation. However, unlike Zigong's salt merchants, who controlled their salt mines and had a chance to promote industrial upgrading, Guizhou's most powerful salt merchants during the republican period were a newly rising group of local distributors who had benefited from Ding Baozhen's reform. To some extent, these merchants' success in the salt trade was more dependent on maintaining relationships with the authorities, and they had more limited bargaining power when policy changed. However, these savvy merchants were no doubt very aware of risks and tended to adopt flexible business strategies. Diversification is a commonly used strategy for merchants to reduce risks or seek out potential synergies. Some studies have noted that the networks of the salt trade were often utilized by merchants to operate their other businesses as well.[6]

[5] Madeleine Zelin, *The Merchants of Zigong: Industrial Entrepreneurship in Early Modern China*, 267–268.

[6] Samuel Adrian M. Adshead, *The Modernization of the Chinese Salt Administration, 1900–1920*, 190–191; Madeleine Zelin, *The Merchants of Zigong: Industrial Entrepreneurship in Early Modern China*, 269–291. Huang Guoxin, *Guojia yu shichang: Mingqing shiyan maoyi yanjiu*, 293–303; Wen Chunlai also discussed such a possible connection

Though the salt merchants in Guizhou rarely got the chance to become involved in salt production, their background granted them the opportunity to control how Guizhou's local products were transported and distributed through the established trade networks. Their diversified investments helped salt merchants to maintain their dominance in the salt trade and facilitated the flow and exchange of commodities between Guizhou and other regions. When the costs of the salt trade rose too high, these investments also provided alternatives for merchants to cut their losses. From late 1930s onward, tobacco became a very promising commodity for salt merchants to overcome the difficulties caused by changing salt administration policies and to reshape the market.

According to a local gazetteer, tobacco was brought to Guizhou by Fujian merchants during the Daoguang Era.[7] Though it became very popular soon after it was first introduced into this borderland province, Guizhou had kept a periphery area for the China's tobacco market when the production of tobacco and related products was industrialized. Purchases of machine-rolled cigarettes were heavily concentrated in the eastern seaboard areas and large cities along the Yangzi River, while Henan, Shandong, and Anhui were the most important planting regions.[8] This situation changed significantly during the anti-Japanese war. These main markets and planting areas were mostly occupied by the Japanese or

between the import of salt and export of minerals, see Wen Chunlai, *Cong yiyu dao jiujiang: Song zhi Qing Guizhou xibeibu diqu de kaifa yu rentong* 从"异域"到"旧疆": 宋至清贵州西北部地区的制度、开发与认同 [From the Foreign Land to the Old Territory: Development and Identity in Northwestern Guizhou From Song to Qing Dynasty] (Beijing: SDX Joint Publishing Company, 2006), 251–261.

[7] Duan Zhao'ao 段兆鳌 ed., *Guiding xian zhi gao* 贵定县志稿 [Draft of Gazetteer of Guiding County] (Guiyang: Guizhou Provincial Library, 1964), reprinted, "Local Products", 70.

[8] These planting regions were selected by the unquestionably dominant tobacco company in China during the republican period, British American Tobacco, after serious field work scouting for suitable plating locations. See Huangfu Qiushi 皇甫秋实. *Weiji zhong de xuanze: zhanqian shinian de zhongguo juanyan shichang* 危机中的选择:战前十年的中国卷烟市场 [Choices in the Crisis: Cigarette Market in Pre-war China] (Shanghai: Orient Press Company, 2015), 26–27. The discussion business networks and strategies of tobacco trade in republican China see also Sherman Cochran, *Big Business in China: Sino-foreign Rivalry in the Cigarette Industry, 1890–1930*(Cambridge, MA.: Harvard University Press, 1980); Howard Cox, *The Global Cigarette: Origins and Evolution of British American Tobacco, 1880–1945* (New York: Oxford University Press, 2000); Benedict, Carol. *Golden-silk Smoke: A History of Tobacco in China*, 1550–2010 (Berkeley: University of California Press, 2011).

severely affected by the war. The tobacco industry in China began to find new opportunities westward.

The government realized that tobacco and related products could be a significant source of tax revenue when cigarettes became more and more popular in the late nineteenth century,[9] and thus the tobacco industry was also their focus in the wartime-controlled economy. The provincial government supported the trial planting of flue-cured tobacco and promoted mass cultivation far before large private tobacco companies such as BAT realized Guizhou's potential as an alternative when the planting regions they were more familiar with encountered problems during the war.[10]

Drawing on historical records from merchants and local officials in Guizhou, this book focuses on changes in the province's business networks: here a term which mainly refers to the linked nodes and ties that support the dissemination of certain commodities. As William Skinner has pointed out in his analysis of the structures of rural markets, one standard market in a rural area, which is established to fulfill the daily needs of people in that area, usually is tied to two or three market towns and there is regular movement of goods and mobile firms between the standard market and intermediate or higher level markets.[11] The two commodities discussed here, salt and tobacco, also were circulated in this kind of market structure. However, these were not only popular commodities in the basic market but also important sources of tax revenue, which brought the state into the picture.

The improvement of the state monopoly system after the Nationalist Government took control of Guizhou also coincided with the fall of the salt business in Guizhou and the rise of the tobacco industry. This book tries to argue that these changes in the salt and tobacco trades were not isolated from each other, and the established networks of the salt trade to some extent contributed to the flourishing of the tobacco industry in

[9] Huangfu Qiushi. *Weiji zhong de xuanze: zhanqian shinian de zhongguo juanyan shichang*, 2–3.

[10] Institute of Economics, Shanghai Academy of Social Sciences ed., *Yingmei yan gongsi zaihua qiye ziliao huibian* 英美烟公司在华企业资料汇编 [Compilation of Materials on British American Tobacco's Enterprises in China] (Beijing: Zhonghua Book Company, 1983), 349–332,349–350,359–360.

[11] William G. Skinner, "Marketing and Social Structure in Rural China, Part I," *The Journal of Asian Studies* 24, no. 1 (1964): 21.

Guizhou during this period. Taking on the perspectives of two dominant players, the local salt merchants of Guizhou and the Nationalist Government, authors in this book try to answer questions such as the following. What were the roles of local merchants and the state in the transformation of the salt and tobacco trades? What role did they have in constructing the supply chain of salt-tobacco in the context of the development of the controlled economy?

Though state-business relations have always been an unavoidable element in research on the business history of China, recent works have begun to go beyond the simplified dichotomy of either reliance or independence and unfold the complexity of the changing relationship and tensions between the state and merchants.[12] Through analyzing the roles that the state and merchants played in the trade network formed by the dissemination of salt and tobacco, as well as the related circulation of money, knowledge, and information in Guizhou, this book looks closely at the dynamics of how the state and merchants can be linked by the flow of certain commodities. Within this theoretical framework, this book aims to trace several processes: how salt merchants in Guizhou strategically dealt with central and local government to sustain their business advantages; how they coped with wartime difficulties, and reshaped their socio-economic networks during this period; and how the nationalist government promoted new financial instruments to better govern markets, regulating businessmen and controlling flows of money and commodities.

It is widely accepted that the agency of merchants is more or less circumscribed by state power.[13] However, economic sociologists have also

[12] Wang Luman, *Money and Trade, Hinterland and Coast, Empire and Nation-State: An Unusual History of Shanxi Piaohao, 1820–1930* (PhD Diss., University of Southern California, 2014), 9.

[13] Studies of institutional economic history have extensively discussed the sources of the state power and its role as resource-supported administrative and coercive organizations that ensure resources are extracted from society. Tilly and Giddens also argue that the state dominates a system of social governance that rationalizes the dominant class's management of society. However, Michael Mann proposes a more dynamic and organic analysis of "what state power is." He argues that there are two types of state power: despotic power and infrastructural power. The former is absolute for a period, a power enjoyed by the dominant class without consultation with other levels of society. However, this power collapses in times of war or dynastic change. The latter type of power is dynamic and sustainable in its influence on other social organizations. It can only work through various consultative, non-bureaucratic institutions. See Otto Hintze, and Felix Gilbert,

argued that when the state uses policies to govern markets, its governance is shaped by established social relations.[14]In Skinner's analysis of two institutions introduced by the communist party after 1949 to socialize rural trade, state trading companies (or state-owned enterprises), and supply and marketing cooperatives, he mentions that patterns of rural trade from the previous market system continued for a few years after their introduction.[15]

It is worth noting that, many economic institutions and economic policies that the communist party implemented after the PRC was founded originated before 1949. Kirby has pointed out that the communist party was not the only Chinese party with a strong interest in national economic planning and the nationalist government laid the foundation for many industrial policies, which were believed to be under the influence of the Soviet Union, and promoted by the communist party during the 1950s.[16] Such continuity is also one of the focuses of Morris L. Bian's analysis of the transformation of Guizhou's regional state enterprises. He reveals that its development, which came about through both war and revolution, was "both radical and transformative and gradual and evolutionary" and emphasizes that the national government, through the particular situation of the wartime crisis, massively transformed Guizhou's

"Military Organization and the Organization of the State", *The Historical Essays of Otto Hintze* (New York: Oxford University Press, 1975), 181; Theda Skocpol, *Social Revolutions in the Modern World* (Cambridge University Press,1994); Charles Tilly, *Regimes and Repertoires* (University of Chicago Press, 2010); Anthony Giddens, "Elites in the British Class Structure," *The Sociological Review* 20, no. 3 (1972): 345–372; Michael Mann, *The Sources of Social Power: Volume 2, the Rise of Classes and Nation-states, 1760–1914* (Cambridge University Press, 2012).

[14] Jan-Hendrik Passoth, and Nicholas J. Rowland, "Actor-network State: Integrating Actor-Network Theory and State Theory," *International sociology* 25, no. 6 (2010): 818–841; Bob Jessop, "Regulationist and Autopoieticist Reflections on Polanyi's Account of Market Economies and the Market Society", New Political Economy 6, no.2 (2001): 213–232.

[15] G. William Skinner, "Marketing and Social Structure in Rural China, Part III," *The Journal of Asian Studies* 24, no. 3 (1965): 363–364.

[16] William C. Kirby, "Continuity and Change in Modern China: Economic Planning on the Mainland and on Taiwan, 1943–58." *The Australian Journal of Chinese Affairs 24*, no. 24 (1990): 124.

industrial economy and established a model of an East Asian developmental state.[17] The state took advantage of the crisis to intervene and restructure the market in a comprehensive manner. However, Bian's study pays less attention to how local business networks are transformed in times of great political and economic change.

The monopolization of commodities also followed a similar trajectory. The communist party established a state monopoly on salt when they set up the China National Salt Industry Corporation during the 1950s, but the process of traditional salt merchants inevitably losing their bargaining power in a more modernized, state-dominated fiscal complex had started before the PRC was founded. By examining the changing power relations between officials and merchants and analysing how this dynamic affected society more broadly, this book also hopes to shed new light on how contemporary China came into being.

With the above concerns in mind, the following chapters begin with a general overview of Guizhou's geography and how that geography shaped its business networks. Chapter 2 shows how the political-geographical division created by its mountainous area has been the most important feature of Guizhou's society and economy. The geographical conditions, the needs of various ethnic groups scattered through this area, and the political designs of the central government gradually formed business networks that linked Guizhou with other parts of China and made it a transportation hub in both a geographical and political-economic sense.

Next, Chapter 3 analyzes Guizhou's local salt merchants, a group of elites that rose after Ding Baozhen's salt reform during the late Qing Dynasty, and the transformation of their business networks under the changing salt administration policies. This chapter shows that, though the relationship between salt merchants and officials was always the key component of the salt trade network, the wartime salt monopoly system brought new challenges for Guizhou's salt merchants and structurally transformed the salt trade network.

Chapter 4 focuses on the development of networks of tobacco trade in Guizhou. It first provides an overview of how the cultivation of tobacco was introduced and proliferated over Guizhou from the Ming Dynasty onward and then focuses on the cooperation and conflict involved

[17] Morris L. Bian, "Redefining the Chinese Revolution: The Transformation and Evolution of Guizhou's Regional State Enterprises, 1937–1957." *Modern China* 41, no. 3 (2015): 313–350.

in the spread of flue-cured tobacco. It shows how, from late 1930s, Guizhou's salt merchants took advantage of their financial instruments, transportation networks, and established government patronage to enter the tobacco industry and enable the integration and expansion of that industry in Guizhou.

Chapter 5 is then a case study of Liu Xiyi刘熙乙, one of the dominant salt merchants in Guizhou during wartime. He controlled the salt trade in northwestern Guizhou and opened the first cigarette factory in Bijie, the economic center of this area. Through analyzing Liu Xiyi's business strategy and business network, this chapter shows the mutual influence between the salt-tobacco road and a particular merchant, and the local merchant community's attitude toward the financial and legal institutional innovations used by the state to mobilize and integrate local resources.

In Chapter 6, the focus moves from merchants to the state. This chapter tries to answer the questions of why and how tobacco became a more important commodity than salt for fiscal revenue and brought about a more stable tax basis during 1940s. It does this by reviewing the fiscal structure of and currency circulation in Guizhou after Ding Baozhen's salt reform.

Finally, Chapter 7 explores a new form of organization promoted by the nationalist government to better control monopolized commodities: the cooperative. Cooperatives were instituted in both salt consumption and tobacco production, but, interestingly, the tobacco production cooperatives were directed by and operated under salt consumption cooperatives. Through close attention to how a tobacco production cooperative was established and managed by a salt consumption cooperative in Guiding, the center of tobacco production in Guizhou, this chapter analyzes how salt merchants and the government reached consensus and cooperation in this new form of economic association, which brought the integration of Guizhou's tobacco industry.

CHAPTER 2

Between Mountain and River: The Formation of a Socio-economic Network in Guizhou

Haoqi Meng

To ensure the security of China's southwest frontier, the area at the edge of Sichuan, bordering on Yunnan, Guangxi, Hunan, and Hubei, became a province called Guizhou in the 11th year of the Ming Dynasty's Yongle period, about 600 years ago.[1] Since then, the political-geographical division of this mountainous space has been the most important feature of Guizhou's society and economy. The geographical conditions, the needs of various ethnic groups scattered in this area, and the political designs of the central government gradually formed business networks that linked Guizhou with other parts of China and made it a transportation hub in both a geographical and political-economic sense.[2] Through a variety

[1] Ren Kecheng 任可澄, "Qianshi Zhi Yi 前事志一(Previous events, part one)," in *Minguo guizhou tongzhi* 民国贵州通志 [A General History of Guizhou, Republic of China], ed. Ren Kecheng 任可澄 et al. (Guiyang: Wentong Shuju, 1948).

[2] A few recent works on the political and economic history of southeast China have realized that Guizhou, as part of China's hinterland, plays an indispensable role in the long-distance flow of capital and commodities. See Wen Chunlai 温春來, *Cong yiyu dao jiujiang: Song zhi Qing Guizhou xibeibu diqu de zhidu kaifa yu rentong* 从"异域"到"旧疆":宋至清贵州西北部地区的制度、开发与认同 [From the "exotic" to the "old frontier": the institution, development, and recognition of the northwest region of Song to Qing

B. Jiang et al., *State, Market and Salt-Tobacco Road in Modern China (1935–1949)*, https://doi.org/10.1007/978-981-97-7654-2_2

of local gazetteers, memoirs, travelogs, and social surveys, this chapter provides a general overview of how Guizhou's business networks developed, focusing especially on how these networks were deeply affected by Guizhou's natural geography and central government control of the province.

1 Networks and Islands: Geography, Transport, and the Legacy of *Tusi* (Chieftains 土司) Politics

Along with the central government's gradually advancing control and development of the southwestern frontier, Guizhou's strategic importance continued to grow in the mind of the state. The establishment of a provincial administration in the province during the Ming Dynasty was most notably aimed at "choking the main road through Yunnan."[3] The state's strategic need to control transportation interacted with the interests of local societies in Guizhou within the province's complex geographical context. These factors have also combined to shape Guizhou's social and trade networks in the modern era, as Guizhou has remained deeply integrated into the central government's governing plan since the Ming and Qing Dynasties.

1.1 Geographic Overview of Guizhou

From the Town of Yuankou along the Qingshui River in the east to Yizikong in the hinterland of the Wumeng Mountains in the west, and from Tongzi and Ganshui in the north to Dushan and Mawei in the south, the total 176,000 square kilometer territory of Guizhou has six mountain ranges. They are the Wuling Mountains, Dalou Mountains, Miao Mountains, Wumeng Mountains, and two branches of the Miao Mountains in the southeast and southwest, namely the Moon Mountains and Mashan Mountains.[4] These mountain ranges are connected by long,

Guizhou] (Beijing: Social Sciences Academic Press, 2019) and James Z. Lee, *The Political Economy of a Frontier: Southwest China, 1250–1850* (Cambridge: Harvard University Press, 2002).

[3] Ren Kecheng 任可澄 et al., *Minguo Guizhou tongshi.*

[4] Guizhoushengshizhiban 贵州省史志办 ed., *Guizhoudilizhi* 贵州地理志 [The History of Guizhou Geography] (Guiyang: Guizhou People's Press, 1994).

vast table lands consisting of the fragmented eastern part of the Yunnan-Guizhou Plateau and ranging from 500 to 1000 meters above sea level. This leaves Guizhou as the only province in China without a large plain to support its economy.[5]

Because of the high topography in the west and the low topography in the east, rivers originating from the eastern Yunnan-Guizhou Plateau cut through the mountainous terrain, forming longitudinal flow areas and V-shaped riverbed channels toward the north, east, and south. The northward and eastward flowing rivers are divided by the Wuling Mountains. Three northward flowing rivers, the Chishui River, the Qi River, and the Wu River join the Yangtze River in Hejiang, Jiangjin, and Fulin, three counties of Chongqing. Meanwhile, the eastward flowing Jinjiang River and Wushui River converge in the Qingshui River in Hunan Province, then flow into Dongting Lake. The southward flowing rivers, which are separated from the other two directions by the Miaoling Mountains, have different headstream regions and flow directions though they eventually join the Xijiang River in Guangxi. The South Panjiang River originates at the western foot of the Wumeng Mountains and flows eastward through the natural border between Guizhou and Guangxi Province, while the North Panjiang River originates at the eastern foot of the Wumeng Mountains and flows along the southwest side of the Mashan and Miao Mountains through southwest Guizhou to join the South Panjiang River, forming the Red River in the upper reaches of the Xijiang River. On the east side, the Duliu River originates at the southern foot of the middle section of the Miaoling Mountains and flows southeastward along the Moon Mountains to Liuzhou in Guangxi Province (Map 1).[6]

With landslides and mudflats made by splitting riverbeds, these longitudinal channels have complicated water conditions for navigation. When mudflats block waterways, passengers are diverted to routes across land in the valleys, and the transit points between water and land become important nodes for the whole flow of traffic, forming a unique and complex

[5] Guizhoushengshizhiban 贵州省史志办 ed., 1994.

[6] Xia Heming 夏鹤鸣 et al. eds., *Guizhou hangyunshi gujindai bufen* 贵州航运史·古近代部分 [Guizhou Ancient Modern Shipping History] (Guiyang: Guizhou renmin chubanshe, 1993).

Map 1 Modern Guizhou road map

pattern of alternating land and water transportation on the east Yunnan-Guizhou Plateau.[7] However, for Guizhou province, these complicated and dangerous routes provide the most convenient access to the outside world and are essential to connecting the Sichuan Basin and the Yunnan-Guizhou Plateau with the Huguang (Hunan and Hubei provinces) and Lingnan regions.

[7] We can easily find complaints about the dangerous traffic condition in Guizhou in early twentieth-century travelogs. The supplies for long travel were usually gained from Bazi, the local name for the small basins and important arable land alongside mountains and rivers. See Ding Wenjiang 丁文江, *Manyou sanji* 漫游散记 [Selected Travelogs] (Kunming: Yunnan renmin chubanshe, 2008), Fang Xianting 方显廷, *Fangxianting huiyilu* 方显廷回忆录 [Memoir of Fang Xianting] (Beijing: the Commercial Press, 2006), and Yan Xiu 严修, *Xunxiangguan shiqian riji* 蟫香馆使黔日记 [A Diary of Working in Guizhou] (Guiyang: Guizhou People's Press, 2019).

1.2 *"Beyond the Main Road, There Are Seedling Hubs of Barbarians"*[8]

In 1368, Zhu Yuanzhang proclaimed the beginning of the Ming Dynasty. During this change of dynasties, as the focus of Emperor Zhu was still on eradicating the remnants of the Mongols in the north of the desert, the southwestern region under his control mostly continued the old system of the previous dynasty. But as the conquest of the remnants of the former dynasty in Yunnan unfolded, the significance of controlling Guizhou's main transport route came to the fore.[9] Thus, along the east–west route in central Guizhou, linking Yunnan and Huguang, the Zhu Ming Dynasty began to establish military garrisons. Under Zhu Yuanzhang's rule, the garrisons in Guizhou were distributed in a pattern of "six upper garrisons," "six lower garrisons," "four western garrisons," and "six outer garrisons," with a wide range of fortress camps under the military garrisons (Map 2).

The establishment of the garrisons was accompanied by a massive military migration, through which the military households settled their own fields.[10] Through this cantonment, the state attempted to solve the problem of difficult recruitment and inadequate payment for soldiers during wartime. The enrichment of the military households at the military garrisons had little to do with the aborigines of Guizhou, and the immigrants' cantonment naturally led to disputes with them. Along with the strong military power of the central government, the immigrants' cantonment gradually took over the areas with superior natural conditions along the main transport routes. Later on, some of the Sichuan, Guizhou, and Hunan *Tusi* (chieftain 土司) of aborigines who were subservient to the central government would also participate in such military conquests and migratory settlements, thus creating residential communities in which inhabitants mainly came from other Han-dominant places, supplemented

[8] "Miao" means the residents outside the rule of the central state. This translation as "barbarians" reflects discrimination against them by the central state.

[9] Traditionally, there were three post roads from the Central Plains to Yunnan—via Qian, via Shu, and via Guangxi—but following the Yuan Dynasty the Qianzhong Road became the first choice of travelers, while the remaining two were gradually abandoned. See Wen Chunlai, *Cong yiyu dao jiujiang*, 117.

[10] Wen Chunlai 温春来, *Cong yiyu dao jiujiang*, 127.

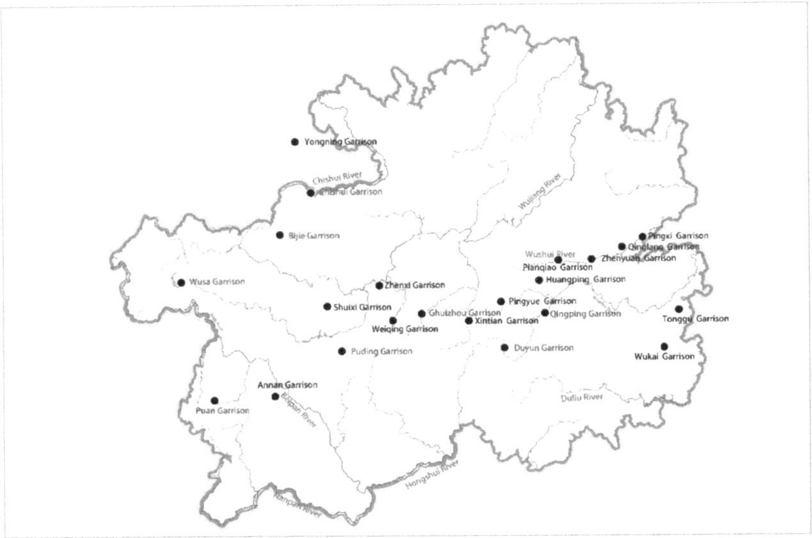

Map 2 Garrisons in Guizhou, Ming

by some aborigines from Sichuan, Guangxi, and Hunan.[11] This occurred mainly in the Chishui River, Qi River, and Wujiang River basins in northern Guizhou, the South and North Panjiang River basins in southwest Guizhou, the lower reaches of the Jin River, Wushui River, and Qingshui River in eastern Guizhou, and the lower reaches of the Duliu River in southeast Guizhou.[12]

Although the Ming Dynasty established a regular provincial administrative body, the *Buzhengsi* (布政司 Provincial administration commissioner), in Guizhou in 1413, the reshuffling of the Sizhou and Sinan *Xuanweisi* (宣慰司 Supervisory Office of Local Authorities) put the Guizhou *Xuanweisi* under the dual control of the *Buzhengsi* and the

[11] The "Ming-Guiding Building Monument," which remains behind the Guiding County God Temple today, introduces the migration of Xiangchu border people to Guiding with the army; see also the record of the migration of Cen surnamed Tusi of Sizhou Province to occupy the South and North Panjiang River basin in Volume one of the "Qiannan Vocational Zhiyi.".

[12] Ortai, *Guizhou tongzhi* 贵州通志 [General Gazetteer of Gzuihou], 1741.

military commanding body, the *Dusi* (都司 regional military commission). This also meant that Guizhou province was formally established. In practice, however, most of the administrative units between the main transport routes continued to be ruled by local authorities.[13] This new way of governance followed the *Tusi* regime.[14] Until the Ming Yongle era, in the Sizhou *Xuanweisi* and Sinan *Xuanweisi* where most of the *Tusi* regimes have been forced to change into local state sectors, there were still large and small 29 governor's departments, that is, the *Tusi* regime under the supervision of *Xuanweisi*.[15] By the end of the Ming Dynasty, Guizhou was still described as follows: "*Beyond the main road, there are seedling hubs of Barbarians.*"[16] The existence of these *Tusi* regimes was partly the result of the central government's continuing use of the *Tusi*'s authority to maintain local stability. This tacit acceptance of *Tusi* regimes was partly due to the fact that Guizhou's most important value lay in its main transport routes, while other areas were of relatively low value and it was less costly to leave them to the *Tusi* administrations; another consideration was that these subservient *Tusi* could help protect the main transport routes.[17] These subservient *Tusi* regimes assumed the responsibility for the state's arch and governance of the major transportation routes to other parts of southwest China. However, their communication with the state was mostly limited to politics and taxation, and they

[13] For a long time after this, with the exception of a few large capitals of provincial state (州*zhou*) along the east–west Yunnan-Xiangjiang route and important passages such as the Sichuan-Yunnan East Road and important garrisons such as Wujiang, Qijiang, and Dushan County.

[14] Zhan Yuqian 翟玉前, *Mingshi Guizhou tusiliezhuan kaozheng* 明史贵州土司列传考证 [Textual Research Biographies of Native Chieftains in the Official Dynamistic History of Ming Dynasty] (Guiyang: Guizhou People's Press, 2008).

[15] *Ibid.*

[16] Guo Zizhang 郭子章, Qiancao 黔草 (Works in Guizhou), ca.1601, volume 11.

[17] Gu Yanwu 顾炎武, *Tianxia junguo libing shu* 天下郡国利病书 [A compilation of the pros and cons of state offices throughout the country], reprint (Shanghai: Shanghai guji chubanshe, 2012). These subservient tusi regimes assumed the responsibility for the state's arch and governance of the major transportation routes to other parts of the southwest. However, their communication with the state was mostly limited to politics and taxation, and they maintained relative independence, with the tusi domains more closely following the self-sufficiency model internally.

maintained relative independence, with the *Tusi* domains more closely following the self-sufficiency model internally.[18]

The situation was different along the middle sections of the Qingshui River, further away from the main transport routes and featuring high mountains and dense forests, where subsistence resources were scarce.[19] Because of the scarcity of arable land, the limited resources for subsistence, and the small populations they could carry, these places became paradises for rebels and descendants of the *Tusi* who did not want to accept the rule of the central government. These places were so restricted in their communication with the outside world that they became so-called "isolated islands." Some inhabitants even gathered in the mountains to destroy the mail routes and "plunder the merchants."[20] In addition to the refusal to communicate with the outside world, the destruction of transport facilities and the blocking of roads by destroying posts continued until the 1940s: most notably on the Yunnan-Xiangjiang Road from Machaiping to Huangping, on the lower section of the Qingshui River from Jianhe to Liuji, and on the middle section of the Duliu River near the Moon Mountain in the Bakai-Rongjiang region, making them feared routes.[21]

The coexistence of these isolated islands with more accessible government-controlled transport routes can also be seen in place names: from the Wushui River down to Zhenyuan County and the middle and lower reaches of the Qingshui River there are many places called "caves (洞 *dong*)," which are the remnants of ethnic minorities' residential areas.[22] In the eastern part of Guizhou, including the Jinjiang River, Wushui River, Qingshui River, and Duliu River basins, there is a longstanding proverb that "the Hmong live in the mountains, the Dong in

[18] On the interactions of the *Tusi* with the major state capitals of Guizhou, see: Ren Kecheng, 1948.

[19] This was especially true in the middle part of the Moon Mountains 月亮山, the whole area of the Leigong Mountains, the main peak of the Miaoling Mountains, and the part of the Chong'an River between Machangping and Huangping.

[20] Guizhou Provincial Archives Collection Guizhou Postal Bureau Archives M58-1–4445 Destruction of Post Road Mail Cabinet Case.

[21] Liu Shifan 刘时范, *Qiandong shibian jiyao* 黔东事变纪要 [Record of riots in eastern Guizhou], Guizhou Provincial Archives, 1943.

[22] *Daoguang Lipingfu zhi* 道光黎平府志 [Local gazetteer of Liping Prefecture in Daoguang period], reprint (Guiyang: Guizhou People's Press, 2010).

the villages and the Han in the streets,"[23] which explains both the spatial distribution of the different ethnic groups in these places and the existence of a considerable number of isolated islands.[24]

1.3 *"Isolated Islands" and the Mobility of Commodities in the Network*

There is a distinct spatial distribution here: the main transport routes as main lines, the habitable tributaries of the river valleys connecting the main transport routes as branches, and the various isolated settlements far from the main transport routes as termini. There is also the pattern of population distribution: the Hmong groups living in the mountains, the Dong people in the cottages, and the Han people in the streets. Since the Ming Dynasty, this basic social structure of networks and isolated islands has been further strengthened by the special pattern of distribution of wealth and goods in Guizhou.

As mentioned earlier, the early Ming Dynasty's desire to use cantonment as a solution to the problem of feeding its army and officials was not very effective. In the short ninety-year period between the establishment of the province in 1413 and the 15th year of Hongzhi (1502), the Ming Dynasty sent salt and rice to nine provinces, including Guizhou Garrison, Bijie Garrison, Wusa Garrison 乌撒卫所 (present-day Weining), Puan Garrison 普安卫所 (present-day Panzhou), Puding Garrison (present-day Anshun), Pingyue Garrison 平越卫所 (present-day Fuquan), Qingping Garrison 清平卫所 (present-day Kaili), Duyun Garrison 都匀卫所 and Chishui Garrison 赤水卫所 (present-day Chishuihe Town). Salt and rice were transported to these places fifteen times, each time with more than 50,000 stones of grain.[25] The extent of the food shortage is evident. As Guizhou could not produce salt, it had to rely on imports from Jiangsu,

[23] Wu Guolin 吴国霖 et al., *Guizhou miaoyi yanjiu* 贵州苗夷研究 [Study on Hmong in Guizhou] (Guiyang: Wentong Shuju).

[24] See Liu Shifan 刘时范, *Qiandong shibian jiyao*, 1943. For an earlier record, see Lingtian 凌剔安, *Xiantong junshi shi* 咸同军事史 [Military history of Guizhou in Xianfeng and Tongzhi Period], 1931, Guizhou Provincial Archives Collection.

[25] *Veritable records of the Ming: Yingzong shilu zhi jintai fulu* 英宗实录之景泰附录 [The records of Jingtai Emperor in the appendix of the veritable records of Yingzong Emperor]. *Xianzong Shilu* 宪宗实录 [Veritable records of Xianzong Emperor]. Xiaozong Shilu 孝宗实录 [Veritable records of Xiaozong Emperor].

Zhejiang, Sichuan, and Guangdong provinces. Despite the government's efforts to ensure the smooth flow of traffic, the natural environment of the mountains and rivers, and the alternating modes of land and water transport in this natural environment, greatly increased the cost of transporting salt and kept the price of salt in Guizhou high for a long time, reaching a peak of a bucket of rice for a pound of salt.[26] The low salt supply had a serious impact on the lives of the inhabitants. As Tian Wen 田雯, a literary figure of the Qing Dynasty, once said, "There is no salt in Guizhou, so the price is high and the people eat lightly."[27] The isolated islands, far from the main roads, were already in a harsh natural environment, and, with the impact of military operations against them, the lack of necessities such as salt and food in these areas was understandable.[28] As a result, the importation and distribution of necessities became an important part of the central government's control and management of Guizhou.

Since the Tang Dynasty, Yanhe County, along the lower reaches of the Wushui River in north-eastern Qianjiang, has been the seat of one of the largest *Tusi* regimes in southwest China, the Tian 田 *Tusi*.[29] Yanhe County is less than 160 kilometers from the nearest salt-producing area, Yushan in Pengshui County 彭水县 in Sichuan Province. Since the Tang Dynasty, the borders of Yanhe 沿河, Pengshui, and the surrounding counties have been shaped and crisscrossed around the salt-producing wells in this area, and the administrative divisions have been deliberately set up to keep the salt areas out of the *Tusi*'s sphere of influence in order to reduce their authority and the risk of rebellion. The situation was similar in the Ming Dynasty. The Yongning Garrison was set up in the Ming Dynasty in order to limit the power of the *Tusi*. The Yongning 永宁 *Tusi*, along with the Shuixi Ans 水西安氏 *Tusi* and Wusa 乌撒 *Tusi*, controlled a large area west of the Yuchi River in present-day Guizhou and up to the large and small Liangshan Mountains in Sichuan, but the Yanjing and Yanyuan in this area were separated to be governed by the central state and controlled

[26] Xue Peixuan 薛培喧 ed., *Gaige yanfa wenti huilu* 改革盐法问题汇录 [Compilation of Questions on the Reform of Salt Law] (Nanjing: yanwu zongju, 1947).

[27] Tianwen 田雯, Qianshu 黔书 [the Book of Qian], 1808.

[28] Liu Shifan, *Qiandong shibian jiyao*, 1943.

[29] Minguo sinan xianzhi gao 民国思南县志稿 [Draft of Local gazetteer of Xinnan County, the Republic of China] (Guiyang: Guizhou People's Press, 2019).

separately.[30] The control of salt and rice was a perfect example of the use of the *Tusi* to guard the main transport routes, as described above. This helped place Guizhou firmly in the hands of the central dynasty, which, in turn, controlled the far reaches of Yunnan, as well as the southwestern and southern regions (Map 3).

Late Ming and early Qing scholar Gu Yanwu 顾炎武 observed that by controlling salt and rice, important resources for people's livelihood along major transportation routes and in *Tusi* regimes, the central state could make *Tusi* regimes dependent on the state while weakening these local regimes. Such manipulation, in turn, further separated migrant settlements from local minority gatherings and influenced the flow of goods and community interaction over time.

In the winter of 1944, one of the largest outbreaks of rinderpest in the southwest of Guizhou during the 1940s occurred in the area of Nidang Town, south of Xingyi County: it killed nearly 100% of the cattle

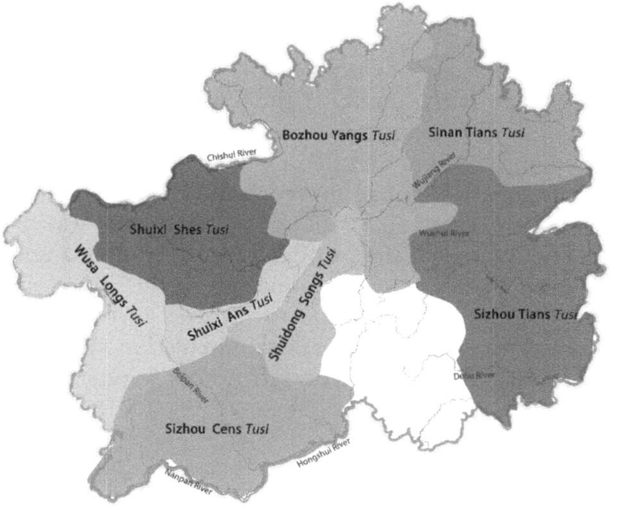

Map 3 Territory of Guizhou *Tusi*, Ming

[30] See Wen Chunlai, 2019.

in the area.[31] What was surprising to control staff was that the rinderpest did not spread northward along the main transport routes to places such as Zhenfeng 贞丰 or Lang Dai 郎岱, but instead, a similar outbreak occurred in Baise County 百色, Guangxi, hundreds of kilometers southward across the Nanpan River 南盘江.[32] Through further investigation, the epidemic prevention personnel found that the merchants from Xingyi 兴义 did not trade along the main transport routes in the Sichuan-Guizhou corridor, but in the Guangxi province. Crude sugar and livestock products trading relationship exists between Nidang 泥凼 in Guizhou and Baise in Guangxi. Residents of Nidang Town often go east along the Nanpan River, passing through Lingyun County to Baise County to trade in the market of Guangxi. This time, rinderpest was spread from Guizhou to Baise, Guangxi through a sick and dead cow processed for beef jerky.[33]

Although the southwestern part of Guizhou was theoretically connected to central Guizhou and even northwestern Guizhou through the Beipan River 北盘江 and passages in the Miao Ling, the spread of the epidemic shows that this area was far less accessible to the people northward along the main road than to the local and those southward to the Baise region of Guangxi. The political forces and the intellectual class that gathered in the important towns along the main transport routes at the time would not have been aware of the existence of this route for the exchange of goods. The reason for this is that the area was once under the jurisdiction of the Cen 岑氏 Tusi of the Sizhou 泗州 in Guangxi, and most of the inhabitants had moved from Sizhou in Guangxi, which is today's Lingyun County 凌云县.[34] This area, which was more closely connected to the area along the NanPanjiang River in Guangxi under the rule of the *Tusi*, was more closely connected to the area along the main transportation route northward than to the area further away from the main transportation route. This localized circulation and the separation of main roads is the product of a combination of long-standing Guizhou traffic control and *Tusi* politics.

[31] See the archives of the Southwest Veterinary Disease Control Office in the Guizhou Provincial Archives of the Republic of China, M66-1–65 Xingyi Rinderpest Report and other correspondence.

[32] Ibid.

[33] Ibid.

[34] Torii Ryuzo 鸟居龙藏, *Xinan zhongguo jixing* 西南中国纪行 [Travel Diary of Southwest China], trans. Yang Zhiqiang 杨志强 (Beijing: The Commercial Press, 2020).

In summary, since the Ming Dynasty, the state's need to further govern Yunnan and control its southwestern borders has increased. Compared to other provinces, despite its geographic complexity, Guizhou had the most effective and convenient access to Yunnan Province. In order to ensure smooth access to Yunnan Province, dynastic power thus penetrated further into Guizhou. The tension between the central state and local regimes created a geographic and economic structure in which Guizhou's multi-directional external networks coexisted with semi-insular communities, and it shaped the patterns of relations between the various ethnic and commercial groups in Guizhou.

2 Political Control, Trade, and the Development of Trade Routes

Despite limited physical control, from the Ming Dynasty onward the central state never gave up on dismantling the local domination of powerful *Tusi*.[35] The central state abolished the old government sectors and established new governing counties in the corresponding regions. This was called "replacing local chieftains with officials" (改土归流 *gaitu guiliu*). In addition to this, the central state constructed new governable infrastructures such as roads and post stations, dredged rivers, and even set up warehouses and salt monopolies deep in the hinterland. This allowed immigrants and descendants of *Tusi* who were subservient to the central state to gradually expand and even develop entrepreneurial enterprises in the regions between the main transport routes; in a sense, it turned them into new frontiers.

The social pattern of "barbarians on all sides beyond the first line" had already been gradually changing before the large-scale forced conversion of local *Tusi* to officials began during the Yongzheng period.[36] In the process, the tributaries and valleys along the Wu River were further developed by local people, and the regions of Zunyi, Dading, and Sinan, formerly under the control of the *Tusi*, were linked together to form a social network of frequent contacts. The marketplaces and temple fairs that cover the middle and lower reaches of the Wu River today span

[35] See: "Guizhou tusi Liezhuan," 贵州土司列传 (Biographies of native chieftains), in Mingshi 明史 (Official dynamistic history of Ming dynasty).

[36] Wen Chunlai 温春来, 2019, 210–226.

Zunyi 遵义, Yuqing 余庆, Fenggang 凤冈, and Sinan 思南, and the scope and depth of trade is unparalleled elsewhere in Guizhou.[37] The subsequent endeavors to turn chieftains into officials during the Yongzheng period brought the further reaches of the Qingshui and Duliu Rivers, which the central state of the Ming Dynasty had no chance for annexing, into the national administration. Through military conscription, the Qing Dynasty set up the Six Frontier Tings (新疆六厅 *xinjiang liuting*)[38] in southeastern Guizhou to control key ports along the river, and dredged the river to link the Qingshui River 清水江 with the middle and lower reaches of the Yangtze through the Yuan River.[39] At the same time, the Chishui River waterway to the north into Sichuan was further opened up, and by the eleventh year of the Yongzheng era (1733) of the Qing Dynasty four major ports of entry for Sichuan salt into Qian were set up, combining several waterways out of Qian and formally forming a salt distribution network with the main route from Hejiang in Sichuan up to the town of Maotai.[40]

With the further development and improvement of transportation in and out of Guizhou, its economic resources have been further mobilized and exploited by the local inhabitants and merchants. Lead mining in northwest Guizhou has been an important strategic industry since the Qing Dynasty, with Guizhou producing anywhere from 67 to 84% of the country's total lead output at various times during the Qing

[37] Ministry of Transportation of National Government in Beijing eds, *Xiangdian xian Guizhou duan yanxian gexian shehijingji diaocha* 湘滇线贵州段沿线各县社会经济调查 [The socio-economic survey of the counties along Guizhou section of Xiang-Dian Line], 1922.

[38] The six prefectural-level administrative units set up by the Qing Dynasty for the control of southern and southeastern Guizhou, mainly for military purposes, were under the responsibility of the nearest prefectural governor, namely the Bazhai ting (part of today's Danzhai County), the Danjiang ting (today's Danzhai County), the Guzhou ting (today's Rongjiang County), the Qingjiang thing (today's Liuchuan Town, Jianhe County, which has been flooded by a reservoir), the Dujiang ting (today's Dujiang Township, Sandu County), and the Taigong ting (present-day Taijiang County). See Minguo guizhou tongzhi jianzhi yange 民国贵州通志·建置沿革 [A general history of Guizhou, Institutional Establishment and Transition, Republic of China], eds. Ren Kecheng 任可澄 et al., (Guiyang: Wentong Shuju, 1948).

[39] Zhang Yingqiang, 2006, 23–39.

[40] *Sichuan yanfa zhi* 四川盐法志 [Gazetteer of Sichuan Salt District], 1882.

Dynasty.[41] The Qingshui River valley, on the other hand, has been an important source of cedar wood and royal Phoebe zhennan wood since the mid-Qing period.[42] In addition to this, Guizhou was also an important manufacturing hub of agricultural products such as tung oil, indigo, tobacco, wild silk, lacquer, and pentandra.[43] By the nineteenth century, Guizhou was the first, fourth, and seventh largest producer of pentandra, tung oil, and indigo, respectively, in China.[44]

The development of local resource in Guizhou was undoubtedly related to the state's attempts to further control and manage the province through economic means, in addition to military and administrative means. Whether conducting military operations or creating additional displaced officials, the administration of Guizhou was costly for the state. Despite the massive move toward replacing local chieftains with officials during the Qing Dynasty, which brought more aborigines into codified households, revenue from land taxation was still insufficient and the local fiscal system relied on assistance from other provinces.[45] Along with the further development of natural resources in Guizhou, the abundant means of production in the province could be exchanged for the necessities of life from other provinces, and sources of taxation were expanded.

A glimpse of the government's interest in this area can be found in the creation of sub-counties. From the Qianlong reign onward, the momentum of land reform slowed down, but new administrative districts

[41] See Wen Chunlai, 2019, 306. Maqi 马琦, *Ghuojia ziyuan: qingdai diantong qianqian kaifa yanjiu* 国家资源:清代滇铜和黔铅开发研究 [National resources: Research on the development of Lead ore in Guizhou, Yunnan Copper mine in Qing Dynasty] (Beijing: People's Press, 2013), 294–298.

[42] See Zhang Yingqiang, 2006.

[43] Guiyangshi junguanhui 贵阳市军管会 (Guiyang Military Adminitrative Committee) ed., (1950) *Guizhou caijing ziliao huibian* 贵州财经资料汇编 [Guizhou Financial Information Compilation] (Guiyang: guiyang junguanhui, 1950).

[44] Zhang Xiaomei 张肖梅, *Guizhou jingji* 贵州经济 [Guizhou Economy] (Chongqing: National Economic Research, 1939).

[45] Zhang Zhongkui 张中奎, Gaitu guiliu yu miaojiang gaizao: Qingdai Xinjiang liuting de wanghua jincheng ji qi shehui wenhua bianqian 改土归流与苗疆改造:清代"新疆六厅"的王化进程及其社会文化变迁 [Turning native rule into regular administration and the conversion of Hmong territories: the construction of "Six Ting of New Frontiers" and the socio-cultural transformation] (Beijing: China Social Sciences Press, 2014).

continued to be set up and divided, such as the sub-counties of Deshengpo under Weining Prefecture in northwest Guizhou, Houping under Yanhe County in north Guizhou,[46] Liuji under Qingjiang Ting 清江厅 in southeast Guizhou, Langdong under Guzhou Ting, Xuedong 雪洞 under Qiongjiang County 邛江,[47] and Yuankou 远口 under Tianzhu County 天柱. By 1911, when the Qing Dynasty collapsed, there were 162 county-level administrative regions in the province, including some military units such as governor's divisions and inspectors, which existed in name only—far more than the 88 that exist today.[48] These administrative districts, at all levels including sub-counties, reach farther into the hinterland than one might think. The sub-county, for example, is located in the Miao Ling 苗岭 in the middle of the lower reaches of the Qingshui River between Jianhe and Jinping County, 98 kilometers from Jianhe and over 100 kilometers from Jinping, which is a four-hour drive from the nearest county today. In the days when there were no roads, this was the furthest area that administration could be extended to. Such sub-counties were set up partly to purge disobedient mountain people, but also to further control the middle section of the Qingshui River, to ensure the cultivation and production of timber and indigo. Similar sub-counties with economic control functions include Deshengpo sub-county 得胜坡, which controls lead and zinc production, and Yuankou sub-county, which controlled gold mining.

Of course, the impact of the influx of immigrants from other provinces on the development of resources in the "vast and sparse land of the Hmong" must not be overlooked in this process. Unlike during the Ming Dynasty, when migration from other provinces was predominantly military, the Qing Dynasty saw a large number of non-military immigrants moving into Guizhou.[49] The immigrants' pursuit of livelihoods

[46] In 1914, Deshengpo sub-county was changed to Hezhang County, Houping sub-county was changed to Houping County, and Houping County was withdrawn in 1941 to be divided into Wuchuan and Yanhe counties.

[47] Qiongjiang County is today's Sansui County, and Xuedong is one of its towns.

[48] Guiyangshi junguanhui 贵阳市军管会 (Guiyang Military Adminitrative Committee) ed., (1950) *Guizhou caijing ziliao huibian* 贵州财经资料汇编 (Guizhou Financial Information Compilation) (Guiyang: guiyang junguanhui, 1950), 10–56.

[49] Cao Shuji 曹树基, *Zhongguo Yimin Shi* 中国移民史 [The history of immigration], volume 6 (Fuzhou: Fujian Education Press, 1997), 156–164.

and the government's need to control Guizhou coincided with the development of Guizhou, and a cooperative relationship gradually developed between them. As well as providing skills and labor for the development of government-supported agriculture and mining, merchants were encouraged by the local officials to move further into the hinterland along the main transport routes: while selling salt, rice, and bolts of cloth to hinterland administrative units, they were able to reach previously inaccessible mountainous areas and to persuade the local people to grow tea, indigo, and tobacco.[50] These persuasions were permitted and encouraged both from a political and commercial point of view: farmers specializing in cultivation were easier to control and tame than mountain people. For the merchants, the development of this trade in the service of politics and the military, even if it was costly, could be rewarded handsomely. Merchants were sheltered in this government-business relationship and profited from the formation of a trade cycle. As we will see in the following chapters, merchants in Guizhou managed their position in the empire and even in the Republic through the development of this service-shelter-profit political and commercial relationship from the modern era onward.

With these incentives, and efforts of government officials and merchants, Guizhou was operating as a transportation hub with several accomplished travel routes as China entered the Republican period.

The most important of the travel routes mentioned above is the east–west corridor running through the center of Guizhou, connecting Kunming in Yunnan and Changsha in Hunan. With Guiyang, the provincial capital of Guizhou in the middle of this route, its east half goes through a series of small basins and along the north foot of the Miao Ling to the first upstream port on the Wushui River, Jiuzhou Town of Huangping County. Here the water conditions become navigable all the way to Hongjiang, the confluence of the Wu River and Yuan River. Then Dongting Lake connects the Yuanjiang River and a variety of important rivers in Hunan and Hubei, including the Xiang River, thus bringing travelers to Changsha, the provincial capital of Hunan Province along

[50] This fact is recorded in the inscriptions behind the Guiding County God Temple. Also see: "Lanfujing Siyan," 蓝福景丝烟 (Memoir of the tobacco shop of Lan family) in Guiding Wenshi Ziliao 贵定文史资料 (Cultural and Historical Materials of Guiding), Lanjinguang 蓝瑾光, series 4, 1987, 177–181.

the Xiang River.[51] The west part of this route first runs through the northern foot of the Miao Ling, enters into the North Pan River Basin via Langdai, and then uses the waterways of two tributaries of the Beipan River to reach Yizikong 亦资孔, the hinterland of the Wumeng Mountains and the west end of Guizhou Province. From Yizigong, the natural conditions make it easy for travelers to cross the Wumeng Mountains and finally arrive at Kunming through the flatlands of the Yunnan-Guizhou Plateau. This grand route across the middle of Guizhou had political and military significance during the Ming and Qing Dynasties. Three of the eight prefectures of Guizhou were on this route, including Zhenyuan county, which controlled east Guizhou and suppressed the Miao's revolts; Guiyang prefecture, the provincial capital and a transportation hub; and Anshun county, which controlled west and southwest Guizhou, and was the residence for the Yunnan-Guizhou Governor during the Qing Dynasty.

The north–south routes are mainly for economic purposes and can be subdivided into east, middle, and west lines, all of which connect with the Yangtze River and its tributaries in Sichuan Province. According to the travelogs written by Westerners during the 1890s, the east line was the main route for Canton merchants to go north to Fuling, and for commodities such as white wax, tung oil, and pith paper to flow into the Lingnan region from Sichuan, Guizhou, and Hunan.[52] Those Canton merchants went up the Duliu River 都柳江 and arrived at Sandu 三都, a port on the upper Duliu River, then used the land pathway near Sandu to cross the Miao Ling and enter into Kaili 凯里, where they could follow the Qingshui River to Huangping and navigate through the Wushui River and its tributary to arrive at Shiqian County in the Wujiang River Basin. The rivers of the Wujiang River System could bring them to their destinations in Sichuan Province.[53] This east line intersects with the east–west corridor mentioned above in Huangping and Zhenyuan, making these two places the most important transportation nodes in eastern Guizhou.

51 See: Torii Ryuzo 鸟居龙藏, *Xinan zhongguo jixing* 西南中国纪行 [Travel diary of Southwest China], trans. Yang Zhiqiang 杨志强 (Beijing: the Commercial Press, 2020).

52 See: Alexander Hosie,Three Years in Western China: A Narrative of Three Journeys in Szechwani, Kweichowi and Yunnan, reprint. (Bangkok: White Lotus, 2001) Zhang Xiaomei 张肖梅, *Guizhou jingji* 贵州经济 [Guizhou Economy] (Chongqing: National Economic Research, 1939).

53 Zhang Xiaomei, 1939.

The middle line is the official road linking Sichuan, Guizhou, and Guangxi, which became the Qiangui Road 黔贵公路 and Chuanqian Road 川黔公路 in the 1930s. It intersects with the east–west corridor at Guiyang and Machangping Town 马场坪镇, which made Machangping, now an ordinary small town along the highway, the destination of the two main routes of the salt trade and commercially prosperous before the 1950s.[54]

The west line has a long history of horse trade dating back to the Song Dynasty. This route follows the North Panjiang River to Zhenfeng County, then uses the pathway through the Miao Mountains to Langdai, where this west line intersects with the east–west corridor. The valley nearby formed by the Wumeng Mountains and the tributaries of the Wujiang River leads travelers to Xuyong 叙永, a county on the border between Guizhou and Sichuan.[55] The west line was not as important as the other two lines, though it was commonly used by smugglers of salt, tobacco, and opium and once was considered by Qing officials to serve as the official route for transporting Yunnan's copper to Guizhou and Guangxi.[56]

However, the route officials finally chose for copper transporting was none of the routes mentioned above. Instead, it traversed the northwest border between Yunnan and Guizhou. Copper was imported via Zhaotong county 昭通 in Yunnan and Weining 威宁 in Guizhou, went along the valleys of the north Wumeng Mountains, and arrived at Bijie. This route was also used for importing salt from Sichuan Province via Xuyong and distributing it in northwest Guizhou.[57]

In 1886, Alexander Hosie set out from Chongqing, followed the Sichuan-Guizhou post road southward, and then turned toward Yunnan, completing a three-year expedition through the three southwestern

[54] See: Lin Xin 林辛, *Guizhou jindai jiaotong shilve* 贵州近代交通史略 (A Brief History of Modern Traffic in Guizhou) (Guiyang: Guizhou People's Press, 1985), chapter 2.

[55] See: Ren Kecheng et al., 1948.

[56] Guizhoushengshizhiban 贵州省史志办 ed., *Guizhoudilizhi* 贵州地理志 (The History of Guizhou Geography), (Guiyang: Guizhou renmin chubanshe, 1994). Wu Xiaogao described his opium trafficking experience in Guizhou Committee of China National Democratic Construction Association ed., Guizhou Gongshangye Shiliao Huibian 贵州工商史料汇编 (Compilation of the industrial and commercial records of Guizhou), 1985.

[57] Ren Kecheng et al., 1948.; About copper and lead、salt, see: Zhao Hengqian 赵亨钤, *Qianchai riji* 铅差日记 (The Diary of a Lead Commissioner) (Guiyang: Guizhou People's Press, 2019); Regarding the Yi *Tusi*, see Map 3.

provinces for commercial activities.[58] He was amazed to discover that a plant called *Tongcao* (Tetrapanax papyrifer 通草) was being grown in both Tongzi and Guiding counties in Guizhou. He found that the local people collected the stalks of *Tongcao* and skillfully peeled and milled them to make a kind of paper for export, without using it themselves; this was the same *Tongcao* paper that was used in Guangzhou to make Western paintings for export to Europe and America. Furthermore, when Hosie traveled to the Duliu River valley, he discovered that the paper and other products, including tung oil, indigo, and wubija, were transported downstream to Liuzhou, Wuzhou, and even Guangzhou via the Duliu River waterway. According to Hosie, Guizhou was connected to the coastal areas of southern China by water at least as early as the nineteenth century.

Contemporary scholars studying the economic history of China's southwestern region are once again comparing economic data to find that Guizhou was linked to east and south China by a well-developed network of land and water transport as early as the nineteenth century and even earlier in the seventeenth and eighteenth centuries.[59] Quantitative historians have focused their attention on the prices of goods in Guizhou, particularly rice and other grains. By analyzing rice price data from eight provinces in Guizhou over 200 years, James Z. Lee has concluded that Guizhou was able to surpass France in the early eighteenth century with a market integration index of 0.43, close to that of the Pearl River Delta and the Yangtze River Delta during the same period.[60] Peng Kaixiang uses over 200 years of grain price data from the Qing Dynasty onward to demonstrate that the fluctuations in grain prices in the state capitals of Guiyang, Anshun, and Zunyi were in line with those of Changsha in Hunan and even Suzhou and Wuxi in Zhejiang. During the Qing Dynasty, he argues, the major state capitals of Guizhou already maintained close commercial ties with the areas along the middle and lower reaches of the Yangtze River through a network of land and water transportation.[61]

[58] See: Alexander Hosie, 2001.

[59] See Li Bozhong 李伯重, *Jiangnan de zaoqi gongyehua* 江南的早期工业化 (Early Industrialization of Jiangnan Region) (Beijing: Social Sciences Academic Press, 2000).

[60] James Z. Lee, The Political Economy of a Frontier: Southwest China, 1250–1850 (Cambridge: Harvard University Press, 2002).

[61] Peng Kaixiang 彭凯翔, *Qingdai yilai de liangjia* 清代以来的粮价 (The Price of Grain Since the Qing Dynasty) (Shanghai: Shanghai People's Press, 2006).

In other words, Guizhou was part of a commercial trade network linked to Jiangnan as early as the mid-seventeenth century.

3 Mobility of Commodities and Local Society in the Republican Period

The administration and development of Guizhou during the Qing Dynasty depended on the state's strong military power and its ability to meet the costs of military operations and administrative measures. Yet, by the beginning of the twentieth century, with weakening military power and a deteriorating financial situation, the state was unable to maintain its already costly administrative units in the hinterland. The state had to abandon a significant portion of its sub-counties, inspectorates, and governor's divisions and turn them into towns or districts. Some counties, such as Liuji, even became villages. By 1914, only 80 county-level administrative units remained in Guizhou.

During the Republican period, although the central state made efforts to restore the administration of Guizhou and the administrative legitimacy of the new state, the kind of commercial network supported by the administrative system during the dynastic period, with the import and distribution of essential goods such as salt as the core, supplemented by the export of mineral and mountain forest products, was continued. These networks formed the basis of Guizhou's commercial network until the 1930s. The salt trading system was the one that led to the continuation, intermingling, and transition of multiple commercial networks. In the Republican period, the traditional salt monopoly system was further strengthened in the turbulent political environment, and a three-tier mechanism for the transportation and distribution of salt was formed and deepened. The Guzhou Ting 古州厅 (later Rongjiang County 榕江县 and its surrounding areas of Bakai 八开, Zhaihao 寨蒿, and Langdong 朗洞), Hongzhou (sub-county) near Liping County, and Liuji town in Jianhe County all became important export terminals for forest products, creating a commercial cycle of Guangdong salt, Huai salt, and Sichuan salt exchanged for local timber, oil, indigo, and minerals.[62] This suggests that "isolated islands" in the political and economic sense were being gradually

[62] See: Liu Shifan 刘时范, *Qiandong shibian jiyao* 黔东事变纪要 (Record of Riots in Eastern Guizhou), 1943.

eliminated in the 1930s. Instead, the commercial network covering the province, with salt at its core, no longer relied solely on the main transport routes and their tributaries, but was fully established through the administrative divisions. The process of deriving and establishing the three-tier shipping and distribution system, and how it reflects and reshapes local merchant networks, will be articulated in Chapters five and six.

The following analysis of relevant observations from the social surveys of the 1930s and 1940s will present a basic picture of the flow of goods in Guizhou after the Republic.

In 1936–1937, in order to complement the construction of the Great Rearguard in Guizhou, a research team led by Liu Dajun 刘大钧 and Zhang Xiaomei 张肖梅 of the National Economic Research Institute conducted a survey of the economy and society of several important counties and cities in Guizhou, and these findings resulted in one of the most comprehensive studies of the economy and society of Guizhou at that time, *Guizhou Economy*.[63] In this study, Zhang specifically studied commodity prices across Guizhou, and she found that prices in Guiyang, Anshun, Zunyi, and other places and counties fluctuate greatly. The prices of commodities in Zunyi, Chongqing, Guiyang, and Changsha fluctuate nearly at the same frequency but the prices in counties extending to both sides of the major transport routes and the surrounding counties of Guizhou, Zunyi, and Anshun fluctuate less.[64] At the same time, an inspection report from the First Administrative Inspectorate of Guizhou showed that prices in Jianhe, Tianzhu, Jinping, and even Liping in the Qingshui River area of southeast China are very low and stable: "Wood is only 1 to 2 yuan per stick, rice is less than 50 cents per quintal … rice and grain is less than one third of that in Guiyang."[65] In other words, in the 1930s and 1940s, prices in rural areas of Guizhou were falling steadily while prices fell sharply in the urbanized core areas. This is why the Guizhou Wood Company, a joint venture between the Guizhou provincial government and the local authorities, taking advantage of the price difference in

[63] Zhang Xiaomei 张肖梅, *Guizhou jingji* 贵州经济 (Guizhou Economy) (Chongqing: National Economic Research, 1939).

[64] Ibid.

[65] Archives of the Guizhou Provincial Department of Civil Affairs in the Republic of China, M8-1-4009 Qiandongxunshibaogao 黔东巡视报告 [Report on the Your of Eastern Guizhou], 1941, Guizhou Provincial Archives.

the delivery network, was so profitable that it made "a profit more than ten times its cost" in 1946 through hoarding in Jinping.[66]

This suggests that, at least in the middle of the twentieth century, many counties and towns on the banks of the Qingshui River were not yet able to keep up with larger cities as far as prices were concerned. Considering that these places were far from the main Yunnan-Hunan corridor and the Sichuan-Qianjiang-Guizhou corridor in terms of transportation conditions, it is evident that their economic ties with the main transportation arteries were not very strong.

What do these seemingly varied findings and observations really tell us?

First of all, almost all studies of central cities and market towns on major transportation routes show that central cities like Guiyang, Zunyi, Anshun, and Zhenyuan were highly economically congruent with these regions because of their high dependence on household goods such as salt, rice, and bolts of cloth from Hunan in the east and the Sichuan basin in the north in the Republican period. By the early twentieth century, a significant change in Guiyang's market supply situation occurred with the rise of the postal transportation system in Guizhou. That is, Guiyang relied on merchants to bring in daily necessities such as department store items and silk from Shanghai or Guangzhou via postal routes; this situation strengthened the ties between important central cities such as Guiyang and the coastal areas in east and south China, further enhancing the economic convergence with these coastal areas.

Secondly, looking at the situation of the market in counties in sub-regional markets, these counties and market towns, which are far from the main routes, are less affected by the transmission of economic fluctuations in the developed eastern region and are more influenced by the local trade circle, showing some independence. For example, in the salt-oil-rice exchange market between Sinan and Pengshui along the lower reaches of the Wu River 乌江, the private salt imported from Sichuan and locally produced oil and rice form a commercial circle of up-and-down circulation and distribution; in the counties of Yanhe, Dejiang, Sinan and the surrounding central market towns of Yingwu Xi 鹦鹉溪, Chaodi 潮底, and Qitan 淇滩, located on the Guizhou side, prices and trade fluctuations are also consistent with Fuling in Sichuan, but different from

[66] Jiang Guosheng 蒋国生 ed., *Guizhou qiye gongsi* 贵州企业公司 [Guizhou's Enterprise Company] (Guiyang: Guizhou People's Press, 2006).

Chongqing.[67] For example, Liping in southeast Guizhou and nearby places like Jinping and Tianzhu form a commercial cycle of timber and fabric with the lower reaches of the Qingshui River in Hunan Province, Hongjiang County 洪江县,[68] so prices and economic fluctuations are in line with Hongjiang and distinguish it from Zhenyuan.[69]

Third, all the above studies fail to point out the characteristics of the economic situation in sub-county market towns and rural areas. However, through an early study of Meitan County in Guizhou published in 1944, we find that scholars studied the structure of rural market towns in Guizhou long before William G. Skinner proposed the Chinese rural market pattern, and this study shows that the sub-county regions of Guizhou at that time had obvious self-circulation phenomenon and their regional economic independence was strong.

In 1944, the Guizhou Agricultural Improvement Institute created a magazine called "China Rural Life." In the inaugural issue of this magazine, "Guizhou Rural Life Special Issue," there was an article signed by "Shou Yu" entitled "Survey of Meitan Township Market." In this article, the author proposed a market radius and its calculation method through a survey of the markets in more than thirty townships in Meitan County and measured the market period of Meitan with a cycle of six days.[70] Through measurement, the author found that the township markets in Maitan County showed obvious spatial stratification, with Yongxing Town in this county as the core and boundaries extending outward every ten miles. The county was roughly divided into three cycles of markets within the county, and each cycle combined five to six market towns. In the same cycle, the earthly branches of the Chinese sexagenary cycle (地支*dizhi*)[71]

67 Ma Zhenkun 马震崑, Minguo sinanxian zhi gao 民国思南县志稿 [Draft of the Gazetteer of Sinan County, the Republic of China] (Guiyang: Guizhou People's press, 2019); also see: J-1–136-11 *Wujiang shangxia wuchanyunsong* 乌江上下物产运送 [Cargo Transportation, Upstream and Downstream of Wujiang River], Pengshui County Archives.

68 Hongjiang District, Huaihua City.

69 Zhangxiaomei, 1939.

70 MG12 *Guizhou nongcunshehuo teji* 贵州农村生活特辑 [Guizhou Rural Life Special Issue], 1944, 101–112. Guizhou Provincial Archives.

71 This is a unit of measurement in the Chinese concept of space–time. Twelve different Chinese character symbols replace different time or space zones. In a temporal sense, twelve is usually a whole cycle. For example, there are twelve hours in a day (each hour corresponds to two hours in the contemporary sense). For the purpose of this article, twelve represents a market cycle. Later chapters will separately address how the Chinese

are used to identify and circulate the market activities; in the market towns of each cycle, merchants stagger each other's trade time. Usually, merchants in smaller market towns trade regularly with the merchants in the nearest larger market town—thus forming a county-level spatial distribution of market towns with the main town as the core and the three-level circulating regular markets within the county.

Merchants rushed back and forth in different cycles of market towns and were able to trade every day.[72] The prices of different markets varied from one cycle to another, with the farthest markets generally being the most expensive for salt and cloth, and the cheapest for rice, local products, and herbs, and the more marginal the market, the more stable the prices.[73] In fact, this highly stratified spatial and temporal distribution of markets is quite common in rural areas of Guizhou.[74]

Thus we can see from the market and economic fluctuations of Guizhou that during the Republican Era, the economy of Guizhou continued to display its previous characteristics of early Modern China: the closer to the central cities of the main transportation routes or the distribution centers of materials, the more obvious the integration of the market into the commercial network. However, it is also important to see that small regional markets were formed below the county level—divergence and convergence of commercial networks existed at the same time. This is characteristic of Guizhou's economy, where markets are highly integrated at all levels, yet local markets maintain their independence. We further argue that this market pattern is embedded in the political geography formed by the power struggle in Guizhou. This is the result of centuries of constant negotiation between the central state and local societies.

concept of time has shaped the geographic distribution of markets and market cycles in the Southwest.

[72] Akinobu Kuroda 黑田明伸, *Huobi zhidu de shijieshi* 货币制度的世界史 [The History of the Monetary System], trans. Heping 何平 (Beijing: China Renmin University Press, 2007).

[73] MG12 Guizhou nongcunshehuo teji 贵州农村生活特辑 [Guizhou Rural Life Special Issue], 1944, 101–112. Guizhou Provincial Archives.

[74] Guiyangshi junguanhui 贵阳市军管会 (Guiyang Military Adminitrative Committee) ed., (1950) *Guizhou caijing ziliao huibian* 贵州财经资料汇编 [Guizhou Financial Information Compilation] (Guiyang: Guiyang junguanhui, 1950), 437–634.

4 Conclusion

Although local uprisings continued, the 463 years of warfare and conversion between the central dynasties and the southwestern *Tusi*, spanning the Ming and Qing Dynasties, ceased between 1413 and the end of the Great Ham Tong Uprising in 1876.[75] During this period, the central state in the Ming-Qing Dynasties completely transformed the disobedient indigenous inhabitants into governable households through three large wars and a massive expansion of the state's territories.[76] The main strategy of these successive conversion wars was surprisingly consistent: the central state attempted to control important transportation arteries and extend territories to both sides of these water and land routes.

Guizhou, which seemed geographically unlikely to be a transportation hub, became a crossroads for the inner frontier of southwest China through the interplay of central state control and local *Tusi* politics. Through trade and warfare, Guizhou also gave rise to a transportation network and commercial network that ran through the province. Geopolitics and economic conflicts and synergies transcended the local society and created these influential transportation and commercial networks.

[75] Lingtian 凌剔安, *Xiantong junshi shi* 咸同军事史 [Military History of Guizhou in Xianfeng and Tongzhi Period], 1931.

[76] Ren Kecheng 任可澄 et al., Minguo Guizhou Tongzhi, 1948.

CHAPTER 3

The Salt Monopoly, Changing Business Networks, and the State's Remodeling of the Salt Trade

Benmo Jiang

It is widely accepted that in China salt administration is an important tool for extending the state's administrative control and keeping government revenue sufficient. However, it always calls for the cooperation of merchants to some extent. Adjustments to salt administration policies lead to adjustments to the government's choice of cooperators and changes to the power structures of merchants.[1]

This feature of salt administration also appeared in the state monopoly system implemented by the nationalist government during the War of Resistance. However, how these state monopoly policies affected the trade

[1] See Niyuping 倪玉平, *Boyi yu junheng:Qingdai lianghuai yanzheng gaige* 博弈与均衡:清代两淮盐政改革 [Game and Equilibrium: Reform of the Lianghuai Salt Administration in the Qing Dynasty] (Fuzhou: Fujian People's Press, 2011); Huang Guoxin 黄国信, *Qu yu jie:Qingdai Xiang Yue Gan jielin shiyan zhuanmai yanjiu* 区与界:清代湘粤赣界邻食盐专卖研究 [Districts and Borders: A Study on Salt Monopoly in the Borders of Hunan, Guangdong, and Jiangxi in the Qing Dynasty] (Beijing: SDX Joint Publishing Company, 2006); Li Xiaolong 李晓龙, "Jindai yanwu jiuchang zhengshui gaige yu guanshang boyi" 近代盐务就场征税制改革与官商博弈 [The Reform of Taxation at Production Place in Salt Industry and the Game Between Officials and Businessmen in Modern China], *Journal of Historical Science* 12 (2020): 41–52.

B. Jiang et al., *State, Market and Salt-Tobacco Road in Modern China (1935–1949)*, https://doi.org/10.1007/978-981-97-7654-2_3

and salt merchants in particular areas, and how this administrative system differed from previous ones for salt merchants, still needs to be discussed further.[2] This chapter analyzes the interaction between changes to salt administration policies and the development of local salt merchants in Guizhou. The first section recounts how local salt merchants became an important group in trade and social affairs in Guizhou during the late Qing and early Republican periods, and the following two sections discuss the changes that the wartime salt monopoly system brought to wholesalers and retailers, respectively.

1 The Rise of Guizhou's Local Salt Merchants

As the central government gradually took control of Guizhou, it also tried to establish administrative control of the salt trade in this border province. The dominant role of Sichuan salt in Guizhou and the four border ports' syndicate system of salt transportation and distribution were gradually developed through the Qing Dynasty.[3] However, it was only after Ding Baozhen 丁宝桢, an official from Guizhou, became the Governor General of Sichuan, and tried to restore the syndicate system after the Taiping Rebellion, that Guizhou's local salt merchants gradually developed into one of the dominant forces in the province's salt trade.

Before Ding's reform, the dominant merchant groups in Guizhou's salt trade were from Sichuan and Shaanxi. The local merchants of Guizhou were normally lower-tier distributors and retailers.[4] Compared to Sichuan and Shaanxi merchants, Guizhou merchants had two major weak points

[2] Tang Mingsheng 唐明胜, *Na yan gui cang: 1800–1960 nianjian zhejiang de yanzheng bianqian yu yanchang shehui* 纳盐归仓: 1800–1960 年间浙江的盐政变迁与盐场社会 [Collecting Salt into Granary, the Changes of Salt Administration and Saltern Society in Zhejiang, 1800–1960] (PhD. Diss., Shanghai: East China Normal University, 2022): 138.

[3] Wu Duo 吴铎, "Chuanyan guanyun zhishimo" 川盐官运之始末 [The Beginning and the End of Official Salt Transportation in Sichuan], *Zhongguo jindai jingjishi yanjiu jikan* 中国近代经济史研究集刊 [Journal of Modern Chinese Economic History Research] 3, no. 2 (1935): 155–56.

[4] There were a few examples of powerful salt merchants in Guizhou before Ding's reform. One was Zhang Chun 張淳 during the reign of Qianlong Emperor. Zhang was born in Renhuai, where was the border port of Ren An. Benefiting from the development of river transportation in Guizhou under the auspices of Guizhou's Governor General, Zhang Guangsi 张广泗, Zhang Chun became a salt tycoon, and his family controlled salt transportation along the Chishuihe River for decades. See Wang Fangjun 王方君, *Qingdai*

regarding accessing to the wholesale business and playing a more important role in Guizhou's salt trade. One was that there was no local salt production in Guizhou, which made it impossible to build a local trade network by controlling local salterns, as Sichuan merchants did. The other weak point, maybe more crucial, was a lack of capital to run any kind of wholesale business; both getting salt certificates and arranging salt transportation from neighboring provinces were very costly. During the 1860s and 1870s, the outbreak of Muslim revolt in Shaanxi, the social upheaval in Sichuan and Guizhou caused by the Taiping Rebellion and other anti-Qing violence drastically impacted the business of Shaanxi merchants and made some of them resign from Guizhou's salt trade.[5] This was a good chance for Guizhou's local merchant to step in. However, when Ding Baozhen and his government tried to rebuild the syndicate system, they found that the new wholesale alliance of Guizhou and Sichuan merchants only had very limited funds, making it hard for them to fill the vacuum left by the Shaanxi merchants.[6]

The main purposes of Ding's reform, as has been discussed in various academic works, was to arrange a competition between Sichuan salt and Lianghuai salt in the Huguang market, and regain control of the stable salt tax revenue from Sichuan salt's production and distribution.[7] To achieve these goals, Ding Baozhen and his team intensified surveillance of the salt trade and altered the former system of salt transportation and

Guizhou yanshang yanjiu 清代贵州盐商研究 [Research on Guizhou Salt Merchants in Qing Dynasty] (Master Thesis, Guizhou University, 2022): 31–37.

[5] Madeleine Zelin, *The Merchants of Zigong: Industrial Entrepreneurship in Early Modern China* (New York: Columbia University Press, 2005): 148; Wu Duo, "Chuanyan guanyun zhishimo," 169–170.

[6] Dingbaozhen 丁宝桢 et al. eds, Zen Fanying 曾凡英, Li Shumin 李树民 and Sun Xiangwei 孙祥伟 reedited and annotated, *Sichuan yanfazhi zhengli jiaozhu* 四川盐法志整理校注 [Collation and Annotation of the Chronicles of Sichuan's Salt Administration] (Chongqing: Southwest Jiaotong University Press, 2019), vol. 13, 343–346.

[7] Madeleine Zelin, *The Merchants of Zigong: Industrial Entrepreneurship in Early Modern China*, 130–157; Wu Xiaoxin 邬晓辛 and Lv Yantao 吕延涛, "Dingbaozhen yu Qingmo Guizhou yanzheng" 丁宝桢与清末贵州盐政 [Ding Baozhen and Guizhou salt administration in Late Qing], *Salt Industry History Research*, 2 (1989): 36–40; Wang Xiaojing 王晓静, "Wanqing chuanyan guanyun shangxiao zhidu de xingsu" 晚清川盐官运商销制度的形塑 (Shaping Sichuan's Salt Marketing System in Late Qing), *Historical Review*, 3 (2021): 110–112; Zhang Honglin 张洪林, *Qingdai Sichuan yanfa yanjiu* 清代四川盐法研究 [Study on Sichuan Salt Administration in Qing Dynasty] (Beijing: China University of Political Science and Law Press, 2012): 140–142,

distribution by implementing official control of wholesale shipments and establishing a General Bureau of Official Transport (官运总局 *guanyun zongju*) in Luzhou. This new system was not only expected by the reformers as an effective way to combat smuggling and optimize tax collection process, but also was designed as part of reformers' larger scheme of expanding the importation of Sichuan salt in Guizhou and Yunnan to cover the loss of giving the salt monopoly quota back to Lianghua salt.[8] Guizhou, Ding Baozhen's home province, became the pilot site for this new system.

Though this official transport and merchant sale system was critiqued because of its high cost and doubtable effectiveness,[9] it provided new opportunities for Guizhou local merchants. Hua Lianhui 华联辉, one of Ding Baozhen's key assistants and advisers regarding salt administration, was believed to be the principal planner of the new official transport system.[10] Hua himself was an experienced salt merchant. He had run his business in Guiyang for years and earned a large amount of money before he was introduced and recommended to Ding Baozhen by another key assistant and Guizhou native, Tang Jiong 唐炯. Under the new system, merchants in the border ports got salt from the salt administration and were allowed to sell it in the regions of Guizhou designated by the branch offices of the Bureau in that port.[11] As a result, salt officials had the power to choose their favored salt merchants. After the reconfirmation of the wholesale salt firms in the border ports, Ren An only had four firms approved by the Bureau of Official Transport to buy salt from their branch office and distribute it into Guizhou. Hua Lianhui and his family controlled two of them: Yonglongyu 永隆裕 and Yongfaxiang 永发祥.[12] Later, these two firms merged together under the name of Yonglongyu.

[8] Wang Xiaojing, "Wanqing chuanyan guanyun shangxiao zhidu de xingsu," 110–112.

[9] Wang Xiaojing, "Wanqing chuanyan guanyun shangxiao zhidu de xingsu," 107–110; Liao Junfei 廖珺霏, "Wang Yuzhao kongan yu Qingmo chuanyan guanyun zhong de duo chong boyi" 王余照控案与清末川盐官运中的多重博弈 [Multiple Games in Wang Yuzhao's Accusation and the Official Transportation of Sichuan Salt in the Late Qing Dynasty], *Salt Industry History Research*, no. 1 (2020): 50–61.

[10] See Zhou Gongshou 周恭寿 eds., *Minguo xu Zunyifu zhi* 民国续遵义府志 [The Continuation Gazetteer of Zunyi Prefecture, the Republic of China] (Chengdu: Bashu Press, 2000), vol. 20, "Biographies" 1, 18b–19a, 37–38.

[11] Zhong Liangxi 钟良曦 and Zhong Changyong 钟良曦, *Chuanyan shilun* 川盐史论 [History of Sichuan Salt], (Chengdu: Sichuan People's Press, 1990), 198.

[12] Wang Fangjun, *Qingdai Guizhou yanshang yanjiu*, 62.

According to Hua Shuren, the great grandson of Hua Lianhui, Yonglongyu had branches in all the important business nodes, such as Maotai, Zunyi, and Tuanxi, along Ren An's trade route to Guiyang, the political center of Guizhou and home of Yonglongyu headquarters. Larger branches were all well equipped with warehouses and provided food and accommodation for their staff.[13]

It is undeniable that Hua Lianhui's role in the salt reform and the trust between him and Ding Baozhen contributed to the dominance of Hua Lianhui and his family in the business of importing Sichuan salt to Guizhou.[14] However, there was also a preference for Guizhou natives in other ports. In Yong An, though some Shaanxi merchants stayed and continued their salt businesses, seven of the thirteen approved wholesale firms belonged to Guizhou merchants.[15]

After the Qing Dynasty ended, the official transport system described above was soon abolished by the military government in Sichuan. According to Deng Xiaoke 邓效可, a supporter of the free trade of salt who briefly served as the head of the salt administration department in Sichuan's military government, this abolishment was a solution to the problems Ding's official transport system had accumulated, and it relieved the suffering of saltern owners, and consumers.[16] In fact, the fierce and continuous conflicts between different warlords in Yunnan, Sichuan, and Guizhou as well as the weak control of the central government in southwestern regions made it impossible to reach a new agreement on the

[13] Hua Shuren 华树人, "Yonglongyu yanhao shulue" 永隆裕盐号述略 (Brief Introduction of Yonglongyu Salt Firm), in Guiyang CPPCC Literature and History Committee ed., *Guiyang wenshi ziliao xuancui* 贵阳文史资料选粹 [Selected Materials of Guiyang Literature and History] (Guiyang: Guizhou People's Press, 2006), vol. 1: 19–26.

[14] Hua Lianhui's brother, Hua Guoying, was the head of the General Bureau of Official Transport. Merchants in the salterns complained of his abusive use of his power to place his relatives in Wang Sanwei Tang's brine well. See Zhong Liangxi and Zhong Changyong, *Chuanyan shilun,* 198.

[15] Yang Tiren 杨体仁, "Yong An yanye yunxiao jiankuang" 永岸盐业运销简况 [Brief introduction of Yong'an salt industry transportation and sales], in *Bijie wenshi ziliao xuanji* 毕节文史资料选辑 [Selected Bijie Literature and History Materials], no. 6 (1988): 55.

[16] Deng Xiaoke 邓效可, "Deng Xiaoke lici Sichuan yanzhengbu zhishu" 邓效可力辞四川盐政部职书 [Deng Xiaoke's Resignation Statement Toward Sichuan Ministry of Salt Affairs], in Jing Taobai 景本白, *Yanzheng geming shi* 盐政革命史 [History of the Salt Revolution] (Beijing: Salt Administration Magazine, 1929), Appendix, 11–23.

distribution of salt tax revenue and destroyed the basis of the official transport system. Under these circumstances, the opening up of free trade in the salterns only helped the warlords better squeeze the wealth from the salterns they controlled.

Thanks to their established networks, the merchants who benefited from the official transport system did not lose their advantages in salt trade when the system ceased. In 1915, the central government in Beijing temporarily took back control over the salt administration in Sichuan and tried to resurrect the previous syndicate system with designated ports and salt quotas. The assigned salt administration official, Yan Anlan 晏安澜, launched a project to mobilize large salt merchants to establish and register salt transportation companies.[17] The surviving thirteen dominant salt firms in Yong An responded to Yan's call and set up the Yongbian Salt Transporation Company to transport salt from Sichuan's salterns and run their wholesale businesses in Guizhou.[18] Unfortunately, only a year later, this company announced its closure because of the National Protection War, and the thirteen firms continued their business independently for a few years.[19] The short existence of Yongbian at least implied that the thirteen salt firms had overcome the difficulties of the regime change and kept their dominance in Yong An's salt trade, actively seeking a new mode to cooperate with salt administration officials.

The Hua Family also sustained its dominance in Ren An. Through participating in the salt reform, the Hua Family had already broadened its influence beyond the salt trade before the end of the official transport system. The second son of Hua Lianhui, Hua Zhihong 华之鸿, was the successor to his father in the family business and the core of the second generation. In addition to further expanding Yongchanglong, Hua Zhihong was sensitive to the changing political climate and actively involved in a series of institutional innovations during the last few years of the Qing Dynasty. He was selected as a member of Guizhou's Consultative Bureau (咨议局 *ziyiju*) and became the president of the chamber of commerce.[20] In 1909, together with two other local elites

[17] Yu Jie 余杰, "Yan Anlan yu Minguo chuqi Sichuan diqu de yanwu gaige" 晏安澜与民国初期四川地区的盐务改革 [Yan Anlan and Sichuan's Reform of Salt Administration in Early Period of Republic of China], *Salt Industry History Research*, no. 3 (2016): 64–69.

[18] Yang Tiren. "Yong An yanye yunxiao jiankuang," 56–57.

[19] Yang Tiren, "Yong An yanye yunxiao jiankuang," 56–57.

[20] Wang Fangjun, *Qingdai Guizhou yanshang yanjiu*, 63–64.

and constitutionalists, Ren Kecheng 任可澄 and Tang Eryong 唐尔镛, he founded a preliminary council for establishing a constitutionalist provincial government. After the 1911 revolution, all the principals in the preliminary council held key positions in the newly established military government in Guizhou; Hua Zhihong, no exception, became the executive of the financial department.[21] Despite facing the problems that every powerful merchant would encounter during this period, such as providing large amounts of money to fulfill the needs of the warlords,[22] Hua Zhihong's political participation helped him in the salt business. Yonglongyu survived during the Warlord Era, while the other two wholesale firms in Ren An, Xiexinglong 协兴隆 and Yishenglong 义盛隆, one owned by the major salt yard owner Li Siyou Tang 李四友堂 and the other jointly owned by Li Siyou Tang and Shaanxi merchants, closed around 1915.[23]

As the different destinies of the Hua Family and Li Siyou Tang suggest, it seems easier for local merchants to deal with the changing political environment during this period. Yong An's Shaanxi firms were struck by the arrest of their leading figure, Zhang Jicheng 张集诚. Zhang had overseen the Yongbian Salt Transportation Company and still dealt with the aftermath of its closure. In 1924, he was detained by a staff officer of Yang Sen 杨森, a warlord of the Sichuan Clique, for no discernible reason and was threatened with corporal punishment. After paying his own ransom and being freed, Zhang soon ceased his business in Yong An and went back to Shaanxi.[24] Zhang's encounter raised anxiety in other Shaanxi merchants regarding their business prospects and broke the monopoly of the alliance of thirteen wholesale firms.[25] At the same time, there were newcomers, normally from Guizhou or the border areas between

[21] Jian Zhen 鉴真, "Guizhou jindai jiechu de qiyejia Hua Zhihong" 贵州近代杰出的企业家华之鸿 [Hua Zhihong, an Outstanding Modern Entrepreneur in Guizhou], *Guizhou dang'an* 贵州档案 [Guizhou Archives], no. 2 (1996): 34–35; Wang Fangjun, *Qingdai Guizhou yanshang yanjiu*, 64.

[22] Hua Shuren mentioned that when the Yunnan Clique controlled Guiyang, the head of their army threatened to burn the city if local merchants did not provide enough money. Hua Zhihong was forced to hand over all the silver dollars stored at Yonglongyu and his private house. See Hua Shuren, "Yonglongyu yanhao shulue", 24.

[23] Wangfangjun, *Qingdai Guizhou yanshang yanjiu*, 62.

[24] Yang Tiren, "Yong An yanye yunxiao jiankuang," 59.

[25] Ibid.

Guizhou and Sichuan, appearing in the salt trade. In Piao'erjing 瓢儿井, the first important node after salt leaving Yong An's border port of Xuyong, there were eight major salt firms around 1900. Among them, the number of salt firms controlled by Guizhou merchants and salt firms controlled by Shaanxi merchants was equal.[26] The total number of salt firms increased to nineteen because of free trade, but only five firms were controlled by Shaanxi merchants during the early republican period.[27] To some extent, this change in the composition of salt merchants who had actual control of major firms can still be attributed to the bond of native place, as large wholesale firms had to keep good relations with warlords and their subordinates, who were normally natives of Guizhou or its neighboring provinces. The remaining Shaanxi merchants also had a close connection to Guizhou natives. Xi Shaoting 席绍庭 was one of the successful Shaanxi salt merchants during the Republican period. Xi was born into a peasant family. When he was thirteen, a famine struck his hometown and he left home to earn a living in Sichuan. He finished his apprenticeship at a salt firm named *Sanyigong* 三益公 in Xuyong,[28] then became the manager of another firm called Gonghecahng 公合长 in Piao'erjing.[29] During the early Republican period, Xi took over Gonghechang as a sole proprietor when the firm faced mismanagement.[30]

26 Mou Yongda 牟永达, "Zhuisu chuanyanye zai Dading Piao'erjing de bada yanhao qianhou" 追溯川盐业在大定瓢儿井的八大盐号前后 [Recollection of the Eight Great Salt Firms in Piao'erjing, Dading], in *Bijie wenshi ziliao xuanji*, no. 6 (1988): 122.

27 Mouyongda 牟永达, "Zhuisu chuanyanye zai Dading Piao'erjing de bada yanhao qianhou," 123.

28 Sources from Dading and Piao'erjing suggest Sanyigong was a Guizhou salt firm, belonging to a commander in the Sichuan Clique name Chen Huiwu 陈辉武 and his family. However, according to the information Yang Tiren provided on Yong An's thirteen major salt firms, Sanyigong was tagged as a Shannxi salt firm. Thus far, there is no clear explanation of this controversy in different sources, but it seems most likely that Xi got his apprenticeship through a network of Shaanxi natives. See Zhang xianqi 张先启, "Xi Shaoting zai Dading piao'erjing ji qita" 席绍庭在大定瓢井及其他 [Xi Shaoting in Dading Piaojing and other], *Dafang wenshi ziliao xuanji* 大方文史资料选辑 [Selection of Dafang Literature and History Materials], no. 6 (1991): 22; Yang Tiren, "Yong An yanye yunxiao jiankuang," 55; Mou Yongda 牟永达, "Zhuisu chuanyanye zai Dading Piao'erjing de bada yanhao qianhou," 122.

29 Zhang Xianqi, "Xi Shaoting zai Dading piao'erjing ji qita," 22.

30 Zhang Xianqi, "Xi Shaoting zai Dading piao'erjing ji qita," 22; Mou Yongda 牟永达, "Zhuisu chuanyanye zai Dading Piao'erjing de bada yanhao qianhou," 122.

Though Gonghechang is tagged as a Shaanxi salt firm in local historical sources, the firm also accepted investments from native merchants throughout its expansion. For example, Gonghechang's Anshun branch, also one of Anshun's four large firms, was owned jointly by Xi and Guizhou merchants. At the same time, Xi was also deeply involved in local social affairs, including a variety of charitable works, which gave him a high reputation in Piao'erjing. In 1921, recommended by Piao'erjing's local elites, he became the leader of the local armed forces and successfully resisted attacks by bandits. Xi's prestige in local society helped him to gain the trust of Zhou Xicheng 周西成 during Zhou's reform to reestablish the government's supervision of designated wholesalers in the salt trade, and it helped him keep his dominant position in Yong An until the central government regained control of salt tax collection in the southwestern provinces.[31]

Though how to evaluate Ding Baozhen's salt reform is controversial, Guizhou's local salt merchants no doubt benefited from this reform. It provided Guizhou merchants with access to the wholesale business and let them more easily build alliances with local administrators as well as political and military power at higher levels. The growing power of Guizhou salt merchants continued after the end of the Qing Dynasty. The unstable environment under warlords' control added risks and made it difficult for these merchants to further expand their businesses but, compared to non-locals, they had better chances of preserving the networks connecting their businesses to social and political resources in Guizhou and along their trade routes.

2 Bundled Wholesalers Under the Controlled Economy

After a series of negotiations with and exerting pressure on the warlords who had taken control of Guizhou, from 1935 to 1936, the central national government gradually regained effective control of the province and began to build Guizhou into a wartime rearguard. Accordingly, the

[31] Xi also was one of the major shareholders of another salt firm, Qianheyong 谦合永, which also became one of Yong An's major wholesale firms and participated in the merging of Yong An salt firms. See Liu Yuyuan 刘裕远, "Yong An de qianqianhouhou" 永岸的前前后后 [The Process of Founding Yong An], *Lixing yuekan* 励行月刊 [Lixing Monthly], 1 (1944): 11; Yang Tiren, "Yong An yanye yunxiao jiankuang," 68.

wartime pattern of increasing state control over the salt trade began to take its shape in Guizhou. In 1936, in the name of preventing profiteering and maintaining a reasonably priced salt supply for the public, the General Salt Administration Bureau of the Ministry of Finance began to regain control over salt merchants and how salt was transported and distributed in Guizhou. The major wholesalers in the four border ports were assigned fixed salt quotas every month. They were required to register with the government and follow delineated transport routes to the designated sales areas. Under this new system, the wholesaler was responsible for transporting the salt into Guizhou and ensuring the salt they transported and distributed could cover the daily needs of their designated sales areas. This was much like the syndicate system during the Qing Dynasty. However, the national government also brought in new measures to strengthen its control as much as possible.

Miao Qiujie 缪秋杰 was the Salt Distribution Commissioner of Sichuan during the late 1930s and became the head of the General Bureau of Salt Administration in 1940. He was one of the major salt technocrats who proposed a plan to organize the border wholesalers and distributors through registration and under the supervision of salt administrative authorities.[32] In his report on the transportation and distribution of Sichuan salt in Guizhou, he claimed that through establishing a united operation organization of salt merchants, shortcomings, such as excessive competition and insufficient capitalization, in Guizhou's salt market could be effectively overcome.[33] Compared to the plans of his predecessors in the late Qing and the Warlords eras, Ding Baozhen and Yan Anlan, Miao's design further strengthened the states' control over the salt trade in two aspects. Whether Ding's or Yan's, their plans focused on ensuring tax collection by controlling the shipment from salterns to border ports, while only loosely regulating how salt was distributed in Guizhou. Miao, with the backing of the central government, began to bring distribution under better control. In Miao's report, he also suggested that branches of the government-approved wholesalers organization should be set up

[32] Li Han 李函 et al., *Miao Qiujie yu minguo yanwu* 缪秋杰与民国盐务 [Miao Qiujie and the Salt Affairs of the Republic of China] (Beijing: China Science and Technology Press, 1990): 140–111.

[33] Miao Qiujie 缪秋杰, "Kaocha chuanyan xingxiao qian an qingxing baogaoshu" 考察川盐行销黔岸情形报告书 [Inestigation Report on Sales of Sichuan Salt to Guizhou], *Yanwu gongbao* 盐务公报 [Salt Bulletin], 1 (1937): 110–111.

in every important center along the trade routes, just as salt firms set up their branches.[34] Miao only provided a vague blueprint for how the salt merchants in each port were to be organized; however, when the new salt administration policy came into effect, this became a more significant difference. The new system required wholesalers to merge into one organization in every border port. That is to say, one border port and the related market only had one organization conducting wholesale business and those who were reluctant to participate in such mergers were not allowed to run salt wholesale businesses of their own. Officially, the organization was called the Joint Trade Office (联合营业处 *lianhe yingyechu*) or the Transport and Distribution Office (运销处 *yunxiaochu*).

In 1941, such an organization in Yong An submitted a charter written by its board of directors to the salt administration department in Guizhou at that time, the Guizhou Salt Administration Bureau (贵州盐务局 *guizhou yanwuju*).[35] This charter includes the composition of the share capital, the subscription method, and information regarding branch offices, showing how the whole organization worked. The charter shows that besides the headquarters in Guiyang, Yong An had branches in Xuyong 叙永, Anshun 安顺, Dading 大定, Bijie 毕节, and Piao'erjing 瓢儿井, subbranches in Weining 威宁 and Shuicheng 水城, and transit stations in Moni 磨尼, Zhijin 织金, and Jichang 鸡场.[36] All the directors on the board were heads of major wholesale salt firms. This board was responsible for reviewing the budgets and accounts as well as approving the staff hired by branch offices.[37] Though evidence shows that the names of each salt firm were still recorded as late as the early 1940s,[38] the charter implies that officially the wholesalers no longer did business using the names of their own salt firms but had to do so in the name of this organization. In many ways, the salt wholesalers did not organize a

[34] Ibid.

[35] "Yong An chuanyan yunxiaoshang gudong dongshihui zhangcheng" 永岸川盐运销商股东董事会章程 [Charter of the Board of Directors of Yong'an Chuan Salt Transporter], July 23,1941, in Si'an yunxiaoshang zai gedi chengli banshichu ji peixiao wenjian 四岸运销商在各地成立办事处及配销文件 [Documents of distributors in four border ports setting up offices in various places and distribution of salt], volume 2, M41-1-3492, Guizhou Provincial Archives.

[36] Ibid.

[37] Ibid.

[38] Yang Tiren, "Yong An yanye yunxiao jiankuang," 118–119.

trade association but were forced to merge into a larger salt firm. Yong An's organization was called the Yong An Salt Firm by the merchants themselves. This also explains why this policy of compulsory merger was commonly known as One Firm for One Port (一岸一商 *yi an yi shang*). In Guizhou, the merchants also used the phrase "bundling merchants together" (捆商 *kunshang*) to refer to the new government-monitored trading mode.

For merchants, these compulsory mergers brought more troubles than benefits. While wholesalers were roughly divided according to the border port where they imported salt from neighboring provinces, merchants in a certain port could be further divided if they controlled different trade routes and had different business networks. Take Yong An, for example: though all the merchants transported salt from Qianwei or Furong Saltern via Xuyong, the merchants following routes to Bijie and the merchants following routes to Piao'erjing could be further divided into two groups with separate markets. During the first few years after the founding of Yong An Salt Firm, the difference between Bijie Group, or Bi Group for short, and Piao'erjing Group, or Jing Group for short, still existed and those two groups had conflicts around how Yong An Salt Firm should work, especially on how to merge their money.[39] Yong An was lucky that these two groups successfully adjusted their structures and maintained relatively stable business as a unified organization after years of struggles.[40] The wholesalers' organizations in other ports faced serious operational problems when they entered the 1940s. Qi An's unified trade office consisted of 28 salt firms, which were further divided into four groups. By October 1939, ten salt firms had quit and the remaining eighteen had divided into five groups. Then, in September 1940, eight salt firms including Xietongyong 协同永, Hekang 和康, Liqun 利群, Dechang 德昌, Fuyuanchang 富源长, Dingsheng 鼎盛, Shenglong 盛隆, and Lihe 利和, split from the organization but continued to do business. In April 1941, the rest of the salt firms and the Guizhou Salt Administration Bureau compromised, breaking the rule of One Firm in One Port. As a result, Qi An had two parallel wholesalers' organizations, each

[39] Yang Tiren, "Yong An yanye yunxiao jiankuang," 71–72; Liu Yuyuan, "Yong An de qianqianhouhou," 10–11.

[40] The charter mentioned above is one of the results of the reorganization in Yong An. Also see Yang Tiren, "Yong An yanye yunxiao jiankuang," 71–72; Liu Yuyuan, "Yong An de qianqianhouhou," 10–11.

with its own salt quota. The ten remaining salt firms reorganized as the First Trade Office of Qi An Sichuan Salt Transport and Sales (綦岸川盐运销第一营业处 *Qi An Chuanyan Yunxiao Diyi Yingyechu*), and the eight previously mentioned salt firms that split off made up the Second Office.[41]

In addition to the compulsory mergers, the tightly controlled profits in this period may have also left merchants feeling bundled. After salt trade became supervised by the government, the selling price of salt had to be approved by the local authority and announced to the public. According to a report on Guizhou's salt administration in 1939, made by the Guizhou Salt Administration Bureau, the net income per market *dan* (市担) was fixed to 2 *jiao* (角) at that time, and all the costs included in the selling price were reviewed by the local authority.[42] The next year, as rising costs[43] added to business difficulties, the registered wholesalers of all the four ports appealed to the General Salt Administration Bureau. They not only asked for a new increased selling price, but also requested a shortened interval for price changes and asked for government support on bank loans.[44] Some of their requests were fulfilled, but more were left waiting for approval from the General Salt Administration Bureau.

Though negotiations between registered wholesalers and the Guizhou Salt Administration Bureau imply that the wholesalers still had some leverage, the bargaining power of merchants was very limited. From the nationalist authorities' perspective, on the one hand, centralized control was necessary to stabilize salt prices and ensure the salt supply during the war, but complete nationalization would be very costly; on the other

[41] Information about the changes of the wholesalers' organization in Qi An is based on Guizhou Provincial Archives ed., *Guizhou shehui zuzhi gailan: 1911–1949* 贵州社会组织概览: 1911—1949 [An Overview of Social Organizations in Guizhou: 1911–1949] (Guiyang: Guizhou People's Press, 1996): 165–166.

[42] *Bensheng ershiba nian yanwu gaikuang* 本省盐务概况 [General situation of salt affairs in this province], July 27 1937, M41-1-8, Guizhou Provincial Archives, 13.

[43] When the national government lost its control of the salterns in the east, Sichuan salt's supply area was broadened. As the production capacity of the salterns could not meet the rising demand, the cost of salt itself rose rapidly during this period. The cost of salt also increased as the war strained manpower and resources. See Ren, "Qi, Fu, Yong si an gongyu kunnan yuqing jiuji gexiang jielue" 仁綦涪永四岸共遇困难吁请救济各项节略 [Petition from four border ports on seeking remedies of shared difficulties), 043-01-0319, Guiyang Municipal Archives.

[44] Ibid.

hand, salt taxes still occupied a key position in terms of fiscal revenue.[45] Consequently, salt wholesalers were significant taxpayers and collaborators in the transportation and distribution of salt, but also subjects for assigning tasks to and squeezing wealth out of. In 1941, to cope with rising prices and inflation, the assessment method of salt taxes was changed from taxation by weight (从量计征 *congliang jizheng*) to taxation by value (从价计征 *congjia jizheng*).[46] After this new assessment method came into effect, the average rate of salt taxes increased drastically.[47] The rise of salt taxes, along with the rising costs of doing business in the salt trade, led to a series of bankruptcies among merchants before a stricter state-run monopoly on salt was implemented in 1942. The Hua family's Yonglongyu in Ren An, which had changed its name to Dingshengheng 鼎升恒, also stopped doing business during this period.[48] When the authority began to nominally take over transportation and wholesale, many more of the remaining merchants chose to quit, as the only way they could continue was to become agents of the government, which would lead to more financial burdens and more government oversight.[49] For those who continued the wholesale business as agents of the government, they not only had to cope with the deterioration of the wartime situation but also faced new competitors such as Daye Trading Company (大业贸易公司 Daye Maoyi Gongsi), which was the government's new collaborator when it came to salt transportation and distribution in Guizhou. Guizhou's local salt merchants believed that, having links with the Shanghai Commercial and Savings Bank, Daye

[45] Man Bun Kwan, "Salt Wars," in Brett Sheehan and Wen-hsin Yeh eds., *Living and Working in Wartime China* (Honolulu: University of Hawaii Press, 2022): 196–198.

[46] State Taxation Administraion ed., *Zhonghua minguo gongshang shuishou shi: yanshui juan* 中华民国工商税收史:盐税卷 [History of Industrial and Commercial Taxation in the Republic of China: Salt Tax] (Beijing: China Financial and Economic Press, 1999): 196–197; Kwan, "Salt Wars," 199.

[47] Ibid.

[48] Hua Shuren, "Yonglongyu yanhao shulue," 19–26.

[49] "Guizhou yanwu guanlichu Li Qinggao zai Guizhou canyihui chengli dahui shang de baogao" 贵州盐务管理处李庆高在贵州参议会成立大会上的报告 [Report by Li Qinggao of Guizhou Salt Administration Office at the Inaugural Meeting of Guizhou Provincial Council], April 25, 1946, in *Sanshisi nian yanwu gaikuang* 三十四年盐务概况 [General Situation of Salt Affairs in the 34th Years of the Republic of China], M41-1–99, Guizhou Provincial Archives.

Company was backed by the well-capitalized Zhejiang and Jiangsu plutocrats and high-ranking central government officials such as H.H. Kung, and this put local merchants at a disadvantage.[50]

It seemed very unwise to continue operating in the salt trade under such circumstances, but there were still some Guizhou wholesalers reluctant to retreat. When the anti-Japanese war ended, Yong An's and the majority of Ren An's designated sales areas were still controlled by Guizhou merchants. One main reason for this might have been expectations of post-war business. According to complaints from salt wholesalers on the free trade policy after the anti-Japanese War ended, the nationalist government had promised to grant them franchise rights once the wartime state monopoly measures were no longer needed. Salt merchants emphasized the hardship they experienced and the efforts they made during wartime to demonstrate their contribution to the nation and urged the government to keep its word.[51] On the other hand, despite the strict monopoly measures and the market upheaval during wartime, the salt trade was still an effective way for merchants to reinforce political ties and get access to other resources. The rise of the Hua family in the salt trade also brought fame and prosperity to local distilled liquor manufacturers in Maotai, a town south of the border port of Ren An. Through Hua Zhihong's promotion, Maotai Liquor earned fame among military and political dignitaries in Guizhou.[52] During wartime, Maotai liquor was popular and a luxury gift choice among the upper class. Wu Xiaogao 伍效高, who was one of the leading merchants in Ren An during the

[50] Wu Xiaogao 伍效高, "Guizhou shiyan yunxiao de huiyi" 贵州食盐运销的回忆 (Memories of Salt Business in Guizhou), in *Guizhou wenshi ziliao xuanji* 贵州文史资料选辑 [Selected Materials of Guizhou Literature and History], no. 17 (1984): 209; Wu Luqin 吴鲁钦, "Jiefangqian Guizhou yunxiao chuanyan gaikuang" 解放前贵州运销川盐概况 [General Situation of Sichuan Salt Transportation and Sale in Guizhou Before Liberation], *Guizhou wenshi ziliao xuanji*, no.3 (1979):149.

[51] Wu Xiaogao, "Qianyan jinshinian zhi yange" 黔盐近十年来之沿革 (Salt Business in Guizhou in the Past Ten Years), *Lixing yueka* 2, no. 1 (1946): 25–26; Wang Zixuan 王子宣, "Shiyan tongzhi yu ziyou" 食盐统制与自由 (Salt Control and Freedom), *Lixing yuekan* 2, no. 2 (1946): 22–23; Ha Zhongying 哈钟英, "Qianyan tongzhishang zai kangzhan qijian suojin zhi yiwu" 黔盐统制商在抗战期间所尽之义务 (The Obligations of the Guizhou Salt Merchants During the Anti-Japanese War), *Lixing yuekan*, 1 (1944): 11.

[52] Guo Zijian, 郭子健, "Jindai zhongguo maotaijiu pinpai de yanjin" 近代中国"茅台酒"品牌的演进 (Evolution of the "Maotai" Liqour Brand in Modern China), *Modern Chinese History Studies* 1 (2022): 83–85.

1940s, mentions in his recollection of the salt business that hundreds of bottles of Maotai liquor were bought by Ren An's salt firm to please the salt administration bureaucrats and celebrities in Sichuan's salt yards and in Chongqing—a form of temporary capital during wartime.[53] This implies that Guizhou's salt merchants were still closely linked with Maotai Liquor's production and distribution even after the Hua family's salt business declined.

For the survivors of the turbulent Warlord Era, the return of the central government did not provide a better environment to further expand their salt businesses. The One Firm for One Port Policy changed the established mode of salt trade and forced salt merchants to rearrange their resources and cooperate with new partners. The state monopoly, with its strict designated salt quotas, met wartime needs; however, under this system, keeping salt supplies stable and salt prices reasonable became not only a moral obligation for salt merchants but also a duty assigned by the government.

3 The Control of Retail and Empowerment of Local Government

Compared with wholesalers, local distributors and retailers received less attention from the salt administration, as they were more scattered. However, in the name of preventing profiteering and maintaining wartime salt supplies, the nationalist government also began to take measures to control the retail end of things. In 1940, two regional regulations targeting salt retail in Guizhou were promulgated: the Rules of Guizhou Salt Shop Management (贵州区盐店管理规则 *Guizhou yandian guanli guize*) and Provisional Regulations of Guizhui Wartime Supervision Committee of Salt Distribution (贵州区各县战时食盐监销委员会暂行章程 *Guizhou gexian zhanshi shiyan jianxiao weiyuanhui zanxing zhangcheng*).

These two new rules were part of the national government's plan for salt rationing, piloted in the Sichuan market from 1939, but they also addressed the anxiety and distrust of the provincial salt authority

[53] Wu Xiaogao, "Guizhou shiyan yunxiao de huiyi", 215.

toward established salt networks.[54] Since the officially approved wholesalers normally only set up their branches and warehouses in regional trading centers in their designated areas, consumers outside these trade centers had to rely on local distributors to further transport and sell salt. In a report written before these two rules were promulgated, provincial salt administrators expressed concern about the difficulties itinerant peddlers and residents faced in buying directly from the bundled wholesalers on account of the alliances between wholesalers and large local distributors.[55] According to the report, most of the wholesalers' salt was being reserved for the large local distributors who tended to open salt shops close to the wholesalers' branches. These distributors then resold the salt and earned the difference in price, which led to a situation where most itinerant peddlers and residents could only buy at a price much higher than the official one.[56] Conceivably, the end customers outside trading centers would face a much higher salt price. The provincial officials saw this as a proof of the need for stronger overall coordination and surveillance by the government, and they decided to issue purchase permits to registered itinerant peddlers and other consumers to break the integration of wholesalers and large local retailers and re-orient salt distribution.[57]

The Rules of Guizhou Salt Shop Management focused on registration. The mandatory registration of salt shops had been practiced in other areas before, but Guizhou's salt shop registration rules were broadened to include peddlers and established much stricter trading requirements. According to the registration rules, legitimate salt retail shops could only sell salt to end consumers, and the geographical scope of their business was restricted to one county.[58] All retailers, including merchants

[54] Reference Room of the General Salt Administration Bureau of the Ministry of Finance ed., *Zhongguo yanzheng shilu* 中国盐政实录 [Records of China's Salt Administration], vol. 1 (1948), "Guizhou", 2.

[55] *Bensheng yanwu gaikuang* 本省盐务概况 [General situation of Salt Affairs in this Province], M41-1–8, Guizhou Provincial Archives.

[56] Ibid.

[57] Ibid.

[58] "Liangzhe guangxinqu yandian guanli guize" 两浙广信区盐店管理规则 [Management Rules for Salt Shops in, Guangxin District, Zhejiang and Jiangxi], *Yanwu Gongbao* 2 (1937): "Regulations", 1–3; "Su wushu yandian guanli guize" 苏五属盐店管理规则 [Management Rules for Salt Shops of the Five districts of Jiangsu], *Faling zhoukan*

with retail stores and peddlers with stalls, had to apply for endorsement from local government and use this endorsement to register with the salt authorities.[59] After registration, the retailers would get their purchase permits to legally buy salt from designated wholesale branches based on the rations of their sales area.[60] These rules defined how rationing was implemented and drew a clear line between wholesalers and retailers with enhanced government oversight. Accordingly, the supervision committee, a new county-level institution for reducing the workload of salt authorities and enhancing county-level salt administration, was created. As the provisional regulation of the supervision committee planned, it was set up in a county where no salt authority resided. It could be involved in any county-level salt administration, including applying for business licenses and purchase permits from a salt authority, setting the ration and retail price for the county, assigning retailers salt transport certificates, and investigating violations of salt regulations.[61] According to the regulation, the committee was composed of seven members, including one member from the county government, one from the county's nationalist party headquarters, one from the county-level party financial committee, and four local elites who had not been involved in the salt business before.[62] The regulation also required that the four local elites should be chosen by the county administrator.[63] Apparently, this new institution further encouraged the county government to exert its power in the salt trade.

Supported by the rationing of salt and related regulations, the county government began to proactively exercise its authority. Zhenfeng 贞丰 County is located near the southeastern border between Guizhou,

法令周刊 [Law Weekly], 350 (1937): "Regulations", 4–5; "Guizhouqu yandian guanli guize" 贵州区盐店管理规则 [The Rules of Guizhou Salt Shop Management], Caizhengbu faling zhangze huibian 财政部法令章则汇编 [Compilation of Ministry of Finance Acts and Regulations]: "Salt", 33.

59 "Guizhouqu yandian guanli guize," 33.

60 "Guizhouqu yandian guanli guize," 33–34.

61 "Guizhouqu gexian zhanshi shiyan jianxiao weiyuanhui zanxing zhangcheng" 贵州区各县战时食盐监销委员会暂行章程 [Provisional Regulations of Guizhui Wartime Supervision Committee of Salt Distribution], Zhonghua minguo fagui jiyao 中华民国法规辑要 [Collection of the Laws and Regulations of the Republic of China], Book 3 (1941): 255–256.

62 Ibid.

63 Ibid.

Yunnan, and Guangxi. During the first few years of the nationalist government's reconstruction of Guizhou's administration, it was left as an unregulated area, and no registered wholesalers had set up branches or transfer stations there. As a result, Zhenfeng's salt supply depended on distributors who brought salt from the nearest wholesaler's branch in Guizhou or transported it from Yunnan.[64] After the nationalist government began to implement salt rationing in Guizhou in 1939, Zhenfeng's local government made a series of efforts to get approval from the provincial administration bureau for a settled salt quota in Yong An's transportation and distribution system and to mobilize local merchants to take on the transportation and distribution of salt. In 1939, Zhenfeng County Government proposed to establish a local organization called the Zhenfeng Salt Distribution Management Office (贞丰食盐经销管理处 *Zhenfeng Shiyan Jingxiao Guanlichu*). Perhaps inspired by the organization of bundled wholesalers, though by name it looked like a governing body, according to the county government's plan, it was in fact a joint-stock firm initiated and supervised by the government calling merchants to subscribe shares.[65] This organization would be responsible for buying salt from wholesale branches in nearby areas such as Anshun and Piao'erjing.[66]

For a county at the periphery of Guizhou's salt monopoly system like Zhenfeng, proactive government involvement helped to guarantee a settled salt quota that could fulfill the daily needs of residents. However, for the county government, there may have been additional motives beyond assuring people's livelihoods and achieving a task assigned by its superiors. After the two new regulations on salt retail were promulgated, Zhenfeng County Government wrote an official letter to the provincial salt administration bureau, complaining of the difficulty of mobilizing local merchants to form a local retail institution.[67] It could be inferred

[64] Letter from Zhenfeng County Government, November 8, 1941 and Zhenfeng County Salt Distribution Management Measures, August 9, 1939, M41-1-3041, Guizhou Provincial Archives.

[65] Zhenfeng County Salt Distribution Management Measures, August, 1939, M41-1-3041, Guizhou Provincial Archives.

[66] Ibid.

[67] Letter from Zhenfeng County Government, November 8, 1941 and Zhenfeng County Salt Distribution Management Measures, August 9, 1939, M41-1-3041, Guizhou Provincial Archives.

from this letter that the management office mentioned above had never been successfully established. At the same time, following the new regulations, Zhenfeng had its supervision committee and began to perform its regulatory duties.[68] Later, when the central government began to implement monopoly shops, retail shops with more meticulous regulatory registration procedures which were part of the nationalization of the salt industry,[69] Zhenfeng County's supervision committee and the county government also actively echoed the higher authority, selecting a local gentry named Tan Qinong 谭岂农 as the organizer of the county's monopoly shop. Tan soon declined the assignment and left the county with the excuse of personal matters. The county government then had to select another organizer, a local merchant called Ran Xinkui 冉鑫奎, to raise funds for opening the county's monopoly shop and transporting salt from the branch office of the Salt Transportation and Distribution Bureau in Anshun. While local merchants and other social elites lacked interest in handling salt retail, there were outside merchants who tried to do retail business in Zhenfeng, creating tensions with the local government. In the official letter mentioned above, Zhenfeng County Government admitted that when the local government failed to mobilize local merchants to form a local retail organization, free trade still existed in Zhenfeng and provided salt to its residents. However, they blamed the main salt supplier in Zhenfeng at that time, merchants from Panxian County, for opening salt shops in Zhenfeng without contacting the local government and thus encouraging high salt prices and smuggling with their profit-driven business style. The county government's difficulty in finding an ideal group of salt merchants to be its agent suggests that it may have placed more importance on maintaining its dominance over salt supply than on building a reasonable retail system for its residents.

The changes among salt retailers in Hezhang 赫章 county followed a similar trend. Salt in Hezhang had long been supplied by itinerant

[68] Ibid.

[69] Yang Tiren, "Yong An yanye yunxiao jiankuang," 109; about the monopoly shop, see Yang Xingqin 杨兴勤, *Zhongguo zhanshi yanwu wenti* 中国战时盐务问题 [China's Wartime Salt Issues] (Chongqing: National Press, 1943); Yang Ting 杨亭, "Shiyan gongmaidian:Kangrizhanzheng shiqi guojia tongzhi de jicing shishi" 食盐公卖店:抗日战争时期国家统制的基层实施 [The Salt Monopoly Shops: the Practice of National Monopoly at the Grass-roots Level During the War of Resistance], *Guizhou wenshi congkan* 贵州文史丛刊 [Guizhou Literature and History Series], 62–68.

peddlers before the Sichuan-Yunnan highway improved the transportation conditions between Hezhang and Bijie. In 1940, with registration documents approved by the Bijie Salt Administration Bureau, three merchants from Bijie opened the first salt shop in Hezhang in a town called Yemachuan 野马川.[70] Then, in the same year, local merchant Liu Yongzhang opened a salt monopoly shop in the county, which implies that this shop was approved by Hezhang County Government. The next year, two of the three Bijie merchants left, and the remaining one, Wang Zhuqing 王竹清, began to cooperate with a local merchant of Yemachuan named Mao Junhui. One year later, Wang also left Hezhang, and Mao found another local business partner, Wei Long.[71] In 1943, Yemachuan's salt monopoly shop got three new shareholders, one from Bijie and two from another town in Hezhang called Pingshanbao 平山堡.[72] The shareholder from Bijie, Wu Junguang 吴俊光, owned half of the shares but was not involved in the local operation, leaving his partners, the Hezhang natives, to handle salt retail in Hezhang and deal with local authorities.[73]

The preference for local merchants in salt retail at the county level and below encouraged more local businessmen to participate in the salt industry and avoid the vertically integrated monopoly of large merchants. However, it was also impossible to ignore how the rising power of local government over salt administration and the lack of limits on its abusive power encouraged local officials to intervene in the salt trade. Local authorities were usually not impartial arbitrators when they had the power to issue purchase permits, examine and approve registration applications, and endorse purchase receipts in legitimate salt transactions. They could only offer facilitation, such as purchase permits or support to open salt shops, to their favored merchants. As a result, wholesalers and distributors at every level had to maintain good relationships with the local government if they wanted to do business smoothly, which led to prevalent bribery. A recollection of salt distribution in Shuicheng County mentions that under the wartime salt monopoly system, the wholesale station in

[70] Long Xianliang 龙宪良 and Xu Renfang 徐仁芳, "Jiefangqian Hezhang shiyan de gouxiao gaikuang" 解放前赫章食盐的购销概况 [General Situation of Salt Trade in Hezhang Before Liberation], *Bijie wenshi ziliao xuanji*, no. 6 (1988): 137.

[71] Ibid.

[72] Ibid.

[73] Ibid.

Shuicheng had to provide one hundred dan of salt to the county government and one hundred dan to the county party headquarters as a bribe every month. The salt would be recorded at the official price in the official accounts but would be redistributed to the black market and sold at a higher price, bringing profit to the local administrative and party officials.[74] A similar operation also took place between salt suppliers in the towns and villages within Shuicheng County.[75] According to estimates, around 30% of Shuicheng's salt quota flowed into the black market in this way and about half of the remaining 70% was sold on black market directly by the officially approved wholesalers or retailers, which means that only 35% of salt was sold at the official price.[76] Accordingly, the cost was passed on to the end consumers.

In the name of balancing wartime salt supplies and fulfilling people's daily needs, the strengthened control of salt retail relied heavily on county officials to govern distribution. Accordingly, actors at the country level and below gradually developed their own distribution networks, with the county governments as their dominant powers. Compared with outside merchants, locals more easily kept contact with local officials, so the increased control of salt retail supported more local merchants stepping into the salt business. As these county-level distribution networks might be incongruous with the already established alliances between wholesalers and distributors and created barriers for top-down integration from the dominant wholesalers, this kind of local merchants-authority alliances had achieved the goals of their business pursuits. However, the strengthened control of retail did not effectively reduce salt hoarding and smuggling. Salt was still siphoned from official channels, but the recipients were now governmental unread business partners.

[74] "Jiefangqian shuicheng chuanyan gouxiao jiankuang," the Literature and History Committee of Shuicheng Special District CPPCC 解放前水城川盐购销简况 [Brief Introduction of Shuicheng Salt Trade Before Liberation], *Bijie wenshi ziliao xuanji*, no. 6 (1988): 173.

[75] Ibid.

[76] Ibid.

4 Conclusion

The rise of Guizhou natives in the province's salt trade occurred under very specific conditions. The late Qing reformer of Sichuan salt production and distribution was coincidentally a Guizhou native, and the social instability of the time had weakened more powerful merchant groups. However, once benefiting from the new policies, Guizhou salt merchants quickly gained acumen and overcame the difficulties of the Warlord Era. When the central government regained control over Guizhou, local merchants may no longer have been favored, but the government still had to rely on their established transportation and distribution networks to maintain salt supplies and earn tax revenue during wartime. The wartime monopoly policy implemented in Guizhou did not directly prevent local merchants from running the salt trade, but tactfully inserted administrative power into their networks. The One Firm for One Port policy restricted the form of wholesalers' operations while empowering local government to control how salt could be distributed. The number of Guizhou natives who participated in Guizhou's salt trade may not have decreased, but their integration and alliances were not encouraged by the monopoly system.

CHAPTER 4

The Early Tobacco Industry in Guiding: Prosperity and Decline

Zhao Zhou and Haoqi Meng

After the outbreak of the Second Sino-Japanese War, Guizhou Province was expected to become an important economic hub in the Chinese interior. To accomplish this, the government fostered the development of agriculture, industry, and commerce. This not only drove the cultivation of new types of tobacco but also changed the structure and scale of the tobacco industry in Guizhou. Instead of primarily processing product for the local market as it had in the past, Guizhou became an important national cigarette production base, planting, processing, and exporting tobacco.

In 1938, the government-backed Guizhou Enterprise Company, together with the Guizhou Provincial Agricultural Improvement Institute,[1] introduced American flue-cured tobacco to Guiding and surrounding areas. This region eventually became the tobacco planting and processing center of Guizhou. At its height, over forty-five cigarette factories, such as Jiuda 久大, Hengxing 恒兴, Huaxiang 华湘, Jianchang 建昌, Xinqian 新黔, and Daxia 大夏, were found in Guiding

[1] Yang Runan 杨汝南 and Hu Rengtong 胡礽同, Guizhou nongzuowu zhi gaijin 贵州省农作物之改进 [Improvement of Crops in Guizhou Province], in *Guizhousheng nongye gaijinsuo* 贵州省农业改进所 [Guizhou Agricultural Improvement Institute] ed. Jiang Guosheng 蒋国生. (Guiyang: Guizhou People's Press, 2006, 539–557).

B. Jiang et al., *State, Market and Salt-Tobacco Road in Modern China (1935–1949)*, https://doi.org/10.1007/978-981-97-7654-2_4

County.[2] Since 1942, the tobacco industry in Guiding has undergone major changes. The planting, processing, and transportation of American tobacco has been included in the tobacco monopoly by the Ministry of Finance[3] and was initially managed by the Guizhou District Tobacco Monopoly Bureau of the Ministry of Finance. Later, it became managed by the Guiding Branch of the Yunnan-Guizhou District Commodity Taxation Bureau and the Guiding Branch of the Yunnan-Guizhou District Direct Taxation Bureau. According to the monopoly policy, all factories engaged in cigarette production are required to register with the monopoly authority and the tax authority. Those who cut tobacco and transport tobacco products must register with the Commodity Tax Bureau and are subject to audits, cost investigations, and requests for sales statistics. In this way, the monopoly authority can levy taxation and fully supervise tobacco production, transportation, and sales.[4]

The introduction and diffusion of American flue-cured tobacco has dramatically influenced the traditional tobacco industry that formed in Guiding during the Jiaqing and Daoguang periods of the Qing Dynasty. In the past, the tobacco business was mainly run by immigrants from Fujian Province and Guangdong Province[5] and typically served the local market. After the introduction of American flue-cured tobacco, merchants from Hunan Province[6] came with skills and capital, setting up new cigarette factories and starting to sell cigarettes to Hunan, Guangxi,

[2] "Organize according to "industry association membership survey statistics", Guiyang Chamber of Commerce Archives in the Republic of China, M43-1-926, Guiyang Municipal Archives, and "Guiding Bureau Guiding County Cigarette Household Survey Form", "Survey Form of Smokers in Guizhou Province", 64. Yunnan-Guizhou District Goods Tax Bureau in the Republic of China, M43-1-10, Guizhou Provincial Archives.

[3] *Guizhou caijing ziliao huibian* 贵州财经资料汇编 [Guizhou Financial Data Compilation], Chapter 1, "*Shenxian caizheng shouzhi qingkuang*" 省县财政收支情况 [Provincial and County Fiscal Revenue and Expenditure], 373, ed. Guizhou Provincial Finance and Economics Commission, 1950, Internal Information.

[4] Measures for the Control of Smoked Tobacco Leaves of the Guiding Office of the Tobacco Monopoly Bureau of the Ministry of Finance, M60-1-8096 Guiding tobacco distribution case, Archives of the Guizhou Provincial Department of during the Republic of China in the Guizhou Provincial Archives, 13.

[5] Duan Zhaoao 段兆鳌 ed., *Guiding Xianzhi gao* 贵定县志稿 [Draft of Gazetteer of Guiding County] (Guiyang: Guizhou People's Press, 2018).

[6] Members of the Guiding County Cigarette Industry Association in the 37th year of the Republic of China, 0-12-12 Guiding County Chamber of Commerce, Guiding County Archives, 15.

and Chongqing. At the same time, the huge potential for profits also drove local merchants to actively participate in various activities such as tobacco purchasing, primary processing, and shredding. Moreover, it attracted other non-local merchants, including salt merchants, to set up factories in Guiyang and offices in Guiding to purchase tobacco and produce cigarettes.[7] These developments, along with the introduction of the tobacco monopoly system, have brought a host of interactions and contradictions among the state, merchants, and localities.

In this chapter, we will describe the development of the tobacco industry in Guiding since the Jiaqing and Daoguang periods of the Qing Dynasty. We will focus on the period after the introduction of American flue-cured tobacco and the management of the tobacco monopoly, exploring the interactions and tensions between the state, merchants, and locals in the process. Especially, we will examine how these actors formed an interest community that enabled the successful diffusion and industrialization of tobacco technology in Guizhou. This chapter is divided into three parts: the first part introduces the early diffusion of tobacco in Guizhou and the development of Guiding's early tobacco industry; the second part describes how Guiding became the center of American flue-cured tobacco planting, processing, distribution, and marketing in Guizhou, as well as the evolution of the tobacco monopoly and registration management system; the third part analyzes the roles of, and interactions between, Guiding's evolving tobacco technology, merchants, and local government, and points out that the successful technological diffusion and industrial development depends on the formation of a state-locality-merchant interest community.

[7] Guiding Branch of the Bank of Guizhou handles money order for purchasing tobacco at Hankou Branch of Guiyang Nanming Tobacco Factory, 0-14-46 Guiding Branch of the Bank of Guizhou. Guiding County Archives.

1 The Early Tobacco Industry in Guiding: Prosperity and Decline

1.1 *The Introduction of Tobacco and the Formation of a Tobacco Planting-Processing Center in Guiding*

Although it is not the earliest county in Guizhou with records of tobacco products being made,[8] Guiding is the earliest county with clear records of a tobacco industry. The third issue of "Draft of Gazetteer of Guiding County" (贵定县志稿 *Guiding xianzhigao*) documents the development of the tobacco industry[9] in Guiding County in detail: "People from Fujian Province and Guangxi Province moved and settled down here, advocated growing tobacco locally. Later, more people joined... Silk tobacco was made and packed into ten dendrobium packs and sold to the towns of Xiasi 下司 and Guzhou 古州[10] in the Daoguang[11] period, Qing Dynasty." According to the Guizhou Tobacco Research Institute, the tobacco strains grown in this period were derived from the Nicotiona species (红花烟草 *honghua yancao*) imported from North America via the Philippines.[12] The mainstream tobacco processing method was to dry the tobacco leaves in the sun, resulting in a dark brown, robe-shaped product. Since there was no standard for the number of days and intensity of sun exposure, the taste of tobacco produced in various locations was diverse

[8] "The earliest tobacco record recorded in "Guizhou Tobacco Chronicles" is the manuscript of Qianlong's "Yuping County Chronicles". But after comparing the original text, we found that it is "烟" instead of "菸", so it is not necessary to use it in doubt. Similarly, in the fourth year of Daoguang's "Songtaoting Zhi", Volume 14. Wuchan also has a record of "tobacco", But the original text is "烟草" instead of "菸草", so there are doubts. The earliest record of tobacco planting is Qing Daoguang's "Sinanfu Continued Chronicles", Volume 3, Food and Local Products, page 82, "Grass" and "Tobacco", "Fengxiangxi Hepengxi The taste of the producer is strong, and the inhalation can make people intoxicated." See Zhou Zuoji 周作楫 et al. ed., Sinan fuxuzhi 思南府续志 [the Continuation Gazetteer of Sinan Prefecture], in Sichuan Provincial Library, Daoguang twenty-one-year edition.

[9] Duan Zhaoao 段兆鳌, *Guiding xianzhigao*, 149–150.

[10] Xiasi is today's Xiasi Town, Kaili City, Qiandongnan Prefecture, Guizhou Province, which is the starting point of Qingshui River shipping; Guzhou is today's Rongjiang County, Qiandongnan Prefecture, a port city of Duliu River.

[11] Around 1820 AD.

[12] Tang Yuanju 唐远驹 ed., *Guizhou shailiangyan* 贵州晒晾烟 [Guizhou sun-cured Tobacco] (Guiyang: Guizhou Science and Technology Press), 2–35.

and often harsh, meaning it could only meet the needs of local markets. In addition, the yield of the dry tobacco leaves per *mu*[13] was only thirty-five kilos.

In the Guangxu period of the late Qing Dynasty, that is, after 1875, in order to overcome the problem of insufficient time of direct sun, a more advanced sun-curing method came into being. This method fixed fresh tobacco leaves with bamboo chips, fully unfolding them for drying and then transferring them for indoor drying. The finished leaves were named yellow sun-cured tobacco for their yellowish-brown appearance. The application of this method eliminated the harsh taste of dried tobacco leaves and made them ripe and mellow while also increasing yield. This served as a foundation for the large-scale tobacco processing industry in Guiding.[14] At the same time, several major producers of smoking tobacco, including Shu Hongxing 舒洪兴, Lan Fujing 蓝福景, and He Quansheng 何全盛, improved their management, hired professional tobacco cutters for material selection and shredding, implemented quality management of rapeseed oil and tobacco leaves, and improved packaging. Gradually, their products were sold to other provinces.[15] "In the early years of Guangxu period,[16] the production and packaging of sun-cured cut tobacco was gradually improved. They is bleached cut tobacco packed in 12.5 kilograms packages, and there is also small-packed cut tobacco that imitates the packing style of the high-end category Golden Orchid cut tobacco from Yongding 永定, Fujian. In the 14th and 15th

[13] One mu equals to 667 square meters.

[14] Tang Yuanju 唐远驹 ed., *Guizhou shailiangyan*, 36–74.

[15] Hu Duankai 胡端楷, Shuhongxing yanzhuang 舒洪兴烟庄 (Shu Hongxing Salt Factory), in *Guiding wenshi ziliao xuanji* 贵定文史资料选辑 [Selected Collection of Guiding Literature and History Materials], Second Series, 59–60, Guiding County Committee of the Chinese People's Political Consultative Conference Cultural and Historical Data Research Committee ed., 1983; He Qingling 何庆铃, Hequansheng yanzhuang 何全盛烟庄 (He Quansheng Salt Factory), in *Guiding wenshi ziliao xuanji* 贵定文史资料选辑 [Selected Collection of Guiding Literature and History Materials], Third Series, 59–61, Guiding County Committee of the Chinese People's Political Consultative Conference Cultural and Historical Data Research Committee ed., 1985; Lan Jinguang 蓝瑾光, Lanfujing siyan 蓝福景丝烟 [Lan Fujing Cut-tobacco], in *Guiding wenshi ziliao xuanji* 贵定文史资料选辑 [Selected Collection of Guiding Literature and History Materials], Fourth Series, 177–181, Guiding County Committee of the Chinese People's Political Consultative Conference Cultural and Historical Data Research Committee ed., 1987.

[16] 1875 AD.

year of Guangxu's reign,[17] the sun-cured cut tobacco industry flourished, with more than 300 sun-cured cut tobacco shops, and they sell to distant markets."[18] The prosperous cut tobacco industry drove Guiding's tobacco cultivation to gradually expand from the surrounding areas to the entire county, and Guiding became a famous tobacco planting and processing center in Guizhou.[19]

1.2 *The Decline of the Guiding Tobacco Leaf Market in the Early Twentieth Century and the Production of Sun-Cured Yellow Tobacco Before the Introduction of American Tobacco*

At the beginning of the twentieth century, imported cigarettes began to have impacts on Guiding's sun-cured cut tobacco market. In 1904, the thirtieth year of Guangxu, the British American Tobacco Company sent staff to Chongqing to promote cigarettes. Since cigarettes were easy to carry and with mild and pleasant flavor, they soon became available in neighboring provinces along the upper reaches of the Yangtze River.[20] Because the taste of sun-cured cut tobacco in Guiding was close to that of the flue-cured tobacco used in cigarettes,[21] the market for sun-cured tobacco was impacted and shrank immediately. "There were more than 300 producers of sun-cured tobacco, because of the imported cigarettes, and the sun-cured tobacco industry in various places has plummeted."[22] At that time, Guiding still used traditional tobacco species: "the local tobacco leaves (named Huayan) were originally Fujian seeds, not American Tobacco. The seeds of local tobacco were improved once ten years ago. The local tobacco seed yields more than the Fujian tobacco seed." The local tobacco leaves were still raw materials for

[17] 1888–1889 AD.

[18] Duan Zhaoao 段兆鳌, *Guiding xianzhigao*, 149–150.

[19] Tang Yuanju 唐远驹 ed., *Guizhou shailiangyan*, 26–35.

[20] Institute of Economics, Shanghai Academy of Social Sciences ed. *Yingmei yan gongsi zaihua qiye ziliao huibian* 英美烟公司在华企业资料汇编 [Compilation of Materials on British American Tobacco's Enterprises in China] (Beijing: Zhonghua Book Company, 1983), 428.

[21] Tang Yuanju 唐远驹 ed., *Guizhou shailiangyan*, 26–35.

[22] Guiding County Cut Tobacco Merchants Association, Guiding tobacco distribution case, Archives of the Guizhou Provincial Department of Construction, M60-1-8096, Guizhou Provincial Archives, 19.

cut tobacco industry.[23] After the demand for local cut tobacco shrank, the dried tobacco leaves were sold to other markets in other region. "Since the Republic of China, tobacco leaf has been transported to high-end Golden Orchid cut tobacco makers in Hongjiang 洪江, Tongren 铜仁, Zhenyuan 镇远, Fazhuang 发庄, and other low-end cut tobacco makers in Anshun 安顺 and Zunyi 遵义."[24] During this period, most of the cigarettes shipped from Guiding to Hunan were local hand-made cigarettes purchased by manufacturers in Hunan to process and sell in imitation of foreign cigarettes.[25] Most of the tobacco planted during this period was North American Nicotiana species introduced from Fujian that had degenerated after several generations of breeding in Guizhou. Even after improvement, Guiding's yield of dried tobacco leaves was only about forty-five kilos *per mu*, which meant that the processor could not realize large-scale production and processing. The processing of raw tobacco to cured tobacco was still mainly dominated by sun-cured technology. Only a small portion of the dried leaves were adopted half sun-cured and half flue-cured technology.[26] Even so, by 1935, Guiding's tobacco[27] output ranked fourth in the country, with an output of about 10.6 million jin in the whole province. Guiding's output made up nearly half of this.[28] As a source of raw materials for export, Guiding continued to play an important role in Guizhou's tobacco industry.

[23] Guiding County Cut Tobacco Trade Association requests compassionate merchants to submit to the Guizhou Provincial Department of Finance, Guiding tobacco distribution case, Archives of the Guizhou Provincial Department of Construction, M60-1-8096, Guizhou Provincial Archives, 24.

[24] Duan Zhaoao 段兆鳌, *Guiding xianzhigao*, 149–150.

[25] Hunan Provincial Chronicles Compilation Committee 湖南省地方志编纂委员会 ed. *Hunansheng zhi dijiujuan gongye kuangchan zhi yancaoye* 湖南省志第九卷·工业矿产志·烟草业 [Hunan Provincial Chronicles Volume 9 Industrial Minerals·Tobacco Industry], (Changsha: Hunan People's Press, 1997), 73.

[26] Tang Yuanju 唐远驹 ed., *Guizhou shailiangyan*, 55–83.

[27] It is local drying tobacco leaves.

[28] "Zhang Xiaomei 张肖梅, Chapter 7 "Agricultural Production, Marketing, Promotion, and Improvement Plan", in *Guizhou jingji* 贵州经济 [Guizhou Economy], (Chongqing: National Economic Research Institute, 1939): 31–32. Please note: the original text is "10.6 million Dan," but the data is too large, it should be 10.6 million Jin.

2 The Rise of Guiding's Tobacco Industry After the Outbreak of the Anti-Japanese War: Technology Introductions and Industrial Development

The outbreak of the Anti-Japanese War brought an opportunity for Guizhou to develop its economy and also created conditions for the rise of Guiding's tobacco industry. In 1937, Wu Dingchang 吴鼎昌, a well-known industrialist, became the chairman of Guizhou, advocating to build the province into an important economic base in southwestern China. To do so, he implemented new policies with both political and economic aspects. The economic policy included two dimensions: finance and industry. In terms of finance, the chairman aimed to reform the tax system to increase fiscal revenue by increasing the proportion of industrial and commercial taxation[29]; in terms of industry, he believed "it is best to have companies jointly established by the government and businessmen, responsible for planning, advocating, and coordinating. This has the benefits of government-run operations without the disadvantages of government-run companies, and have the convenience of commercial operations."[30]

Following these new policies, the Guizhou Provincial Government, the Resources Committee of the Ministry of Economic Affairs, local Guizhou industrialists, the Bank of China, and other national banks jointly founded Guizhou Enterprise Company.[31] This company successively established a number of enterprises across industries including ceramics, hardware, textiles, tobacco, and others. Among them, Guizhou Tobacco Company was a subsidiary of Guizhou Enterprise Company with a mission of "promoting, improving and increasing tobacco production in the industry."[32] Its production was based in Hankou Xieji Tobacco Factory (汉口协记

[29] Wu Dingchang 吴鼎昌, *Huaxi suibi chubian* 花溪随笔初编 [Huaxi Essays ·Volume 1], (Guiyang: Guizhou Provincial Printing Office, 1943): 13. Information collected by Guizhou Provincial Archives.

[30] Ibid.

[31] Wu Dingchang 吴鼎昌, *Huaxi suibi xubian* 花溪随笔续编 [Huaxi Essays ·Volume 2] (Guiyang: Guizhou Provincial Printing Office, 1943): 28. Information collected by Guizhou Provincial Archives.

[32] GuiZhousheng danganguan 贵州省档案馆 ed, *Guizhousheng qiye gongsi* 贵州省企业公司 [Guizhou Provincial Enterprise Company], Volume II, *Guizhou yancao gonsi*

烟厂 *Hankou xieji yanchang*). With technical support regarding American tobacco cultivation from the Guizhou Provincial Department of Construction, the company aimed to select suitable planting sites for American tobacco in order to form a local flue-cured tobacco planting and processing base in Guizhou. With this introduction and promotion campaign, Guiding County was selected as the field to initiated projects for tobacco improvement and promotion by the Guizhou Provincial Government.

2.1 *Introduction and Scale-Up of American Tobacco: The Role of Technological Adaptation and Industrial Finance*[33]

The Guizhou Provincial Agricultural Improvement Institute, which was affiliated with the Guizhou Provincial Department of Construction, introduced American tobacco for trial planting through the Central Agricultural Experimental Institute in 1938, and actively searched for planting bases that could be extended after the trial planting was successful.[34] The introduction of American tobacco plantation in this province began in 1938. In that year, the Agricultural Improvement Institute conducted a comparative experiment on varieties of American tobacco. The results showed that "Virginia Bright Leaf" was high-yielding and good quality. This experiment facilitated the development of the tobacco industry in Guizhou, as these newly introduced American tobacco varieties were able to achieve a yield of 125 to 200 kilograms of dry tobacco leaves *per mu*. And they were more suitable for baking in barns. Compared to sun-drying, the flue technology is easier to control and to scale up. These

zhangcheng 贵州烟草公司章程 [Articles of Association of Guizhou Tobacco Company], (Guiyang: Guizhou People's Press, 2003), 1200.

33 For the part about industrial finance supporting the development of the cigarette industry, please refer to the analysis of the fiscal part mainly focused on the tobacco industry in Chapter 5.

34 Yang Runan and Hu Rengtong 杨汝南, 胡礽同, "*Guizhou nongzuowu zhi gaijin*" 贵州省农作物之改进 [Improvement of Crops in Guizhou Province], in *Guizhousheng nongye gaijinsuo* 贵州省农业改进所 [Guizhou Agricultural Improvement Institute], ed. Jiang Guosheng 蒋国生 (Guiyang: Guizhou People's Press, 2006), 539–557.

features of the new tobacco species were the basis for large-scale industrial production of cigarettes.[35]

As the traditional center of tobacco planting and processing in Guizhou, Guiding had succeeded in planting and processing sun-cured local tobacco varieties. These local tobaccos not only had a close taste to the American tobacco leaves, but were also similar in terms of preferred environment, irrigation requirements, planting density, and field management.[36] This made it almost barrier-free, technically, for tobacco farmers in Guiding to switch to American tobacco. Therefore, Guiding County was able to stand out among the traditional local tobacco production areas in Guizhou and was favored by the Guizhou Provincial Agricultural Improvement Institute and Guizhou Tobacco Company. Starting in 1940, the Guizhou Agricultural Improvement Institute cooperated with the Guizhou Tobacco Company to promote tobacco in Guiding County. "This is a joint endeavor by the Guizhou Enterprise Company and our institute, and it was very welcomed by farmers."[37] "improving local tobacco, producing and selling cigarettes is the only business of our company. The former is cooperated by the Enterprise Company and the Agriculture Improvement Institute with a special fund allocated this year.[38] Guiding was selected as the promotion area for American tobacco, and more than 500 acres[39] of American tobacco were planted." After one year's efforts, American tobacco achieved large-scale cultivation in Guiding, and the output of tobacco reached about two million kilos[40] that year.

In addition to the diffusion of agricultural skills, industrial financial institutions also participated in supporting farmers to plant American tobacco. Rural financial credit institutions represented by the Guiyang branch of the Farmers Bank of China, took the opportunity of promoting

[35] Guizhousheng fuquan yancao kexue yanjiusuo 贵州省福泉烟草科学研究所 ed, *Guizhou kaoyan zaipei* 贵州烤烟栽培 [Guizhou Flue-cured Tobacco Cultivation] (Guiyang: Guizhou People's Press, 1979), 4–10.

[36] Tang Yuanju 唐远驹 ed., *Guizhou shailiangyan*, 12–20.

[37] Yang Runan and Hu Rengtong 杨汝南, 胡礽同, "*Guizhou nongzuowu zhi gaijin*," 539–557.

[38] Refers to 1940.

[39] GuiZhousheng danganguan 贵州省档案馆 ed, *Guizhousheng qiye gongsi*, 1205.

[40] Yang Runan and Hu Rengtong 杨汝南, 胡礽同, "*Guizhou nongzuowu zhi gaijin*," 539–557.

the establishment of credit cooperatives in the rural areas of Guiding to increase credit support for the cultivation of American tobacco in rural areas of Guiding. They not only expanded the planting area of American tobacco with loans, but also actively helped establishing barns.[41] By doing this, it helped farmers to do primary processing in their fields. In 1941, the Guiyang Sub-branch of the Bank of China began supporting Guiding County's cooperative treasury[42] with one-year short-term loans to grow American tobacco in Luobeihe 洛北河, Matu Town 马图乡, Beiguan Town 被关乡, Wangdachong Town 王大冲乡, Xiaozhai Town 小寨乡, and Jiuzhi Town 旧治乡.[43] From 1941 to 1946, more than six million Yuan in loans for American Tobacco production in Guiding was approved through the cooperative treasury and cooperative organizations.[44]

2.2 The Exit of Sun-cured Cut Tobacco Manufacturers and Formation of an American Tobacco Industry

Abundant and high-quality[45] tobacco leaves had laid the foundation for Guiding to establish a number of tobacco enterprises. After Guizhou

[41] Hu Qingming, Li Guangze 胡庆明, 李光泽, "*Jianjie guiding xinpudiqu zhongzhi de kaoyan*" 简介贵定新铺地区种植的烤烟 [Introduction to flue-cured tobacco grown in Xinpu area of Guiding], in Guiding wenshi ziliao xuanji 贵定文史资料选辑 (Selected Collection of Guiding Literature and History Materials), Series 3. Guiding County Committee of the Chinese People's Political Consultative Conference Cultural and Historical Data Research Committee ed., 1985, 57–58.

[42] Tian Jinfeng 田锦凤, Guizhou jiefangqian de hezuoshiye 贵州解放前的合作事业 [Cooperative undertakings before the Liberation of Guizhou], in *Guizhou jinrong huobishi luncong* 贵州金融货币史论从 [Guizhou Finance and Currency History Collection], ed. Guizhou Provincial Institute of Finance (Guiyang: People's Bank of China Guizhou Branch, 1986), 172–185.

[43] "Farmers Bank's case of increasing loans for American tobacco cultivation in Guiding County," in Guizhou Provincial Department of Construction, M60-1-9254, Guizhou Provincial Archives.

[44] Liu Daokui 刘道揆, "*Guiding de meiyan shichang*" 贵定的美烟市场 [Guiding American Tobacco Market], in *Guiding wenshi ziliao xuanji* 贵定文史资料选辑 [Selected Collection of Guiding Literature and History Materials], Series 4. Guiding County Committee of the Chinese People's Political Consultative Conference Cultural and Historical Data Research Committee ed., 1987, 169–173.

[45] Guizhousheng fuquan yancaokexue yanjiusuo 贵州省福泉烟草科学研究所 ed, *Guizhou kaoyan zaipei*, 4–10.

Tobacco Company produced Penguin brand (企鹅牌) cigarettes[46] with American tobacco leaves grown in Guiding County in 1941 and became very popular, more local businessmen in Guiding were inspired to invest in tobacco production and processing. "In recent years, local visionaries have seen this trend and thus established a number of cigarette factories,[47] such as Jiuda[48] 久大 and Jisheng[49] 济生 in 1941–1942," taking advantage of the high-quality tobacco leaves. Traditional silk cigarette merchants also benefited from using the American tobacco leaves to make shag.[50]

However, in 1942, Guiding's tobacco planting and processing industry faced new changes. The national government began to monopolize industries such as tobacco, alcohol, tea, sugar, and salt during the war.[51] The Ministry of Finance's Tobacco Monopoly Bureau Guiding Office and the Guiding Branch of the Yunnan-Guizhou Area Goods Tax Bureau were established. They immediately imposed strict control over the entire tobacco industry in Guiding, from planting to production and processing.[52] At the same time, the Guiding County Government formulated local tobacco industry development measures according to the ninth article of the "Regulations for the Control of Smoking Leaves by the Guiding Office of the Ministry of Finance's Tobacco Monopoly Bureau,"

46 Guizhousheng danganguan 贵州省档案馆 ed, *Guizhousheng qiye gongsi*, 1205.

47 The Guiding County Cigarette Industry Association petitioned to reduce patent taxes, 0-7-13, 1, Guiding County Archives holds the archives of Guiding County Tobacco Monopoly Office during the Republic of China.

48 Zhang Yizhi 张贻之, "*Wo suozhidaode jiuda yanzhuang*" 我所知道的贵定久大烟庄 [What I know about Guidingjiu Dayangzhuang], in *Guiding wenshi ziliao xuanji* 贵定文史资料选辑 [Selected Collection of Guiding Literature and History Materials], Series 3, ed. Guiding County Committee of the Chinese People's Political Consultative Conference Cultural and Historical Data Research Committee, 1985, 46–49.

49 Jisheng Tobacco Factory Suspension Report in Guiding County Tobacco Monopoly Office, 0-7-14, Guiding County Archives, 174–175.

50 He Qingling 何庆铃, "*Hequansheng yanzhuang*" 何全盛烟庄 [He Quansheng yanzhuang], in *Guiding wenshi ziliao xuanji* 贵定文史资料选辑 [Selected Collection of Guiding Literature and History Materials], ed. Series 3. Guiding County Committee of the Chinese People's Political Consultative Conference Cultural and Historical Data Research Committee, 1985, 59–61.

51 Guizhou Provincial Finance and Economics Commission ed., *Guizhou caijing ziliao huibian*, 373.

52 Measures for the Control of Smoked Tobacco Leaves of the Guiding Office of the Tobacco Monopoly Bureau of the Ministry of Finance, in Guizhou Provincial Department of Construction, M60-1-8096, Guizhou Provincial Archives, 13.

which stated that "shag tobacco shops are not allowed to use baked tobacco leaves to make shag." The new measure consisted of nine articles, which strictly prohibited shag merchants from participating in the business of tobacco leaves and related products. All the enterprises that processed tobacco were required to establish factories locally: "all registered cigarette factories, except for the Enterprise Company that can transport outside the county, should set up factories in the county."[53] This regulation strictly prohibited shag merchants from processing and exporting roasted tobacco made from American plants. They were limited to using sun-cured tobacco for processing, which meant that they were effectively excluded from the industry.

From the perspective of industrial structure, the purpose of these regulations, with their strong local protection and preference for the cigarette industry, was to establish a tobacco processing industry chain based on flue-cured tobacco and cigarettes. These new regulations from the Guiding Tobacco Monopoly Office raised strong dissatisfaction and opposition from the traditional local shag tobacco merchants. The Guiding County Cut Tobacco Business Association, an organization of these merchants, appealed to the Guizhou Provincial Government twice to request changes to the regulations[54]; they were especially concerned with the regulation that prohibited sun-cured cut tobacco merchants from entering the flue-cured American tobacco market. They argued that "this tobacco leaf was originally a local specialty seed that was improved and has been sold outside of Guizhou for many years. As long as national taxes are paid, they can go to the market without barrier. How can they (local authorities) ignore the livelihood of thousands of people by following the interests of one or two big cigarette merchants?" These merchants believed that they were all taxpayers and that the authorities were showing a bias toward a certain group.

Data on tobacco taxation in Guizhou before the implementation of the monopoly system in 1942 provides some notable context here. We found that since the abolition of the provincial tax on tobacco sales in September 1936, as long as cut tobacco products circulating within the

[53] "Guiding County Council Resolution No. 79," in Guizhou Provincial Department of Construction, M60-1-8096, Guizhou Provincial Archives, 20.

[54] "Smoke No. 7; Submitted on November 6, the 31st year of the Republic of China" in Guizhou Provincial Department of Construction, M60-1-8096, Guizhou Provincial Archives, 19–24.

province and imported cigarettes from other places paid business taxes at the raw material purchasing or factory location stage, no other taxes were levied. Instead, a yearly unified tax of 168,000 yuan was paid to the Ministry of Finance of the National Government.[55] This means that local sun-cured cut tobacco merchants in Guizhou did not actually have to pay taxes except when purchasing raw materials. In contrast, cigarette manufacturers based locally had to pay business taxes to resident tax collectors from the direct tax bureau,[56] and the business tax rate on cigarette factories was as high as 60%.[57] Moreover, starting in 1942, the central finance also deducted 50% of the local business tax revenue to the county-level finance.[58] Therefore, both the central and local governments received much more revenue from cigarette factories than from cut tobacco merchants, who paid a 40% tax rate on goods.[59] In addition, cut tobacco merchants were usually small scale with low output, making it difficult for them to form large-scale operations and generate significant tax revenue like cigarette factories. Therefore, it makes sense that the cut tobacco merchants' opposition could not change the authorities' decision to exclude them from the American tobacco industry. Eventually, the tobacco industry in Guiding County was divided into two parts: first, American tobacco trade, roasted tobacco production and processing, and cigarette factories' establishment and production were subject to the admission and daily management of the Guiding Tobacco Monopoly Office, and their taxes were handled by the direct tax bureau; second, the

55 Zhang Xiaomei 张肖梅, *Guizhou jingji*, 1–2. The original book subscription fee was 240,000 yuan, but according to the fiscal revenue statistics table in the "Guizhou Financial Information Compilation", it was only 168,000 yuan.

56 Guizhou Provincial Finance and Economics Commission ed., *Guizhou caijing ziliao huibian*, 406–417. In 1944, there were still local tax bureaus that levied tobacco specialty tax and transaction tax, which were directly owned by the local county Department of Finance.

57 "Instructions on uniform collection of patents from factory residents," in Guiding County Branch of the Yunnan-Guizhou District Direct Taxation Bureau, 0-17-138, Guiding County Archives, 12–15.

58 Ma Yinchu 马寅初, "Chapter 2 Division of Central Taxes and Local Taxes," in *Caizhengxueyuzhongguocaizheng—lilunyuxianshi* 财政学与中国财政—理论与现实 [Public Finance and Chinese Finance—Theory and Reality] (Beijing: The Commercial Press. Reprinted, 2006), 186–188.

59 "Details of patent tax on raw materials for processing native tobacco," in County Government, M-1-5843, Sansui County Archives, 16.

traditional cut tobacco merchants could only process traditional sun-dried tobacco under the management of the Guiding Branch of the Yunnan-Guizhou Area Goods Tax Bureau.[60] The cigarette industry was also strictly limited to using sun-cured tobacco leaves,[61] and strict tax rates were set to control it. In this way, a relatively closed flue-cured tobacco/cigarette industry chain was formed.

The local tobacco factories were subject to the administration of the Monopoly Office and the Direct Tax Bureau. These organizations' duties included the following: adjusting monopoly tax rates according to the costs of local tobacco factories, investigating the costs and verifying the prices of the tobacco factories, registering and changing the registration of the cigarette factories, registering the trade of tobacco and its products, and, most importantly, preventing tobacco smuggling. Among them, the Guiding Office was given the discretion to adjust tax rates according to costs and the market conditions. By doing so, they expected that the local cigarette factory would not be at a competitive disadvantage.

Because of this discretion, the Guiding County Cigarette Industry Association thought that the monopoly tax was too high and could be reduced after negotiation with the Tobacco Monopoly Office and Direct Tax Bureau. For example, in June 1943, the Guiding County Cigarette Industry Association applied for a reduction of patent taxes based on comparisons with the neighboring provinces of Hunan and Guangxi.

> Recently, we received letters from various cigarette factories in the county saying that the tax amount of the new monopoly certificate is too high and asking for a reduction. We found that the cigarettes consumed in this county over the years are non-local products, and local manufacturers and merchants have suffered huge losses. In recent years, local merchants with insight have seen this and they have set up cigarette factories to protect their rights. Although the quality of their products is still inferior to imported ones, they seem to be no worse than those produced in other counties in the province. However, due to the sharp increase in patents fees, the selling price is high and it is not easy to sell. If we do not urgently attempt to protect them, it will be difficult for local products to compete with foreign tobacco products, and it will be impossible for them

60 "Treasury Instructions on Tax Rates and Jurisdiction," in Guiding County Tobacco Monopoly Office, 0-7-58, Guiding County Archives, 49–50.

61 Same to note 58.

> not to close down. The only way to save them is to temporarily suspend the implementation of new patent fees. If patents fees have to be increased, they should also consider the situation in Guangxi and Hunan. Otherwise, there is no future for cigarettes in this county. Therefore, we respectfully list all the reasons for the reduction of patents fee as above. Please judge whether it is feasible.[62]

The Guiding County Tobacco Monopoly Office and the Direct Taxation Bureau later made a decision to "reduce the tax to 60%"[63] after comparing the monopoly tax rate and collection situation in neighboring provinces, which eased the tax payment pressure faced by local cigarette factories.

The Guiding Office of the Tobacco Monopoly Bureau of the Ministry of Finance also implemented a differentiated policy for the export of local planted American tobacco and its products. The management of the export of American tobacco raw materials was very strict, while the export of cigarette products only adopted a filing system. For example, in June 1943, when Guiding Huadun Cigarette Factory shipped two kinds of cigarettes (Baota and Jinque) to Kunming, they only needed to fill out a transportation application form to verify the quantity.[64] During the same period, the export of cigarettes by other individuals, enterprises, or cooperatives also only required an application form.[65] In contrast, in May 1943, merchants from Hunan and Guangxi who had purchased permits from the Xianggui District Branch of the Tobacco Monopoly Bureau of the Ministry of Finance were not allowed to ship raw tobacco leaves purchased from Guiding. They needed to resubmit their applications to the Guiding Office for shipping permits. After the Tobacco Monopoly

62 "Submission from Guiding County Cigarette Industry Association to apply for reduction of monopoly tax," in Guiding County Tobacco Monopoly Office, 0-7-13, Guiding County Archives, 1–5.

63 "Guiding Cigarette Monopoly Office's Order on Reducing the Tax Rate on Cigarette Monopoly," in Guiding County Tobacco Monopoly Office, 0-7-12, Guiding County Archives, 101.

64 "HuaDun Tobacco Factory applies for filing of transportation bill for exporting Kunming cigarettes," in Guiding County Tobacco Monopoly Office, 0-7-3, Guiding County Archives, 14–18.

65 "Guanghua, Jisheng Tobacco Factory, and Peng Fuqing applied for filing of transport orders for cigarettes exported to Kunming, Guiyang, and other places," in Guiding County Tobacco Monopoly Office, 0-7-3, Guiding County Archives, 19–21.

Bureau of the Ministry of Finance verified the quantity and grade of the materials, they could be transported.[66] The approval process might take as long as four months. These regulations essentially prohibited the export of raw tobacco leaves.

This strict control over exporting raw materials even applied to Guizhou Tobacco Company's licensed purchase and sales. In November 1944, the Tobacco Monopoly Office of Guiding County filed a case against the Guiding Office of Guizhou Tobacco Company for illegally transporting American tobacco leaves out of the county. They detained Wu Weisheng 吴渭生 (the director of the office) and Lin Zhiyuan 林至远 (the transporter) on the grounds that Guizhou Tobacco Company had transported tobacco leaves without obtaining a transport permit and that the permitted mileage of the transport vehicles was only valid from Guiyang 贵阳 to Longli 龙里. They confiscated 970 *jin* of tobacco leaves from the Guiding Office of Guizhou Tobacco Company. After negotiation by the Guiding Warehouse of Guizhou Tobacco Company and the Bank of Guizhou Headquarters, the administrative penalty was imposed on the grounds of "failure to declare tax in advance," and only 300 *jin* of tobacco leaves were confiscated in the end.[67]

Under this strict control of the export of raw materials and monopolizing of the supply chain, eight of the twenty-one tobacco processing enterprises in Guiding enjoyed relatively high profit margins.[68] According to statistics from the Guiding Office of the Tobacco Monopoly Bureau of the Ministry of Finance, by 1945, before the victory of the Anti-Japanese War, the average gross profit margin of the cigarette factories in Guiding reached 19.29%.[69]

[66] "Cigarette factories in Hunan and Guangxi provinces holding Hunan-Guizhou District purchase permit certificates must re-apply for correspondence and correspondence with purchase and shipment permission certificates," in Guiding County Tobacco Monopoly Office, 0-7-12, Guiding County Archives, 8–16.

[67] "Punishment process for the case of Guizhou Tobacco Company's Guiding Office not transporting and selling tobacco leaves in accordance with regulations," in Guiding County Tobacco Monopoly Office, 0-7-1, Guiding County Archives, 1–15.

[68] "List of cigarette franchisees in November 1944 prepared by the Guiding County Chamber of Commerce," in Guiding County Tobacco Monopoly Office, 0-7-36, Guiding County Archives, 34–36.

[69] "Cost and profit statistics of cigarette manufacturers in Guiding District in 1944," in Guiding County Tobacco Monopoly Office, 0-7-12, Guiding County Archives, 158–164.

2.3 *The Growth of the Local Cigarette Market: The Investigation of Smuggled Sun-cured Cut Tobacco and the Promotion of Cigarettes*

The administrative monopoly and control outlined above not only created a relatively closed industrial environment for the local flue-cured tobacco/ cigarette industry, but also severely suppressed the consumption of sun-cured cut tobacco products. The investigation of illegal behaviors, such as using American tobacco leaves as raw material for cut tobacco, increased the market for cigarettes. After the implementation of the Flue-cured Tobacco Leaf Management Measures in 1942, in order to participate in the production of American tobacco leaves, traditional cut-tobacco manufacturers, including Shu Hongxing Tobacco Factory (舒洪兴烟庄) and He Quansheng Tobacco Factory (何全盛烟庄), transformed to cut tobacco for cigarette companies.[70] These changes hit the already shrinking sun-cured cut tobacco manufacturing hard, and the price of sun-cured cut tobacco quickly soared. Some individual cut tobacco manufacturers took risks by buying low-end cigarettes to dismantle[71] or directly buying American tobacco leaves to cut and sold these privately to make huge profits.[72] Such behavior was intolerable to the monopoly and tax authorities. The monopoly agency set up a special anti-smuggling office to crack down on these activities, which also indirectly hit the consumer market for cut tobacco. By the end of the Anti-Japanese War, the cut

[70] Hu Duankai 胡端楷, "Shuhongxing yanzhuang" 舒洪兴烟庄 [Shu Hongxing yanzhuang], in *Guiding wenshi ziliao xuanji* 贵定文史资料选辑 [Selected Collection of Guiding Literature and History Materials], Series 2, ed. Guiding County Committee of the Chinese People's Political Consultative Conference Cultural and Historical Data Research Committee, 1983, 59–60; He Qingling 何庆铃, "Hequansheng yanzhuang" 何全盛烟庄 [He Quansheng Tobacco Factory], in *Guiding wenshi ziliao xuanji* 贵定文史资料选辑 (Selected Collection of Guiding Literature and History Materials), Third Series, ed. Guiding County Committee of the Chinese People's Political Consultative Conference Cultural and Historical Data Research Committee, 1985, 59–61.

[71] "Wang Xinghua, manager of the Minsheng Cigarette Factory, reported the case of Luo Zifan in the south of the city who used cigarettes to secretly dismantle shredded tobacco and sell it," in Guiding County Tobacco Monopoly Office, 0-7-9, Guiding County Archives, 8–10.

[72] "Yang Xuehai's case of privately selling shredded American tobacco," in Guiding Branch of the Yunnan-Guizhou District Goods Taxation Bureau, 0-11-26, Guiding County Archives, 129–132.

tobacco market had almost disappeared, and the local sun-cured tobacco varieties and technology finally vanished in 1957.[73]

At the same time, various types of cigarettes were being vigorously promoted. Factory staff often gave cigarettes as gifts when they went to local administrative agencies for business.[74] Cigarette factories also actively promoted cigarettes as employee benefits to various consumer cooperatives, which grew the local market for cigarettes in Guiding.[75] By 1948, the local cigarette market accounted for 30% of the cigarette production in Guiding County.[76]

2.4 After the Monopoly: The Tax-Based Management Model and the Role of the Chamber of Commerce in Guiding County

After the victory of the Anti-Japanese War in 1945, the strict control of the tobacco industry in Guiding was relaxed. First, the registration of tobacco factories was no longer the responsibility of the Guiding Office of the Tobacco Monopoly Bureau of the Ministry of Finance. With the reorganization of the taxation system of the Ministry of Finance of the Nationalist Government, the Guiding Branch of the Direct Taxation Bureau of the Hunan, Guizhou, and Guizhou Districts (湘桂黔区) of the Ministry of Finance was established. And from October 1945, administrative issues such as applications for reorganization, suspensions of business, and relocations of cigarette factories in Guiding were all handled by this newly established office.[77]

[73] Tang Yuanju 唐远驹 ed., *Guizhou shailiangyan*, 12–20.

[74] Hu Duanzheng 胡端正, "Wo renguidingxian lianshe jingli de Qianqian houhou" 我任贵定县联社经理的前前后后 [The story behind my appointment as manager of the Guiding County Association], in *Guiding wenshi ziliao xuanji* 贵定文史资料选辑 [Selections of Guiding Cultural and Historical Materials], Series2, ed. Cultural and Historical Materials Research Committee of Guiding County Committee of Chinese People's Political Consultative Conference, 1983, 24–34.

[75] "Letter from Ouya Cigarette Factory to promote cigarettes to Guizhou Bank Colleagues Cooperative," in Guiding Branch of the Bank of Guizhou, 0-14-4, Guiding County Archives, 33.

[76] Guizhou Provincial Finance and Economics Commission ed., *Guizhou caijing ziliao huibian*, 423.

[77] "Guiding Hengxing Cigarette Factory applied for reorganization and re-recruitment of shareholders," in Guiding Branch of the Hunan-Guangxi-Guizhou District Direct Taxation Bureau of the Ministry of Finance, 0-10–66, Guiding County Archives, 92–92.

Due to the end of the Anti-Japanese War, many non-locals began to return to their hometowns. The strategic importance of Guizhou decreased. The economy was depressed, and consumption shrank. The cigarette industry in Guiding also faced market shrinkage and depression. Cigarette factories such as Jiuda[78] 久大, Yuqian[79] 豫黔, and many others ceased operations or closed down. Some merchants who served tobacco cutting also closed down due to a sharp decline in the downstream demand.[80]

At the same time, the Guiding Branch of the Direct Taxation Bureau of Hunan, Guangxi, and Guizhou Districts launched an investigation and collection campaign regarding the business taxes of the tobacco industry. They conducted business tax inspections of tobacco factories, requesting them to suspend operations, which forced many factories to choose bankruptcy and liquidation.[81] By the end of 1945, a report from the Guiding County Cigarette Industry Association showed that, due to the suspension of business and the impact of the Qiannan Incident (黔南事变 *qiannan shibian*) in 1944, more than half of the tobacco factories in Guiding had closed.[82]

By January 1946, the Guiding Branch of the Direct Taxation Bureau of Hunan, Guangxi, and Guizhou Districts began to implement the Ministry of Finance's "Regulations on Domestic Tobacco and Alcoholic Tax." According to the new regulations, tobacco and its associated products

[78] Zhang Yizhi 张贻之, "Wo suozhidao de jiuda yanzhuang", 46–49.

[79] "Investigating the case of the Henan-Guizhou Tobacco Factory's application for tax payment due to business suspension," in Guiding Branch of the Hunan-Guangxi-Guizhou District Direct Taxation Bureau of the Ministry of Finance, 0-10-66, Guiding County Archives, 81–83.

[80] "Minxing Cigarette Shop's Application for Suspension of Business," in Guiding Branch of the Hunan-Guangxi-Guizhou District Direct Taxation Bureau of the Ministry of Finance, 0-10-66, Guiding County Archives, 97–98.

[81] "Defuji Tobacco Store was unable to bear the tax burden and filed for bankruptcy," Guiding Branch of the Hunan-Guangxi-Guizhou District Direct Taxation Bureau of the Ministry of Finance, 0-10-47, Guiding County Archives, 212–214.

[82] "The Guiding County Chamber of Commerce applied for exemption from the 1944 business tax for the cut tobacco and cigarette industries," in Guiding Branch of the Hunan-Guangxi-Guizhou District Direct Taxation Bureau of the Ministry of Finance, 0-10-47, Guiding County Archives, 108–113.

could be sold freely after paying taxes.[83] As a result, the tobacco industry and its management in Guiding County entered a new stage. Since the tobacco and products in Guizhou had formed a stable consumer group and market during the war, many manufacturers who moved inland, such as Huaxiang 华湘 Tobacco Factory, were not eager to move back, and even began to expand investment and production under the new relatively relaxed monopoly management regulations.[84] By the end of 1947, Guiding Tobacco Industry had eight major cigarette manufacturers, including Ouya[85] 欧亚, Xinmin 新民, Datong 大同, Lianhua 联华, Jufeng 聚丰, Huafeng 华丰, Jincheng 金城, and Zhonghua 中华, with a total capital of 7,884.3 million yuan and an annual production of 5,508,000 large boxes of cigarettes.[86] It became the second largest center of tobacco industry in Guizhou Province after Guiyang.

Due to the frequent restructuring of the financial system by the National government, from 1948 onward, except for patent taxation which was collected by the Guiding Tax Collection Office of the Ministry of Finance and State Taxation Bureau, the other administrative matters including tobacco factory registration were managed by the Chamber of Commerce in Guiding County (CCGC).[87] Establishment, suspension of business, and reorganization were also handed over to the CCGC. The CCGC was dominated by tobacco manufacturers and merchants from Hunan. Most of them had many years of experience in the industry and were familiar with the cigarette market, its technologies, and its sales

[83] "Instructions promulgated and implemented by the Ministry of Finance's 'Domestic Tobacco and Alcohol Regulations,' in Guiding Branch of the Hunan-Guangxi-Guizhou District Direct Taxation Bureau of the Ministry of Finance, 0-10-42, Guiding County Archives, 76–80.

[84] Ou Shouqi 欧寿祺, "Guiding ouya yanchang jianchang qianhou" 贵定欧亚烟厂建厂前后 [Before and after the establishment of Guiding Ouya Tobacco Factory], in *Guiding wenshi ziliao xuanji* 贵定文史资料选辑 [Selections of Guiding Cultural and Historical Materials], Series2, ed. Cultural and Historical Materials Research Committee of Guiding County Committee of Chinese People's Political Consultative Conference, 1983, 20–23.

[85] Restructured from Huaxiang Tobacco Factory.

[86] Guizhou Provincial Finance and Economics Commission ed., *Guizhou caijing ziliao huibian*, 146. Please note: 1 large box = 10 Small box = 120 Piece = 1200 Pack = 24,000 cigarettes.

[87] "Guiding County Chamber of Commerce issues and withdraws Youde Tobacco Shop business license," in Guiding County Chamber of Commerce, 0-12-8, Guiding County Archives, 19–20.

networks.[88] This enabled the coordinating function of the chamber of commerce to be fully exerted, and it not only approved admission into the industry but also represented the cigarette industry in Guiding County in direct negotiations with the Guizhou Provincial Department of Finance and the Guiding County Government regarding the rationality of tax collection procedures and special product taxes. In 1949, it successfully convinced the Guizhou Provincial Department of Finance to simplify the tax inspection procedures for cigarettes entering the Guiyang market.[89] In the same year, it also successfully removed cut tobacco from the county government's special product tax list.[90] Thus far, the tobacco industry in Guiding County has formed a management model combining self-discipline of the industry association and monopoly tax collection by the authorities.

3 Continuation and Fragmentation: The Conclusive Remarks on Interaction and Tension Between the Country Government and Local Merchants

The history of tobacco planting and processing in Guiding from the Jiaqing (1700–1820) and Daoguang (1821–1850) period of the Qing Dynasty, when tobacco was first introduced to the county, up until 1949 shows that tobacco planting and production underwent major technological and organizational changes, such as the introduction of new technologies and the intervention of state power. However, the industry did

[88] "Staffing of Guiding County Cigarette Industry Association in 1948," in Guiding County Chamber of Commerce, 0-12-12, Guiding County Archives; Also see Wang Ming 王明, "Wo canjia kaiban guiding yucheng yanhang de diandi huiyi" 我参加开办贵定裕成烟行的点滴回忆 [My memories of participating in the establishment of Yucheng Cigarette Store in Guiding], in *Guiding wenshi ziliao xuanji* 贵定文史资料选辑 [Selections of Guiding Cultural and Historical Materials], Series4, ed. Cultural and Historical Materials Research Committee of Guiding County Committee of Chinese People's Political Consultative Conference, 1987, 174–176.

[89] "Documents from the Guiding County Chamber of Commerce on simplifying the procedures for entering the market of cigarettes," in Guiding County Chamber of Commerce, 0-12-8, Guiding County Archives, 12.

[90] "Documents from the Guiding County Chamber of Commerce on adjusting the objects of special product tax," in Guiding County Chamber of Commerce, 0-12-13, Guiding County Archives, 12.

not experience serious disruption. Rather, a new American tobacco leaf-cigarette industry was formed based on the successful transplantation and adoption of new technologies. But if we look deeper into the industry, we find that the traditional production entities, consisting mainly of traditional cut tobacco merchants, were either eliminated from cigarette processing or transformed into a part of its chain, while the cigarette merchants from Hunan became the main entities of the industry. This replacement of industry entities despite industrial continuity also marked the disappearance of the original group of local industrial and commercial practitioners dominated by merchants from Fujian and Guangdong. The interactions and tensions between the state, merchants, and localities under this seemingly contradictory trend in Guiding's tobacco planting and processing history are consistent with the conditions of successful technological transplantation in the early stage of industrialization in developing economics.[91]

3.1 Importing Technology[92]

Unlike most agricultural-industrial complex technology, which takes years to diffuse, the introduction and the eventual diffusion of American cigarettes in Guiding was nearly complete in a very short time. It started in 1940 and began to scale up in 1941; after 1942, the local government and merchants began to invest in large-scale industrial production. This rapid technology diffusion and industrial development was possible not only because Guiding County was endowed with the natural environment for it but also an enabling institutional environment. We use the induced technological innovation model developed by Hayamizu and Ratan in 1985 as our analytical framework here. This model aims to illustrate how, in the early stages of industrialization, technological innovation and introduction progress smoothly along a path of saving labor and utilizing increased capital. And we see that the production conditions of

[91] Yujiro Hayami and Yoshihisa Godo, "Chapter 6 Pattern and Sources of Technological Progress," in *Development Economics: From the Poverty to the Wealth of Nations (Third Edition)* (New York: Oxford University Press, 2005), 188–190.

[92] Yujiro Hayami and Vernon W. Ruttan, "Factor Prices and Technical Change in Agricultural Development: The United States and Japan, 1880–1960," *Journal of Political Economy* 78, no. 5 (1970): 1115–1141.

American Tobacco leaves were in line with this law: with the same labor input, American Tobacco could produce more tobacco leaf products.

Comparison of American Tobacco and Traditional Tobacco

Variety	*Input per Mu*				
	Labor (person)	*Capital(Franc)*	*output(Kilos)*	*Capital/labor Ratio*	*Labor Productivity*
American Tobacco	10	400	125	40	12.5
Sun-dried Tobacco	20	283	45	14.15	2.25

It can be seen that American tobacco planting is a typical production technology that favors labor saving and capital utilization. The application of this technology is in line with the needs of large-scale industrial production in the early stage of industrialization. In terms of their planting environments, there is no difference between the local sun-cured tobacco and American tobacco in Guiding,[93] so technical and economic barriers are almost non-existent in introducing American tobacco.

Of course, the enabling technology and economic inputs do not always lead to the successful introduction of technology. The theory of induced technological innovation argues that the success of technology introduction requires several conditions: capital support, including a series of industrial financial supports[94]; technology to trigger the development of industry and bring high profits[95]; and sufficient technical personnel and human capital. Looking at the prosperity of the Guiding American tobacco industry, as the flue-cured tobacco industry, we can see that these conditions were met one by one in the interactions between the state, locality, and merchants.

[93] Tang Yuanju 唐远驹 ed., *Guizhou shailiangyan*, 12–20.

[94] Alexander Gerschenkron, "Economic Backwardness in Historical Perspective," In The Globalization and Development Reader: Perspectives on Development and Global Change (Second Edition), ed. J. Timmons Roberts, Amy Bellone Hite, Nitsan Chorev (Oxford: Blackwell, 2014), 62–78.

[95] Same to note 92.

3.2 *Changes in Industrial Structure*

After the cut tobacco manufacturers were eliminated from the industry by the monopoly regulations, Guiding's American tobacco/flue-cured cigarette production manufacturers reached an average gross profit rate of 19.29%. These American tobacco manufacturers formed a monopoly power[96] over upstream American tobacco acquisition and also had certain pricing power in the downstream market. Based on the price and cost data of eight tobacco factories in Guiding in 1944,[97] we found that the average cost-plus rate[98] was 1.2–1.36,[99] which means that these tobacco factories could exercise 20–36% premium power on prices, implying considerable control over the market. Thus, a certain premium ability and higher average profit margin gave Guiding's cigarette industry a higher expected profit, which attracted subsequent manufacturers to join. In fact, after 1946, manufacturers such as Huaxiang, Xinmin, Datong, Lianhua, Jufeng, Huafeng, Jincheng, and Zhonghua joined Guiding's cigarette industry, and at most there were forty-five factories.

3.3 *Introduction of Industrial Finance: Planting and Production*[100]

From 1942 to 1949, five banks successively set up branches or offices in Guiding, including the Farmers Bank of China (中国农民银行 *zhongguo nongmin yinhang*), Bank of Communications (交通银行 *jiao-tong yinhang*), Cooperative Treasury (合作金库 *hezuo jinku*), Bank of China (中国银行 *zhonghuo yinhang*), and Bank of Guizhou (贵州银行 *guizhou yinhang*). They not only provided farmers with planting loans,[101] but also commercial credit for tobacco leaf acquisition and tobacco

[96] Liu Daokui 刘道揆, "Guiding de meiyan shichang," 169–173.

[97] "Cost and profit statistics of cigarette manufacturers in Guiding District in 2014," in Guiding County Tobacco Monopoly Office, 0-7-12, Guiding County Archives, 158–164.

[98] Jan De Loecker, Jan Eeckhout, and Gabriel Unger G, "The Rise of Market Power and the Macroeconomic Implications," *The Quarterly Journal of Economics* 135, no. 2 (2020): 561–644.

[99] Zhang Yizhi 张贻之, "Wo suozhidaode jiuda yanzhuang," 46–49.

[100] For more details on this section, please refer to Chapter 4 on Tobacco Taxation and Finance.

[101] Same to note 96.

factory financing.[102] These commercial loans covered all aspects of the tobacco industry in Guiding County, from planting to curing, purchase, storage, shredding, and even cigarette processing. The conditions for obtaining funds were convenient, ranging from overdraft credit loans to mortgage and pledge loans. This provided a good financial environment for the development of local tobacco industries.

3.4 Human Capital Advantages

In addition to local farmers' expertise in planting tobacco, the development of the tobacco industry in Guiding County also benefited from the cigarette industry practitioners, mainly from Hunan, who moved in after the Anti-Japanese War broke out. These practitioners had mostly set up factories in Changsha 长沙, Changde 常德, and other central areas where the cigarette industry was well developed and flooded into Guiding after the tense situation in Hunan in 1944.[103] More than 2000 skilled workers were brought in during this period.[104]

By 1948, more than half of the members of the Cigarette Industry Association, under the guidance of Guiding County Chamber of Commerce, were from Hunan, and only Ma Fujiu was from Guiding among the six directors. At this time, the Guiding County Chamber of Commerce's Hunanese industrialists and merchants played a crucial role. Among these industrial and commercial players, the larger ones, such as Ouya Tobacco Factory (欧亚烟厂 *ouya yanchang*), Yucheng Tobacco Company (裕诚菸行 *yucheng yanhang*), and Xinmin Tobacco Factory (新民烟厂 *xinmin yanchang*), have retained production bases and sales networks in Changsha, Changde, Hunan, and other places and provided the necessary human capital for their business expansion through the linkage between Guiding and Hunan, filling the personnel gap required for local industry development in very short time frames.[105]

102 "Letter of financing for Asia American Tobacco Company," in Guiding Branch of the Bank of Guizhou, 0-14-38, Guiding County Archives, 139.

103 Ou Shouqi 欧寿祺, "Guiding ouya yanchang jianchang qianhou," 20–23.

104 Hunan Provincial Chronicles Compilation Committee, ed., *Hunansheng & nbsp; zhi dijiujuan gongye & nbsp; kuangchan & nbsp; zhi yancaoye* 76–84.

105 Ibid.

4 The Collusion of State, Locality, and Merchants: The Rise of List-Style Infant Industry

Based on an analysis of the failed import substitution policy in Latin America, development economists generally believe that the development model proposed by List, which consciously sets up barriers to protect specific local industries and then removes them, will eventually lead to inefficient industrial conspiracy.[106] That is, local merchants and merchants from the new industry will eventually form an alliance to maintain high monopoly profits, while the industry itself cannot be fully developed: this is called the "List Trap."[107] However, the development and growth of the tobacco industry in Guiding show us that, in the context of wartime, interaction between the state, localities, and merchants that were not deliberately designed promoted the rise of the cigarette industry around American tobacco and the processing of flue-cured tobacco. To some extent, this is a case of the rise of a List-style infant industry, but it is not a model that can be generalized.

[106] Yujiro Hayami and Yoshihisa Godo, "Chapter 8 Market and State," in *Development Economics From the Poverty to the Wealth of Nations (Third Edition)* (New York: Oxford University Press), 250–256.

[107] Ibid.

CHAPTER 5

Merchant on the Salt-Tobacco Road: Liu Xiyi's Business Strategy and Business Network

Benmo Jiang

Starting with almost nothing, Liu Xiyi became the most prominent merchant in Guizhou during the 1930s and 1940s. The salt trade was Liu's initial business interest and enabled him to build his wealth. However, his focus shifted to other industries during the 1940s, and Nanming Tobacco Factory became one of his most important business achievements during this period. Through a four-part chronological account of Liu Xiyi's rise in the salt trade and in the tobacco industry, including an analysis of his business strategy and business network, this chapter tries to show the mutual influence between the salt-tobacco road and this particular merchant; more broadly, it aims to explore the local merchant community's attitudes toward the financial and legal institutional innovations used by the state to mobilize and integrate local resources.

1 Liu's First Involvement in Salt Business

In 1906, Liu Xiyi was born into an impoverished peasant family in a poor mountainous valley in Bijie County. The family originally cultivated land rented from Tusi to make a living. Due to banditry, however, they fled

B. Jiang et al., *State, Market and Salt-Tobacco Road in Modern China (1935–1949)*, https://doi.org/10.1007/978-981-97-7654-2_5

to the walled county town of Bijie and began running small businesses.[1] Liu Xiyi received several years of private schooling both in the countryside and in the county town. In 1929, he chose to follow his parents into business. With money he borrowed from his relatives he bought cloth in the Bijie's county town and sold it to the countryside, then used his profits to buy opium and sold it to dealers in the county town.[2] At that time, Qianfeng firm (黔丰字号 *qianfeng zihao*) was the main supplier of opium in Bijie. This firm was owned by Liu Wanquan 刘玩泉, who was one of Bijie's wealthiest merchants. Liu Xiyi, with his excellent social skills and business acumen, built a good friendship with Pu Shaowen 蒲绍文, the manager of the firm, and with Liu Wanquan himself.[3] Since Liu Xiyi and Liu Wanquan shared the same family name, though they might not be blood relatives, the latter treated Liu Xiyi as a junior in the family. Liu Xiyi gradually ended his business as a county-level peddler and began taking advantage of Qianfeng firm's opium business to visit various regional commercial centers and ports like Guiyang and Hankou. He bought other profitable commodities in these cities and sold them in Bijie.

According to the recollection of Lai Yongchu 赖永初, another famous Guizhou businessman, around 1935, Liu Xiyi told him that for getting rich quickly, he wanted to upgrade and expand his business network throughout the whole province by connecting with political forces and business talents from inside and outside Guizhou.[4] Also in 1935, The

[1] Liu Yuyuan 刘裕远, "Liu Xiyi de fajia yu shuaibai" 刘熙乙的发家与衰败 [The Rise and Fall of Liu Xiyi], in Guizhou gongshang shiliao huibian 贵州工商史料汇编 [Compilation of Historical Materials of Industry and Commerce in Guizhou], ed. Guizhou Committee of China National Democratic Construction Association, no.1 (1985): *Guizhou zhengxie wenshi ziliao cungao xuanbian* 23.

[2] Because Bijie is located at the junction of Yunnan, Guizhou and Sichuan, it was the opium distribution center at that time. After receiving the opium in Bijie, the merchants transported it to Guiyang and other places for sale.

[3] Liu Yuyuan, "Liu Xiyi de fajia yu shuaibai," 23–24; Liu Yuyuan & Tang Bin 唐斌, "Gongshang shiye jia Liu Xiyi" 工商实业家刘熙乙 [Liu Xiyi: An Industrialist], in *Guizhou zhengxie wenshi ziliao cungao xuanbian* 贵州政协文史资料存稿选编 [Selected Manuscripts of Guizhou CPPCC Literary and Historical Materials] (Guiyang: Guizhou People's Publishing House, 2006), vol. 3, 75–76.

[4] Chen Fende 陈棻德, "Cong xiaoshanfan dao dashangjia: dui Liu Xiyi facia zhi mi de pojie" 从小商贩到大商家——对刘熙乙发财之"谜"的破解 (From Small Peddler to Big Merchant: The Decipherment to the "Mystery" of Liu Xiyi's Fortune], *Guiyang wenshi congkan* 贵州文史丛刊 (Guizhou Literature and History Series), 4 (2005): 23.

Central Government of Nationalist Party began to take effect control and then implemented a "six-year anti-opium program" to control and restrict opium cultivation and opium transportation. Although the specific means of implementing the program were adjusted according to the actual situation and financial needs, and the Nationalist government was not completely antagonistic to the opium merchants,[5] the morally ambiguous nature of opium and the uncertain future of the trade made it clear that Liu Xiyi would have to look elsewhere to support his ambitions.

So, in 1936, Liu Xiyi became formally involved in salt transportation. Together with Liu Wanquan and a Bijie merchant called Guo Ju'an 郭举安, he opened the Xinji Salt Firm (新记盐号 *xinji yanhao*). Xinji had branches in Shuicheng and Dading, with a share capital of more than 10,000 yuan, of which Liu Xiyi owned 60%. This made him the manager of Xinji. According to a report from the managing sectors of the Salt Administration Bureau before the merger of various salt firms in Yong An, the strongest salt firm at this time was Qianxintong Salt Firm (谦信通盐号 *qianxintong yanhao*), with a capital of about 100,000 yuan, and the capital of other strong salt firms in Yong An ranged between 30,000 and 40,000 yuan. Among dealers in Anshun and Xingyi, capital varied from 3000 to 10,000 yuan.[6] It can be seen that Xinji was not outstanding in Yong An. According to the recollection of Liu Xiyi's brother and important trading partner, Liu Yuyuan, after the establishment of Xinji, the company quickly rose to the top among the salt companies in Bijie,[7] relying on concessions to retailers and farmers who carried salt.

According to one of Liu Xiyi's collaborators, Wu Xiaogao, a major opium trader from Anshun, the salt trade was not an attractive venture for opium traders. Opium could be purchased locally in Guizhou and taken to nearby larger trading ports such as Guiyang and Anshun, where it could be sold out easily in the market with high profits. In contrast,

[5] See Qin Heping 秦和平, "Yuoguan sanshi niandai zhonghouqi Guizhou jinyan yundong de youlai ji qi renshi" 有关30年代中后期贵州禁烟运动的由来及其认识 [The Origin and Understanding of the Anti-opium Movement in Guizhou in the Middle and Late 1930s), *Guiyang wenshi congkan* 贵州文史丛刊 [Guizhou Literature and History Series], 3 (2001): 58–59.

[6] Miao Qiujie 缪秋杰, "Kaocha chuanyan xingxiao qian an qingxing baogaoshu" 考察川盐行销黔岸情形报告书 [Inestigation Report on Sales of Sichuan Salt to Guizhou], *Yanwu gongbao* 盐务公报 [Salt Bulletin], 1 (1937): "Appendix", 107.

[7] Liu Yuyuan, "Liu Xiyi de fajia yu shuaibai," 24–25.

the capital for salt transportation generally took three to four months to recover and required significant investment.[8] From the standpoint of most opium traders, opening Xinji did not seem to be a particularly wise investment at that time, so why Liu Xiyi saw salt transportation as an opportunity to expand his territory?

First of all, it was easier for a businessman like Liu Xiyi, who had little involvement in new industries, to get started in a traditional industry like the salt trade than to invest in a new type of business. In the same way, Wu Xiaogao, who was also looking for a way to avoid the anti-opium campaign, first invested in a hardware factory but later decided that it was more stable to run a salt business. He then cooperated with Liu Xiyi and Sun Yunqi 孙蕴奇 to take over salt transportation in Ren An.[9]

Secondly, from the time the warlord Zhou Xicheng took control of Guizhou, his financial needs and those of other warlords led to the implementation of a recognized merchant system (认商制 *renshangzhi*) of tax subscriptions, with each port being prepaid for a quota of salt by a fixed number of salt firms. However, due to political turmoil and military conflicts between the warlords, the salt tax money for each port was often controlled by the military forces that gained controll of each area, and the salt system became very chaotic. In 1935, the Red Army Long March passed through Guizhou, and the people in the north of the province fought against the salt merchants under the influence of the army. These rebels, large and small, destroyed salt warehouses at various stations and impacted the power structure of the salt merchants. By the end of 1935, more than half of the Ren An firms had gone bankrupt.[10] In the case of Yong An, if we compare the list of subscribing merchants in 1930 with the list of salt companies that were formed in 1937, when the "one merchant for one port" policy was officially implemented, we see considerable changes (see the table below). This situation favored newcomers

[8] Wu Xiaogao 伍效高, "Guizhou shiyan yunxiao de huiyi" 贵州食盐运销的回忆 [Memories of Salt Business in Guizhou], *Guizhou wenshi ziliao xuanji* 贵州文史资料选辑 [Selected Materials of Guizhou Literature and History], no.17 (1984): 207.

[9] Wu Xiaogao, "Guizhou shiyan yunxiao de huiyi," 207.

[10] Wu Luqin 吴鲁钦, "Jiefangqian Guizhou yunxiao chuanyan gaikuang" 解放前贵州运销川盐概况 [General Situation of Sichuan Salt Transportation and Sale in Guizhou Before Liberation], *Guizhou wenshi ziliao xuanji* 贵州文史资料选辑 [Selected Materials of Guizhou Literature and History], no.3 (1979): 146–149.

with capital, like Liu Xiyi. After starting in salt transportation, he quickly gained a firm foothold in this business.

Comparison of Yong An's subscribing merchants in 1930 and Yong An's twenty-one salt firms in 1937

Subscribing merchants in 1930		*Twenty-one salt firms merged under the "one merchant for one port" system in 1937*	
Name of salt firm	Name of manager	Name of salt firm	Name of manager
吉盛镕 Jirongsheng	樊耀堂 Fan Yaotang	公合长 Gong Hechang	张集贤 Zhang Jixian
裕顺成 Yushuncheng	黄芝荣 Huang Zhirong、焦静斋 Jiao Jingzhai、孙荣斋 Sun Rongzhai	?盛 (the letter of the name of the firm is unclear)Sheng	李岷光 Li Minguang
信昌 Xinchang	李茂南 Li Maonan、徐赞尧 Xu Zanyao	恒泰永 Hengtaiyong	程 少怀 Cheng Shaohuai
益厚公 Yihougong	袁朝鸣 Yuan Chaoming、张茂勋 Zhang Maoxun、彭信孚 Peng Xinfu	泰记 Taiji	费继成 Fei Jicheng
吉义长 Jiyichang	冯锡镛 Feng Xiyong、何云青 He Qingyun	云福长 Yunfuchang	李复初 Li Fuchu
衡协祥 Hengxiexiang	曾任民 Zeng Renmin、葛贤宾 Ge Xianbin	德厚长 Dehouchang	
隆裕 Longyu	unknown	谦信通 Qian xintong	王渭清 Wang Weiqing
恒合昌 Henghechang	unknown	信成 Xincheng	彭信孚 Peng Xinfu
		仲记 Zhongji	刘治中 Liu Zhizhong
		德福昌(井) Defuchang (Ging Group)	孙蕴奇 Sun Yunqi
		永福祥 Yong fuxiang	李彬华 Li Binhua
		新记 Xinji	刘熙乙 Liu Xiyi
		宏盛 Hongsheng	李岷光 Liminguang
		谦合永 Qianheyong	张集贤 Zhang Jixian
		德泰昌 Detaichang	杨继和 Yang Jihe
		谦信通 Qianxintong 聚诚 Jucheng	钟文光 Zhong Wenguang

(continued)

(continued)

Subscribing merchants in 1930	*Twenty-one salt firms merged under the "one merchant for one port" system in 1937*	
	益厚 Yihou	郑壁光 Zheng Biguang
	同福永 Tong Fuyong	李厚芳 Li Houfang
	德福昌(毕) Defuchang (Bi Group)	陈有钧 Chen Youjun

Source "Ge an renshang paihao jijingliren xingming yilanbiao" 各岸认商牌号暨经理人姓名一览表 (List of registered brands and manager names), *Guizhou yanwu yuekan* 贵州盐务月刊 (Guizhou Salt Monthly), 1 (1930): 117; Liu Yuyuan, "Yong An de qianqianhouhou" 永岸的前前后后 (The process of founding Yong An), *Lixing yuekan*, 1 (1944): 11.

On July 1, 1937, in accordance with the National government's regulations, twenty-one salt wholesale firms in Yong An were merged into the Yong An Sichuan Salt Joint Operator (永岸川盐联合运营商 *yongan chuangyan lianhe yunyinshang*), which later became the Transportation and Distribution Office of Official Salt of Guizhou Yongbian Sales District (贵州永边销区官盐运销营业处 *Guizhou yongbian xiaoqu guanyan yunxiao yinyechu*). After the implementation of a salt monopoly in 1942, the salt transportation of the four ports was entrusted to the wholesale merchants, who were under dirigiste policy, in the form of a commission. Finally, the official name of the Yong An salt office was changed to the Official Salt Commissioned Transporters Business Office of Sichuan-Guizhou Yong An Salt Sales Area (*chuanqianyong yunxiaoqu guanyan weituo yunshang yinyechu* 川黔永运销区官盐委托运商营业处), though it was called Yong An Salt Firm in daily use. After the merger, Yong An Salt Firm continued to be divided into Jing group (井组) and Bi group (毕组) according to their respective region. The Jing group covered business from Xiaohe, through Piao'er Jing, Dading, Puding in Zhijin, Anshun, and Xingyi, with Li Fuchu as the manager of the whole group. The Bi group's business scope was from Chishui River through Bijie, Weining, Shuicheng to Panjiang. It was managed by Zheng Biguang.[11]

11 See Sun Yunqi 孙蕴奇, "Cunqian yongan xiaoqu guanyan weituo yunshang yingye gaishu" 川黔永岸销区官盐委托运商营业概述 [Overview of the Official Salt Commissioners's Business in the Sichuan-Guizhou Yong An Sales Area], *Lixing yuekan* 1 (1944):

As mentioned in previous chapters, under the dirigisme policy, the restrictions on salt merchants were greatly increased. Price adjustments were subject to the approval of the Salt Administration Bureau in Guiyang, and warehouses were collectively managed by supervisors sent by the Bureau. Soon after the implementation of the "one merchant for one port" system under controlled economy, the July 7th Incident occurred and escalated the Second Sino-Japanese War. With the escalation of war, salt merchants encountered more difficulties in terms of capital, manpower, and transportation, and thus needed to maintain closer contact with the Salt Administration Bureau to discuss ways of dealing with this situation. At a board meeting of Yong An Salt Firm in 1938, Liu Xiyi proposed setting up an office in Guiyang in order to stay in touch with the Bureau. The board approved this proposal and elected Liu Xiyi as the director of the office and Sun Yunqi as the deputy director.[12] In 1939, the Guiyang Office of the Guizhou Yong An Official Salt Transportation and Distribution Office (贵州永边官盐运销营业处贵阳办事处 *Guizhou yongbian guanyan yunxiao yinyechu Guiyang banshichu*) was officially established, and Liu and Sun moved to Guiyang to take up their posts. They negotiated all tasks with the Salt Administration Bureau in Guiyang.

In 1940, the Guizhou Salt Office convened a meeting for the development of the salt business in the four main ports. In addition to discussing measures to deal with the merchant's common operational problems at that time, those at the meeting also approved the motion of a temporary merging of two groups in Yong An to facilitate the business.[13] In the introduction to the Yong An salt merchants later written by Sun Yunqi, the merger of the two groups was justified in two ways: the Yong An people felt merging would allow them to concentrate their capital strength, and they received an order from the salt authorities to merge the two groups.[14] In reality, it is more likely that Liu, Sun, and other

14; Liu Yuyuan, "Yong An de qianqianhouhou" 永岸的前前后后 [the Process of Founding Yong An], *Lixing yuekan*, 1 (1944): 11.

[12] Liu Yuyuan, "Liu Xiyi de fajia yu shuaibai", 25.

[13] *Guizhou Yanwu Banshichu ershiba nian zhaoji si an xiaoshang gaijin huiyilu* 贵州盐务办事处二十八年召集四岸销商改进会议录 [Proceedings of the improvement meeting of Guizhou Salt Office and the Four Border Ports Distributors, 28th Year of the Republic of China], 043-01-0319, Guiyang Municipal Archives, 49.

[14] 孙蕴奇, "Chanqian yongan xiaoqu guanyan weituo yunshang yingye gaishu," 14.

Guiyang offices first proposed the merger, obtained the approval of the salt authorities, and then used the endorsement of the salt authorities to push it forward. The merger of the two groups was not formally completed until May 1941, when the head office of the Yong An operation was moved from Xuyong to Guiyang, with Liu Xiyi as manager and Sun Yunqi as associate manager. Following this, the Yong An salt wholesalers formed an organizational structure with Liu Xiyi and Sun Yunqi at its core, Guiyang as the center, branches set up at various important nodes of salt transportation, and an office in Chongqing,[15] the capital of Nationalist government during the war.

2 The Making of the Corporate Groupe of Yong An

As discussed in Chapter 3, the Nationalist government's dirigisme policy regarding salt transportation and distribution imposed more restrictions on the salt merchants than the previously recognized merchant system, and the profits of salt merchants were kept low. However, compared to the previous chaos under warlords, the political situation in Guizhou had become more stable after the central government was able to take strong control of the province. As a result, the centralized control of the salt business was actually a double-edged sword. As long as there was enough money to keep this business going, it provided more opportunities for salt merchants to strengthen their ties with the local military and other powerful individuals, and to gain new sources of funding outside of the state-controlled salt trade. By taking advantage of this, though the escalation of the war and the tightening of government control over salt as a strategic material added to the difficulty in running salt business, Yong An Salt Firm not only managed to maintain its operations under the auspices of Liu Xiyi, but also expanded its business widely after the 1940s, participating in the establishment of new institutions such as the Jukang Bank (聚康银行 *jukang yinhang*), the Ren An Limin Salt Firm (仁岸利民盐号 *ren'an limin yanhao*), and the Yumin Salt Well Company (裕民盐井公司 *yumin yanjing gongsi*).

[15] See "Chuanqianyong yunxiaoqu guanyan weituoshang yingyechu zhiyuan lulibia", 川黔永运销区官盐委托运商营业处职员履历表 [Résumé of the Staff of the Official Salt Commissioned Transporters Business Office of Sichuan-Guizhou Yong An Salt Sales Area], *Lixing yuekan* 1 (1944): 35–43.

As mentioned earlier, the main difficulties for salt wholesalers were the high cost, the high risk, and the slow return of capital, which meant they had to invest continuously to cover their losses and maintain normal operations. Seeking more financial flexibility, after the center of Yong An's salt operation was moved from Xuyong to Guiyang, Liu Xiyi began to plan financial institutions to absorb social lobbying capital and also to provide guarantees for salt merchants to borrow from other banks.[16] Thus, he and his long-time trading partner, Liu Wanquan, took over the name of Chongqing Jukang Native Bank through Li Jiyun, a Guizhou businessman in Chongqing, and reorganized it as a modern bank. Then with the support of Wang Boqun 王伯群, a Guizhou socialite who had some influence in the relevant political circles and was the president of Daxia University at that time, Jukang Bank was soon successfully registered with the Ministry of Finance.[17]

Just when Liu worked to establish his modern bank, a risky opportunity came knocking on the door. The wholesalers' organization of Ren An was dissolved and wholesalters "resigned from the port" due to their inability to replenish capital into salt trade. The border trading port of Ren An, Hejiang, was very close to Xuyong, the border trading port of

[16] At the same time, Liu Xiyi may also have connected the funds in his other businesses with Yong An's operations. For example, after Liu Xiyi stationed in Guiyang due to the need for Yong An's business, he took advantage of the shortage of wartime supplies and the soaring prices, and opened Jishi Firm in Guiyang. He bought gauze from Shaoguan, Guangzhou, and shipped it to Guizhou through Hunan and Guangxi for wholesaling, so as to make huge profits. In addition to Liu Xiyi's own funds, the company also was invested by other shareholders of Yong An. From the existing source, the operation and success of Jishi Firm cannot have been possible without the help of Wang Wenzhao, an employee of the Guizhou Highway Bureau that Liu Xiyi made friends with. Wang Wenzhao had a relative who served as the head of the tax bureau in Changsha, and provided convenience for the transportation of goods from Hunan to Guizhou. In Guizhou Province, in addition to setting up a general office in Guiyang, Jishi also set up a branch office in Bijie, which was managed by Wang Weiqing, then president of the Bijie Chamber of Commerce, with the assistance of Liu Yuyuan. It can be seen from the above table that before the formation of Yong An Salt Firm, Wang Weiqing was the manager of Qianxintong, while Liu Yuyuan has been involved in Liu Xiyi's various businesses. It can be speculated that part of the operation of Jishi relied on the transportation network of Yong An Salt, and Wu Xiaogao also adopted a similar method after taking over Ren An. See Liu Yuyua, "Huiyi Liu Xiyi jingshang de jingli" 回忆刘熙乙经商的经历 (Recollections of Liu Xiyi's business experience), in *Guizhou wenshi ziliao xuanji* no. 17 (1984), 203; Liu Yuyuan & Tang Bin "Gongshang shiye jia Liu Xiyi," 77; Wu Xiaogao, "Guizhou shiyan yunxiao de huiyi," 214–215.

[17] Liu Yuyuan and Tang Bin, "Gongshang shiye jia Liu Xiyi", 81.

Yong An. Salt business of these two trade routes could be integrated. One proof is that once Ren An and Yong An were designed to transport salt from different salterns and Ren An's salt was cheaper. As a result, Yong An's salt merchants were troubled by the encroachment of Ren An's salt on business in Yong An, as in general, the salt from Yong An's designated saltern did not sell well in Guizhou during that time.[18] After the central government imposed control on the salt industry, the types and quantities of salt sold in each port were readjusted and more strictly controlled, but since the routes of the sales areas were largely based on the already established and mature salt transportation routes, mutual influence between Ren An and Yong An remained.

However, Liu had a strong competitor on taking over Ren An's salt business. Daye Company (大业公司 *daye gongsi*), a subsidiary company of one of the most powerful Chinese commercial banks at that time, the Shanghai Commercial Saving Bank, and believed to be backed by the central government, was ready to take over Ren An and had already received the support of the General Salt Administration Bureau.[19] Before Daye Company attempted to take over Ren An's business, there were already cases where original salt wholesalers in Qi An and Fu An resigned due to operational difficulties and were taken over by the same company. With such a background, it is obvious that Daye successively took over Qi An, Fu An, and Ren An in an attempt to form a monopoly on salt transportation in Guizhou, and it was only a matter of time before it began to

[18] Song shu 宋树 et al. eds., *Xuyongxian zhi* 叙永县志 (Local Gazetteer of Xuyong County), 1933, vol. 7, "Salt Industry", *Xinxiu fangzhi congkan* 新修方志丛刊 [Newly Revised Local Gazetteers Series] reprinted (Taipei: Taiwan Student Book Company, 1962), vol. 2, 567.

[19] "Ren An jiangyou Daye Gongsi jishang jieban" 仁岸将由大业公司集商接办 [Ren An will Be Handled by Daye Company], *Yanwu yuebao* 盐务月报 [Salt Monthly], 5 (1942): "chronicle", 35.

squeeze the original local state-controlled business of Yong An.[20] Therefore, winning over Ren An's salt business was not only to expand Liu Xiyi's business landscape but also to protect his interest in Yong An.

Liu Xiyi, and his Yong An business partners soon proposed that "the salt Guizhou people eat should be run by Guizhou merchants", and joined hands with a number of Guizhou celebrities to negotiate with the Chongqing authorities to leave the business of Ren An to local Guizhou merchants. In this process, another Guizhou political figure in Chongqing, Deng Hanxiang 邓汉祥, the secretary general of the Sichuan provincial government, was also involved.

However, the capital of the merchants in Yong An alone was not enough to rely on to establish Jukang Bank and compete with Daye for Ren An. So Liu Xiyi thought of Wu Xiaogao, whom he had met in the opium trade in the past. Wu was running a hardware factory in Guiyang at that time. Due to a lack of political backing, when the hardware factory was forced to merge with Guizhou Enterprise Company, a Guizhou provincial enterprise under the leadership of Wu Dingchang, Wu Xiaogao had to withdraw after the merger. Consequently, Wu attempted to find new business opportunities to invest in. Through Wu Xiaogao, Liu Xiyi was able to reach other Anshun opium traders with significant capital.

According to Wu Xiaogao's recollection, Jukang Bank and the establishment of Limin Salt Firm (利民盐号 *limin yanhao*) in Ren An was planned by Liu Xiyi, Wang Boqun, Deng Hanxiang, and other merchants who had some preliminary ideas. Wu agreed to join, and then he and Liu Xiyi went to find the most powerful local businessman in Anshun, Shuai Canzhang 帅灿章. They persuaded Shuai to join them, and at the same time contacted other Anshun merchants to collaborate. After all these negotiations, Liu Xiyi, Wu Xiaogao, and Shuai Canzhang were the initiators and invited other business people to discuss the establishment of Jukang Bank and the issue of taking the salt business in Ren An over from Daye Company. They finally raised 10 million *yuan* to run Jukang

[20] According to the recollections of several Guizhou salt merchants, Daye's attempt to monopolize salt transportation was the consensus of local salt merchants at that time. See Liu Yuyuan & Tang Bin "Gongshangshiyejia Liu Xiyi", 81; Wu Luqin, "Jiefangqian Guizhou yunxiao chuanyan gaikuang," 149; Wu Xiaogao, "Guizhou shiyan yunxiao de huiyi," 209; the basic information about Daye Company can also see "Jieshao Daye maoyi gongsi" 介绍大业贸易公司 [Introducing Daye Trading Company], *Jingji daobao* 经济导报 [Economic Herald], 3 (1947): 24.

Bank first and then set up Guizhou Renji Limin Salt Firm (贵州仁记利民盐号 *Guizhou renji limin yanhao*).[21]

Through the efforts of Wang Boqun and Deng Hanxiang, and with the support of local public opinion in Guizhou, Liu and his partners finally gained the support of Wang Boqun's brother-in-law, He Yingqin 何应钦, who had enough bargaining power in the central government and could directly negotiate with the Minister of Finance, H. H. Kung. Besides meeting the specific requirements raised by Daye, local merchants also offered salt quota of Ren An's designated area in South Guizhou to be operated by Daye Company in the negotiation. Daye finally compromised and the Limin Salt Company was able to successfully take over Ren An.[22]

Since the Anshun merchants, such as Wu Xiaogao, had no experience in handling salt transportation, Limin Salt Company was initially operated mainly by personnel from Yong An. In line with the business needs of Yong An and Ren An, the business scope of Jukang Bank continued to grow. In addition to the main management office in Guizhou, the bank set up branches in Guiyang, Chongqing, Changsha, Anshun, and Wuzhou, and offices in Bijie, Wutongqiao, Neijiang, Duyun, and other important nodes of salt transportation.[23] The establishment of Jukang Bank and Limin Salt Company not only prevented Yong An's salt transport from being annexed by the Daye Company but also brought the salt transportation business in western Guizhou under Yong An merchants' control and strengthened the connection between Guizhou and important commercial ports outside the province. This enabled the Yong An salt merchants under Liu Xiyi's leadership to consolidate and rationally deploy their various resources.

At the same time, Liu also kept seeking the opportunity to involve Yong An in the development of salt wells to achieve the vertical integration of production, transportation, and marketing together. He had been very close to this goal by participating in the preparation and establishment of the Yumin Salt Well Company (裕民盐井公司 *yumin yanjing gongsi*). The salt well of Yumin Salt Well Company was located in Azatun, Shuicheng County, near Bijie, and was originally owned by the Wang

21 Wu Xiaogao, "Guizhou shiyan yunxiao de huiyi," 207–208.

22 Wu Xiaogao, "Guizhou shiyan yunxiao de huiyi," 207–208; Liu Yuyuan, "Liu Xiyi de fajia yu shuaibai", 26.

23 Liu Xiyi & Jiang Zhengqi 蒋徵琪, "Jukang yinhang gaikuang" 聚康银行概况 [Overview of Jukang Bank], *Lixing yuekan*, 1 (1944): 15–18.

family of the Shuicheng gentry. The salt well was re-developed in 1940 due to transportation difficulties during the war and the short supply of salt in Sichuan. The Yumin Salt Well Company was officially incorporated in 1942, with its head office in Guiyang and an engineering office in the Shuicheng to handle the specific tasks of opening the well and boiling the salt. Although it is not known exactly when Liu Xiyi became involved, he was the managing director and general manager of the company after it was established, and he solved the company's lack of funds, so he no doubt was the central figure in the Yumin Salt Well Company. At least until 1944, the salt well's excavation was still underway, and Liu Xiyi led journalists from the Central Daily News, the China Times, Guizhou Daily, and other media outlets to visit and report on the site. Unfortunately, the salt well suffered an accident later, and neither Liu Xiyi nor Mi Junmu 糜君牧, the manager of Yumin Salt Well Company, could raise more funds to maintain it, so the well gradually fell into disuse.[24]

As we can see, during this period, when the wartime situation was becoming increasingly tense and state control was escalating, the high risk made many dominating salt wholesalers begin to quit salt business. However, thanks to Liu Xiyi's reflexible use of his business network, Yong An merchants were able to expand their power and become one of the major business groups in Guizhou province. Opening the above-mentioned enterprises took advantage of the social influence of Guizhou's military and political elites and successfully absorbed the extensive capital of the Anshun opium traders; in turn, these enterprises became strong links between politics and business. After the establishment of the Jukang Bank and Ren An Limin Salt Company, respectively, Wang Boqun and Deng Hanxiang served as the chairman of the board of directors. Both men had shares in the two places with no actual investments but could participate in the dividends when there was a surplus in the accounts.[25] The Yumin Salt Well Company was also formally established with the support of Han Wenhuan 韩文焕, the deputy commander of the Guizhou

[24] Information about Yumin Salt Well Company, see "Guizhou Yumin yanjing gongsi" 贵州裕民盐井公司 [Guizhou Yumin Salt Well Company], *Guizhou qiye jikan* 贵州企业季刊 [Guizhou Enterprise Quarterly] 2, no. 2 (1942): 171–172; Liu Xiyi, "Guizhou Yumin yanjing gongsi gaikuang" 贵州裕民盐井公司概况 [Overview of Guizhou Yumin Salt Well Company], *Lixing yuekan* 1 (1944): 22–23; Liu Yuyuan, "Huiyi Liu Xiyi jingshang de jingli," 27.

[25] Wu Xiaogao, "Guizhou shiyan yunxiao de huiyi," 210.

military control district and head of the security forces, then Han served as the chairman of this company.[26] According to Wu Xiaogao, the Limin Salt Company too included some shareholders with official backgrounds, such as Wang Wenxiang 王文湘 (wife of He Yingqin and sister of Wang Boqun), Gu Jishu 谷纪书 (brother of later Guizhou provincial chairman Gu Zhenglun 谷正伦), and Han Yunbo 韩云波 (cousin of Han Wenhuan), who were invited to join the company not for financial capital but for the social influence of their names and backgrounds.[27]

Although Anshun opium merchants also invested extensively in these enterprises,[28] their voice was not as strong as that of the leading figures of Yong An, such as Liu Xiyi. The capital backing of Jukang Bank was independent of funds running the transportation and distribution sectors in Ren An and Yong An, but the main shareholders were basically the same group of people. However, the core figures of Yong An, such as Liu Xiyi and Sun Yunqi, had investments in all three places, while Anshun merchants such as Wu Xiaogao only invested in the Jukang Bank and Limin Salt, with only indirect influence on Yong An through the Jukang Bank.

The Anshun opium merchants led by Wu Xiaogao accounted for 80% of the investment in Ren An, but because they had no experience in salt transportation, the actual operation of Limin Salt Company was still dominated by the personnel of Yong An for a long time after its establishment.[29] Wang Yukai 王裕凯, who at one time served as director secretary at Jukang Bank, once said, "Yong An, the mother, gave birth to a big sister (Jukang) with a little brother (Ren An)." This mother–children

[26] Liu Yuyuan & Tang Bin "Gongshangshiyejia Liu Xiyi," 79.

[27] Wu Xiaogao, "Guizhou shiyan yunxiao de huiyi," 210.

[28] Shuai Canzhang 帅灿章 and Wu Xiaogao also invested in Yumin Salt Well Company. Like Liu Xiyi, they are the executive directors of Yumin Salt Well Company, but Shuai did not participate in the actual operation of the company. See "Guizhou yumin yanjing gongsi," 172.

[29] There was a conflict between Liu Xiyi and Sun Yunqi, the Yong An merchants from Bijie and Dading, and Wu Xiaogao and other Anshun opium traders who had newly participated in the salt buniness about the managerial authority issue of Ren An. At first, under the mediation of Wang Boqun, the two sides reached a tentative settlement, see Wu Xiaogao, "Guizhou shiyan yunxiao de huiyi," 215–216.

analogy was also recognized by Liu Yuyuan.[30] It can be seen that the promoters and actual controllers of the Jukang Bank and the Ren An Limin Salt Company were the Yong An salt merchants led by Liu Xiyi, and it can also be said that Liu Xiyi used the funds of the Anshun opium merchants to achieve the expansion of Yong An. This situation laid the groundwork for conflict between the Anshun merchants and the Bijie and Dading merchants, especially with the leader of the latter, Liu Xiyi.

3 Xinqian Enterprise Company (新黔企业公司 *xinqian qiye gongsi*) and the Two "Xinqian Cigarette Factories"

As can be seen from the discussion above, the expansion of Yong An merchants was initially centered on salt transportation. On one hand, these merchants attempted to develop local salt wells in Guizhou and integrate production, transportation, and distribution; on the other hand, they established their own financial network and expanded the scope of transportation and distribution under their control by taking over Ren An. In 1939, under the planning of Wu Dingchang, the chairman of Guizhou Province at that moment, Guizhou Enterprise Company (*Guizhou qiye gonsi* 贵州企业公司) was set up. It was a joint-stock limited liability company run by the provincial government and local merchants, providing a new way for Liu Xiyi to closely associate with political forces.

In 1941, Liao Xingxu 廖兴序 became the inspector of the Fourth Administrative District of Guizhou (第四行政区 *disi xinzhengqu*),[31] soon establishing a connection with Liu Xiyi and investing in the Yumin salt well.[32] Liu and Liao gathered local elites from Bijie, including Huang Tong 黄通, director secretary of the special bureau (专署秘书主任 *zhuanshu mishu zhuren*), Zhao Fazhi 赵发智, head of the construction department and director of the Fourth District Agricultural Improvement Institute, Li Siqi 李思齐, Head of the Education Department, and

[30] Liu Yuyuan, "Mantan ren yong ju qian gui xin (xing)" 漫谈仁永聚黔贵新(兴) [Sketches on Ren An, Yong An, Jukang Bank, Qianren Company, Guizhou Bank, Xinqian Company and Zhongxing Enterprise Company], *Lixing yuekan* 2, no.1 (1946): 65.

[31] The Fourth Administrative District has jurisdiction over 5 counties including Bijie, Dading, Qianxi, Weining, and Shuicheng, and the commissioner's office is stationed in Bijie County.

[32] "Guizhou yumin yanjing gongsi," 172.

Wu Songping吴颂平, a local gentry.[33] This group began to cooperate in setting up a joint enterprise company in the Fourth District, following the model of the Guizhou Enterprise Company.

In 1944, after a year of preliminary planning, Xinqian Enterprise Company, the District-supported enterprise of the Fourth District, was officially established. The company planned to develop printing, cigarette, textile, animal husbandry, and mining business in the Fourth District. Its capital consisted of official shares, including shares from the Special Bureau of the Fourth District, the Fourth District's Farm, the county-level governments of the Fourth District, and the Finance Committee (财委会 *caiweihui*), and commercial shares, including shares from various firms, institutions, merchants, and other local elites, with a total of nearly 300 shareholders in the name of institutions and natural persons.[34] Among them, Liu Xiyi alone contributed 1.4 million currency, more than the sum of all the official shares. According to Liu Yuyuan's recollection, part of Liu Xiyi's investment in Xinqian Enterprise Company was funded by Yong An. A close connection between Xinqian Enterprise Company and the salt business in Yong An was evident. After the establishment of Xinqian Enterprise Company, it soon joined with Yong An Salt Firm and other companies that had close ties with the salt business in Yong An to create an internal publication called *Lixing Monthly* for inter-company communication.[35] In addition, Liu Yuyuan was appointed as the head of the Chongqing offices of six institutions: Yong An Salt Firm, Ren An Limin Salt Company, Jukang Bank, Qianren Company, Guizhou Bank, and Xinqian Enterprise Company. The six institutions issued joint appointment letters.[36] From Liu Yuyuan's point of view, the five institutions other than Guizhou Bank were developed by Yong An.[37]

[33] Liu Yuyuan, "Huiyi Liu Xiyi jingshang de jingli," 209.

[34] See "Xinqian qiye gongsi faqiren biao" 新黔企业公司发起人表 [Founding Members of Xinqian Enterprise Company], "Xinqian qiye gongsi gudong biao", 新黔企业公司股东表 [Shareholders of Xinqian Enterprise Company], in Xinqian Gonsi dengji wenjian Xinqian Gonsi dengji wenjian 新黔公司登记文件 [Xinqian Company Registration Documents], M61-1-7333, Guizhou Provincial Archives, p4, p61; Liao Xingxu 廖兴序, "Xinsheng de xinqian qiye gongsi" 新生的新黔企业公司 [The Newborn Xinqian Enterprise Company], *Lixing yuekan* 1 (1944): 19.

[35] Liu Xiyi, "Chuangkanci" 创刊词 [Preface], *Lixing yuekan* 1 (1944): 1.

[36] Liu Yuyuan, "Mantan ren yong ju qian gui xin (xing)," 64.

[37] Liu Yuyuan, "Mantan ren yong ju qian gui xin (xing)," 64–65.

Thus, Liu Xiyi's investment in Xinqian Enterprise Company was a plan to incorporate Xinqian into Yong An's business, thereby expanding Yong An's influence from the salt industry to more industries and forming a concerned group under his control. Moreover, the most prominent cigarette factory under Xinqian Enterprise Company exemplifies Liu Xiyi's personal investment style of distributing financial risks.

According to Liao Xingxu's introduction of Xinqian Enterprise Company in the *Lixing Monthly*, the cigarette factory named "Xinqian" was one of the first endeavors in operation after the company's establishment. It was combined with the Fourth District Farm's plan to promote the cultivation of American tobacco in the region.[38] As early as the fall of 1941, Liu Xiyi had been producing cigarettes under the name "Xinqian Cigarette Factory" in the Sanyi Temple in the Shuangjing Monastery of Bijie. This Xinqian Cigarette Factory was initially a hand-rolled cigarette factory, with about twenty employees. Later, the factory gained two small cigarette rolling machines, and the number of employees increased to more than one hundred. The factory produced several types of cigarettes, including Lianzhu 联珠牌, Lingfeng 灵峰牌, and 555, which were distributed to various temples in Bijie to sell.[39] There is no clear evidence that the Xinqian Cigarette Factory of Xinqian Enterprise Company was established by taking over Liu Xiyi's Xinqian Cigarette Factory,[40] but there is some succession between the two factories of the same name. Both employed Luo Binhou 罗彬侯 as manager and, in September 1944, the Xinqian Enterprise Company responded to the request of the Guizhou Branch of the National Industrial Association (*quanguo gongye xiehui guizhousheng fenhui* 全国工业协会贵州省分会) to

[38] Liao Xingxu, "Xinsheng de xinqian qiye gongsi," 20.

[39] Liu Yuyuan 刘裕远, "Liu Xiyi de fajia yu shuaibai", 29–30; Guizhou Provincial Chronicle Compilation Committee ed., *Guizhou sheng zhi yancao zhi* 贵州省志·烟草志 [Chronicles of Guizhou Province, Tobacco] (Guiyang: Guizhou People's Press, 2002), 184.

[40] For example, in the record of the textile business of Xinqian Enterprise Company, it is listed that the property, equipment and goods of the Minsheng Factory jointly established by the government and merchant in Bijie will be transferred into Xinqian for reorganization. See "Xinqian qiye gufen youxian gongsi disanci gudong dahui huiyi jilu" 新黔企业股份有限公司第三次股东大会会议记录 [Minutes of the Third General Meeting of Shareholders of Xinqian Enterprise Company], in Xinqian gonsi chexiao dengji wenjian 新黔公司撤销登记文件 [Xinqian company Deregistration Documents], 60-1-4370, Guizhou Provincial Archives, 43.

investigate the company's products, stating that the cigarettes produced by the Xinqian Cigarette Factory were also branded 555.[41]

Guizhou Enterprise Company's investment in the tobacco industry has provided a good example of how the support of official power is conducive to the optimal allocation of resources in cigarette production to achieve industrial upgrading. In Xinqian's case, they even had an experienced tobacco expert. Zhao Fazhi 赵发智, graduated from the Department of Agronomy of Southeast University in Nanjing and was the head of the Fourth District Farm. Zhao had worked as the director of the provincial agricultural experimental farm before, studied flue-cured tobacco and flue-cured technology, and established the first flue-curing house in Guizhou. Thus, it can be said that he had considerable experience and connections regarding tobacco cultivation and processing.[42] However, this time Liu seemed to have no interest in following the strategy of Guizhou Enterprise Company and further upgrading Xinqian Cigarette Factory. In 1943, when Liu and Liao were planning to open this enterprise company, Liu gave Xinqian Cigarette Factory's two cigarette machines to his opium trading partner Li Wenshang 李文裳 as an investment,[43] as Li Wenshang had opened a cigarette factory called Nanming in Guiyang in partnership with others.[44] The Xinqian Cigarette Factory, a subsidiary of the Xinqian Enterprise Company, was a hand-rolled cigarette factory with a reduced number of employees.[45] The change from a machine-rolled cigarette factory to a hand-rolled cigarette factory did not cause difficulties in the production of Xinqian cigarettes but, rather, may have facilitated it. After Xinqian Enterprise Company was established in 1944, the company soon increased the factory's capital from one and a half million yuan to five million yuan. At the time the Xinqian Enterprise

41 Bijie juanyanchang chanpin diaochabiao 毕节卷烟厂产品调查表 [Survey Form of Cigarette Factory Products], i043-01-0869, Guiyang Municipal Archives.

42 Zhuofu 拙夫, "Renwu jieshao:Wu Xiaogao" 人物介绍:伍效高 [Profile: Wu Xiaogao], *Lixing yuekan* 2, no. 2 (1946): 62.

43 Liu Xiyi and Li Wenshang previously jointly opened Yisheng, which was engaged in opium trading, see Liu Yuyuan, "Liu Xiyi de fajia yu shuaibai," 25.

44 Liu Yuyuan, "Guiyang Naming Yanchang zhuiyi" 贵阳南明烟厂追忆 [Remembrance of Guiyang Nanming Tobacco Factory], in *Nanming wenshi ziliao xuanji* 南明文史资料选辑 [Selected Materials of Nanming District Literature and History), no.2 (1984), 41–45.

45 "Xinqian qiye gufen youxian gongsi disanci gudongdahui huiyi jilu", M60-1-4370, Guizhou Provincial Archives, 43.

Company decided to go into bankruptcy, the hand-rolled cigarette factory still had a surplus, and was the only industry of the Xinqian Enterprise Company that was still profitable,[46] while another subsidiary cigarette factory Xinqian Enterprise Company set up in Guiyang, machine-rolled, had been losing money due to high production costs.[47]

The hand-rolled cigarette industry was more sustainable during wartime. Compared to machine-rolled cigarettes, hand-rolled cigarettes were produced on a smaller scale and were more troublesome for the government to manage. Indeed, before the July 7 Incident, the nationalist government intended to ban hand-rolled cigarettes due to their small scale, scattered production, serious rate of counterfeiting, and high tax supervision costs. However, after the July 7 Incident, the major commercial ports in Southeast China fell one after another, making it difficult to transport machine-rolled cigarettes to inland provinces. The state no longer wanted to outlaw hand-rolled cigarette, and instead tried to facilitate taxation by strengthening their regulation.[48] Even so, the management and taxation of hand-rolled cigarettes, which were sold in smaller numbers and lower price, were minimal. Guizhou had enforced monopoly policies since 1943 in accordance with the state's tobacco monopoly regulations, under which the tax and fees paid for producing and distributing machine-rolled cigarettes were much higher than hand-rolled cigarettes.[49]In this situation, hand-rolled and machine-rolled cigarettes entailed quite different business models, and running a machine-rolled cigarette business was not necessarily better than hand-rolled cigarettes as far as profitability was concerned.[50] In addition, the original cigarettes produced by Liu Xiyi's Xinqian Cigarette Factory were suspected of imitating the British American Tobacco Company (i.e.,

46 Ibid.

47 Ibid.

48 Chen Hongyou 陈洪友, *Minguo shiqi henan shougongjuanyan yanjiu (1912–1949)* 民国时期河南手工卷烟研究 [Study on Hand-rolled Cigarettes in Henan During the Period of Republic of China (1912–1949)] (PhD diss., Nanjing: Nanjing University, 2012], 120–127.

49 Ibid.

50 Discussion on the reverse substitution of hand-rolled cigarettes for machine-made cigarettes,see Huangfu Qiushi 皇甫秋实, *Weijizhong de xuanze:zhanqian shinian de zhongguo juanyan shichang* 危机中的选择: 战前十年的中国卷烟市场 [Choices in Crisis: Cigarette Market in Pre-war China] [Shanghai: Oriental Press, 2016], 118–138.

the 555 brand) and the Nanyang Brothers Tobacco Company (e.g., the Lianzhu brand).[51] The cigarettes produced by Xinqian Enterprise Company's Xinqian Cigarette Factory were also suspected of being imitations of these brands,[52] and their sales range was limited to Bijie and the surrounding areas, which shows that the production and sales scale of the Xinqian Cigarette Factory may have been more suitable for the production of hand-rolled cigarettes.

Of course, the change in Xinqian Cigarette Factory's business model was to a large extent related to the structure of Xinqian Enterprise Company. On the one hand, although the operating structure of Xinqian Enterprise Company imitates that of Guizhou Enterprise Company, the nature of the shares attributed to it is different.[53] According to the documents submitted by Xinqian Enterprise, the company's official shares amounted to 981,000 yuan, the commercial shares accounting for 1.4 million yuan, followed by 1 million yuan for Liu Yuyuan, and 1 million yuan for Wu Xiaogao. The proportion of commercial shares to official

[51] Lianzhu brand is one of the main products of Nanyang Tobacco Company,see Shanghai Institute of Economics, Chinese Academy of Sciences, and Institute of Economics, Shanghai Academy of Social Sciences eds., *Nanyang xiongdi yancao gongsi shiliao* 南洋兄弟烟草公司史料 [Historical Materials of Nanyang Brothers Tobacco Company] (Shanghai: Shanghai People's Press, 1960), 244; the 555 brand/"Three Five" (State Express 555) is a product of Ardath Tobacco Co. See "Xuzhan shending shangbiao di 1357 hao" 续展审定商标第1357号 [Renewal of the Approved Trademark No. 1357],in *Shangbiao gongbao* 商标公报 [Trademark Gazette], Issues 161–162,"Renewal of Approved Trademark", 31.

[52] According to the reply from Xinqian Enterprise Company to the Guizhou Branch of the National Association of Industry and Commerce, Xinqian Cigarette Factory produced two types of cigarettes. In addition to the "Three Five Brand" and the "Diamond Brand". The Diamond brand is also registered by Nanyang Brothers Tobacco Company. See Bijie juanyanchang chanpin diaochabiao 043-01-0869, Guiyang Municipal Archives.; Quanguo shangbiao zhuce suoyin 全国商标注册索引 [National Trademark Registration Index], Part I, 649.

[53] Proportion of capital contributed by provincial enterprises see Lu Liangzheng 卢征良 & Zhu Yingui 朱荫贵, "Kangzhan shiqi shengying qiye gongsi xingzhi yanjiu" 抗战时期省营企业性质研究 [The Character of the Provincial Enterprises in Modern History], *Social Science*, 9 (2020): 155–156; about provincial enterprises can also see Zhang Zhongmin 张忠民, "Luelun kangzhan shiqi neidi shengqu qiye gongsi de zhidutezheng" 略论抗战时期内地省区企业公司的制度特征 [A Brief Discussion on the Institutional Characteristics of Enterprises and Corporations in Inland Provinces and Regions During the Anti-Japanese War], *Shanghai Journal of Economics* 9 (2004): 72–78; Morris L. Bian, "Redefining the Chinese Revolution: The Transformation and Evolution of Guizhou's Regional State Enterpriese," *Modern China* 41, no. 3 (2015): 317–321.

shares in Xinqian Cigarette Factory was much higher.[54] Thus, Xinqian Enterprise Company was a joint venture between the government and social elites in the Fourth Administrative District, but in terms of capital composition, it was different from other public enterprises of this period, such as Guizhou Enterprise Company, in which the proportion of government shares to commercial shares was much higher, and the government was in full control of the company's management. On the other hand, although the core of Yong An, such as Liu Xiyi and Liu Yuyuan, wanted to make Xinqian Enterprise a part of the "Yong An Group," the influence of the government at all levels of the Fourth District, and on the board of directors and supervisory board of Xinqian Enterprise could not be ignored. As can be seen, the operation of Xinqian was largely based on Liu Xiyi's ability to maintain good relations with the heads of government agencies at all levels within the Fourth District.

These two characteristics outlined above determined the instability of Xinqian Enterprise Company's operating structure: although Xinqian Enterprise Company was established as a joint-stock company under the Company Law, when it dissolved the arrangement for the company's assets was to return the shareholders' shares and the dividends, while Liu Xiyi alone bore the losses of the company. It should be noted here that the actual operation of Xinqian Enterprise Company was different from that of a joint-stock limited company in the modern economics sense. Liu Xiyi was willing to accept such an arrangement because he had some pressure to ask other shareholders, especially the official shareholders, to share the loss.[55]

As mentioned before, Liu Xiyi invested the two cigarette machines from the Xinqian Cigarette Factory into the private Nanming Tobacco Factory as production materials partly in consideration of his own assets instability, the result of a joint venture between government and business. In 1940, the Guizhou Tobacco Company, a provincial enterprise under the Guizhou Enterprise Company, was opened. This enterprise also had only three medium-sized cigarette machines. Later, private machine-rolled cigarette factories appeared in Guizhou, most of which had been reorganized and reestablished due to Japan's "Ichigo Offensive". Most

[54] "Xinqian qiye gongsi gudong biao", 61.

[55] Xinqian qiye gufen youxian gongsi disanci gudongdahui huiyi jilu, M60-1-4370, Guizhou Provincial Archives, 43.

of the machines used in these private factories, originally from Hunan province, were small cigarette-rolling machines.[56] These machines were a precious production material at that time. If the Xinqian Cigarette Factory had changed from a purely private cigarette factory to a joint venture company and being co-funded by the local government and local merchants, the ownership of cigarette machines would probably have been changed.

To sum up, reallocating the cigarette machines from the Xinqian Cigarette Factory into the operation of the Nanming cigarette factory, and reverting the Xinqian Cigarette Factory back to manufacturing hand-rolled cigarettes, was Liu Xiyi's strategy for adapting to local conditions and spreading out risk on the experience he had accumulated in cigarette production. In terms of results, Xinqian Enterprise Company was discontinued a year after its establishment due to poor operation, making it a failed project for Liu Xiyi. However, due to the flexible business strategy he adopted, Liu Xiyi was left with room to readjust Yong An's business and continue to develop cigarette production in Guizhou.

4 Nanming Cigarette Factory Beyond Yong An Business

After the investment from Liu Xiyi, Nanming Tobacco Factory switched from producing hand-rolled cigarettes to producing machine-rolled cigarettes. In 1944, the factory received investments from Wu Xiaogao, Shuai Canzhang, Dai Ziru 戴子儒, and others. The total capital of Nanming Tobacco Factory after this infusion was 70 million yuan: of which Liu Xiyi's and Liu Yuyuan's shares accounted for 50%, Wu Xiaogao and other Anshun merchants accounted for 25%, and Li Wenshang and Zeng Yunqing 曾韵青, the original founders of the factory, accounted for 25%. Among them, Liu Xiyi was the chairman, Zeng Yunqing was the manager, and Li Wenshang was the factory manager. Nanming Cigarette Factory had more than 400 employees and produced two types of cigarettes, Sanjiao 三角牌 and Xiniuwang 犀牛王牌. As the tobacco factory produced flue-cured tobacco locally in Guizhou, the good quality

[56] Li Minzhang 黎敏章, "Guizhou yancao gongye zhi jueqi" 贵州烟草工业之崛起 [The Rise of Guizhou Tobacco Industry], in *Nanming wenshi ziliao xuanji* 南明文史资料选辑 [Selected Materials of Southern Ming Dynasty's Literature and History], no. 20 (2001): 59–61.

and reasonable price made these two brands of cigarettes produced by Nanming Tobacco Factory popular not only in the counties of Guizhou but also in the counties of Yunnan and Sichuan, which border Guizhou.[57]

In November 1945, Liu Xiyi, Liu Yuyuan, Zhao Fazhi, and others began to establish Zhongxing Enterprise Limited Company (中兴企业股份有限公司 *zhongxing qiye gufen youxian gongsi*), which was formally established in June of the following year. The main shareholders of Zhongxing included the Liu brothers, Zhao Fazhi, Luo Huibai 罗惠白, Sun Yunqi, Wu Songping, and others. Five of them were elected as the managing directors, Liu Xiyi, Zhao Fa Zhi, Zhang Zhiqi 章志齐, Sun Yun Qi, and Qian Jingxing 钱景星, with Liu Xiyi as the chairman and Zhao Fazhi as the general manager. From the composition of the staff, it is easy to see that, in addition to Yong An's original connections, the local elites of Bijie who had participated in Xinqian Enterprise Company, Zhao Fazhi, and Wu Songping, were also involved. However, these people were all involved as individuals, and Zhongxing Enterprise Limited Company was a purely private enterprise.[58] In Liu Yuyuan's account, Zhongxing was the successor of Xinqian in the Yong An Group. The change from Xinqian to Zhongxing was made by these merchants in response to the local political and socio-economic situation, and also as a way to restructure their business.[59] According to the report on the founding of Zhongxing and the introduction of its director Luo Huibai, the purpose of Zhongxing was "to operate various industries, develop local resources, and promote the economic development of the province," as well as "to bring prosperity to the countryside and promote the rejuvenation of people's livelihoods." When the company was established, there were already branches in Shanghai, Kunming, Anshun, Bijie, and Dading, and offices in Panxian, Zhijin, Qianxi, Shuicheng, Chongqing, Anjiang, Changsha, Hankou, and Hong Kong.[60] In contrast

[57] Liu Yuyuan, "Guiyang Naming yanchang zhuiyi," 43–44.

[58] "Zhongxin qiye faqiren biao" 中兴企业公司发起人表 [Founding Members of Zhongxing Enterprise Company], Zhongxing qiye gongsi dengji wenjian 中兴企业公司登记文件 [Zhongxing Enterprise Company Registration Documents], M60-1-7350, Guizhou Provincial Archives, 7.

[59] Liu Yuyuan, "Mantan ren yong ju qian gui xin (xing)," 64–65.

[60] Luo Huibai 罗惠白," Zhongxing qiye gufen youxian gongsi gaikuang" 中兴企业股份有限公司概况 [Overview of Zhongxing Enterprise Co., Ltd.], Lixing yuekan 2, no. 3 (1946): 37–38.

to Xinqian, Zhongxin's business scope was no longer limited to Bijie and the surrounding areas. However, although the designated business of the company included cigarettes, Zhongxing did not choose to invest in the Nanming Tobacco Factory or any other tobacco business, citing the stagnant traffic and financial difficulties caused by the current political and socio-economic situation, and instead used the funds for import and export trade, buying and selling pig bristles, tung oil, cotton yarn, newsprint, and other business.[61]

On the other hand, also in 1946, Liu Xiyi and several other major shareholders of Nanming Tobacco Factory, Shuai Canzhang, Dai Ziru, Zeng Yunqing, and Li Wenshang, reorganized the factory with additional capital and established Zhonglong Industrial Limited Company (中隆实业股份有限公司 *zhonglong shiye gufen youxian gongsi*). Although Zhonglong's scope was quite broad, including the exploitation of mineral deposits, improvement of farming and animal husbandry, transportation and marketing of agricultural and mineral products, domestic and foreign trade, and various production businesses, the most direct purpose of establishing Zhonglong was to expand and optimize the production scale of Nanming Tobacco Factory and to expand the production and marketing network of local flue-cured tobacco and cigarettes in Guizhou overall.[62] The address of Zhonglong Industrial Limited Company was where the Guiyang Nanming Tobacco Factory was previously located. Zhonglong planned to set up a factory in Hankou and offices in Chongqing, Shanghai, Luxian, Kunming, Chengdu, Guiding, Xuchang, Hong Kong, and Guangzhou. The locations of the offices—Guiding, Luxian, and Xuchang were important cigarette production areas, while the rest were the most important commercial ports in Southwest, South, and East China—show that Zhonglong's planning was completely centered on cigarette production and sales.[63]

After Zhonglong was established, the company built a new machinery storehouse near the original factory site in Guiyang to accommodate new equipment and leased another house as a staff dormitory and warehouse; at the same time, the company managers also actively set up the factory

[61] Ibid.

[62] Zheng Yuanmo 郑远谟, "Zhonglong shiye gufen youxian gongsi gaikuang" 中隆实业股份有限公司概况 [Overview of Zhonglong Industrial Co., Ltd.], Lixing yuekan 2, no. 5 (1947): 46.

[63] Ibid.

in Hankou. Both factories were mechanized. The factory in Guiyang had four cigarette rolling machines, three cigarette cutting machines, one knife grinding machine, one cigarette breaking machine, one lathe, and a newly purchased boiler and frying drum; while the Hankou branch factory had three cigarette rolling machines and one cigarette cutting machine.[64] In early 1947, under the planning of Liu Xiyi, Zhonglong set up another branch of Nanming Tobacco Factory in Chongqing, which was larger in scale than the one in Hankou in terms of personnel. The funds for the three Nanming tobacco factories partly came from the shareholders of Zhonglong, partly came fromthe funds of local merchants in these three places. The funds for the three tobacco factories were independent of each other. However, the Liu brothers held 50% of the shares in each of the three factories, thus firmly establishing themselves as the main voices in their operation. All three tobacco factories had Liu Xiyi as their director, and Li Wenshang, Zeng Yunqing, and Zeng Wensheng, Zeng Yunqing's brother, were their managers.[65]

It is evident that the Liu brothers were deeply involved in the establishment and operation of Zhonglong Industrial Limited Company and the two new Nanming tobacco factories, but did not intend to incorporate Nanming Tobacco Factory into the Yong An group again. Instead, they tried to develop another business group, independent of Yong An, based on cigarette production.[66]

In 1948, Anshun-born military general Gu Zhenglun replaced Yang Sen as the chairman of Guizhou's provincial government, and also became the head of the security forces, taking military and political power in Guizhou. After Gu took office, because he had conflicts with Liu Xiyi, he had Liu arrested and imprisoned for having internal account books at Guizhou Bank. Although Liu Xiyi was eventually released from prison and fled to Chengdu to avoid trouble, due to the persecution of Gu Zhenglun and the devaluation of gold yuan vouchers at that time, most of Liu's industries related to Yong An lost money. The industries that Gu

[64] Ibid.

[65] Zheng Yuanmo, "Zhonglong shiye gufen youxian gongsi gaikuang," 46; Liu Yuyuan, "Guiyang Naming yanchang zhuiyi", 43–44.

[66] An example of the opposite is the Bank of Guizhou. Liu Xiyi acted as an personal investor and manager of the bank, but in fact his share capital came from Yong An. Liu Yuyuan also regarded this bank as an institution closely related to Yong An. This later caused big trouble for Liu Xiyi.

Zhenglun thought needed to be continued, such as the Jukang Bank, were handed over to the Anshun merchants Wu Xiaogao and Deng Ruofu. The Yong An group, without Liu Xiyi as its core, disintegrated.[67] During this period, the Nanming Tobacco Factory continued to operate under its original structure because it was independent of Yong An, and Liu Xiyi remained chairman of the three tobacco factories in Guiyang, Chongqing, and Hankou.[68]

5 Conclusion

As discussed in Chapter 3, the Nationalist government was able to control Guizhou relatively effectively in 1935, and it began to adopt a strict salt distribution mechanism. The government first reverted to the official supervision and merchant sale (*guandu shangxiao* 官督商销) model and then introduced stricter salt monopoly policies in 1942 based on wartime needs. As a result, the profit margins of salt shippers were gradually reduced. They were subjected to more pressure from the government in both transportation and sales, and the original transportation and distribution structure and its participants were constantly changing. Under these circumstances, Liu Xiyi was still able to keep the operation of the Yong An Salt Firm stable for a long time, and gradually developed a business group based on the salt transportation of the firm, with the Yong An merchants as the core. This would not have been possible without Liu Xiyi's personal capability to examine situations, adopt flexible business strategies, and develop diverse operations according to changes in the business environment. In the process of maintaining and developing Yong An, Liu Xiyi continuously integrated and optimized the human resources, materials, and capital in his established network.

After the 1940s, Liu Xiyi invested in cigarette production. The government was encouraging cigarette production and sales to develop the tobacco industry, but, more importantly, Liu felt that there would be a mutual influence between the investment in cigarette factories and the stable operation of Yong An, and the promising tobacco business would further Yong An's development through the flow of people and capital.

[67] Wu Xiaogao, "Guizhou shiyan yunxiao de huiyi," 217; Liu Yuyuan & Tang Bin, "Gongshangshiyejia Liu Xiyi", 84–86.

[68] Liu Yuyuan, "Liu Xiyi de fajia yu shuaibai," 35.

However, Liu Xiyi always had doubts about whether the tobacco industry should be part of Yong An group's business, and after the failure of Xinqian Enterprise Company, there was a conscious effort to further divide salt transportation from cigarette production. This decision to diversify and spread out risk allowed the Nanming Tobacco Factory to continue to operate under Liu Xiyi's control when the Yong An group was in crisis, thus leaving Liu Xiyi with the hope of a comeback despite suffering many setbacks.

The organizational structure of salt transportation and cigarette production under Liu's leadership provides a complex example of the role of corporate hierarchies and social networks in the development of modern enterprises. Regarding this issue, previous studies have noted that the development of Chinese enterprises during the Republican period involved a combination of social networks and the modern corporate system.[69] Such characteristics can certainly be seen in Liu Xiyi's salt transportation and cigarette factory ventures. However, in addition to Liu Xiyi's own preference for corporate forms and management structures, the policies pursued by the state during wartime and the company's particular situation also influenced the operation of its enterprises—enterprises such as the Xinqian Enterprise Company, which claimed to have been established in accordance with the Company Law. In the society of that period, the implementation of a limited liability shareholding system was the hallmark and trend of corporate modernization, However, in actual business operations, the external protection mechanisms and internal motivation to maintain such a form of business were not always sufficient. The case of Liu Xiyi offers the opportunity to more deeply understand the business strategies and limitations of Chinese entrepreneurs in this context.

[69] Sherman Cochran, *Encountering Chinese Networks: Western, Japanese, and Chinese Corporations in China, 1880–1937* (Berkeley: University of California Press, 2000), 177–185; Bian Linan (Morris Bian), "Xifang xuejie zuijin sishinian dui zhongguo qiyeshi yanjiu de pingshu" 西方学界最近四十年对中国企业史研究的评述 [A Critical Examination of Western Studies of Chinese Business and Economic History], *Economic and Social History Review*, 4 (2018): 115–117.

CHAPTER 6

From Salt to Tobacco: Reforms of the Salt Tax and Tobacco Tax in Guizhou's Fiscal Revenue

Haoqi Meng

1 Introduction

Guizhou has had a financial problem since the province was established, and it is one of the most important problems restricting local economic development.[1] Due to a scarcity of cultivated land and underdeveloped industry and commerce, Guizhou has been unable to make ends meet. How to increase fiscal revenue of all kinds to meet fiscal expenditures has been the core problem that the rulers of Guizhou have strived to solve. From the third year of Emperor Yongzheng in the Qing Dynasty (1725) to 1949,[2] the structure and composition of the province's fiscal revenue underwent many changes, gradually becoming less unstable and getting on the right track. Among them, the most significant change in Guizhou's fiscal system has been that tobacco taxation has replaced salt taxation as the main source of fiscal revenue. This subverted a fiscal and taxation system that had relied on the province's salt since Ding Baozhen's period.

[1] Ren Kecheng 任可澄 et al. eds., *Minguo Guizhou tongzhi* 民国贵州通志 [A General History of Guizhou] (Guiyang: Wentong Press, 1948), "Qianshi zhi" 前事志 [Previous Events], vol. 20, 19.

[2] Ibid.

B. Jiang et al., *State, Market and Salt-Tobacco Road in Modern China (1935–1949)*, https://doi.org/10.1007/978-981-97-7654-2_6

This chapter focuses on the main components of Guizhou's fiscal revenue before 1949, including funds from other provinces,[3] and analyzes the transformation of Guizhou's fiscal revenue from relying on salt taxation to relying on tobacco and tobacco industry taxation. It reveals the basic logic behind Guizhou's fiscal revenue availability transition from salt to tobacco. The availability of fiscal revenue refers to (1) the local government's ability to collect taxes from merchants; (2) the merchant's ability to pay taxes while maintaining a certain amount of profit. Guizhou's primary fiscal revenue sources have gradually shifted from commodity trade relying on small businesses and small transactions to industrial and commercial production centered on credit and large transactions. The transition from salt finance to tobacco finance reflects this logic.

This chapter is divided into three main sections. The second section describes and analyzes the development of Guizhou's system of salt finance. It introduces the changes in Guizhou's fiscal revenue structure before and after Ding Baozhen's reform and how the salt tax was established as the core of that structure; then, it analyzes the institutionalization of Guizhou's salt tax finance system after the reform, and how this institutionalization integrated with the existing problems in the monetary system, and gradually led to specific taxation difficulties for local governments. The third section of this chapter focuses on the establishment and basic logic of the fiscal revenue based on tobacco business and the tobacco industry from the late 1930s to the middle and late 1940s. This is followed by a third section concluding remarks.

2 Difficulties and Logics of Fiscal Revenue Dominated by the Salt Tax

2.1 *The Salt Tax Agreement and the Prototype of Salt Finance: Elaborate Design or Political Compromise (1882–1916)*

In 1876, Ding Baozhen, the governor of Sichuan at the time, began to rectify Sichuan's salt administration and try to eliminate the backlog of salt storage. He faced two problems: first, after the Taiping Rebellion

[3] The co-payment refers to the system in which the financial deficit is supported by a fixed part of the financial revenue of other provinces, and it is a form of transfer payment in the Qing Dynasty's finance. See Ren Kecheng et al. eds., *Minguo Guizhou tongzhi*, "Qianshi zhi", vol. 29, 3.

ended, the scope of salt sales in Sichuan returned to the area in Yunnan, Guizhou, Sichuan, and southern Shaanxi, just as before the turmoil; the second problem was the backlog of salt in Guizhou (the traditional main sales area) which was difficult to sell.[4] Restoring and increasing the sales of salt in Guizhou, ensuring the collection of salt taxes to realize the rectification of the salt administration, and increasing fiscal revenue became the starting points of Ding Baozhen's salt sector reform.[5]

Ding Baozhen's reform of the salt sector started with the sale of salt in Guizhou. This salt law reform, known as "official transportation and merchant sale" (官运商销 *guanyun shangxiao*) or "official supervision and merchant sales" (官督商销 *guandu shangxiao*), was divided into two steps. First, Ding separated production and sales in the ports where Sichuan's salt entered Guizhou. In this model, salt was consigned and transported by the local government and sold by local merchants. He recruited salt merchants from Sichuan, Guizhou,[6] and Shaanxi to form a transportation and distribution alliance to receive and transport salt produced in various salterns in Sichuan; at the four Guizhou border ports (Xuyong, Hejiang, Jiangjin, and Fuling), Guizhou salt merchants were responsible for retransfering this salt to various parts of the province. Ding negotiated with the Chief Secretary of Central State in Guizhou (*guizhousheng buzhengsi shu* 贵州省布政司署) to calculate total salt consumption based on the per capita daily salt consumption of 5 *qian* (钱) in Guizhou Province. Secondly, the Sichuan salt monopoly organization, Sichuan Salt and Tea Committee (四川盐茶道 *Sichuan yanchadao*),[7] collected taxes from producers at the salterns and distributors at the border ports of Guizhou according to quantity. At the same time, the various tariffs and *likins* 厘金 in the process of salt transportation and

[4] Madeleine Zelin, *The Merchants of Zigong: Industrial Entrepreneurship in Early Modern China* (New York: Columbia University Press, 2005), chapter 6.

[5] Huang Guoxin 黄国信, *Guojia yu shichang: Mingqing shiyan maoyi yanjiu* 国家与市场: 明清食盐贸易研究 [State and Market: Salt Trade of Ming-Qing Period] (Beijing: Zhonghua Book Company, 2019), 116–142.

[6] Hua Sshuren 华树人, "Yonglongyu yanhao shulue" 永隆裕盐号述略 [Brief Introduction of Yonglongyu Salt Firm], in *Guiyang wenshi ziliao xuancui* 贵阳文史资料选粹 [Selected Materials of Guiyang Literature and History] (Guiyang: Guizhou People's Press), Guiyang CPPCC Literature History and Learning Committee ed. vol. 1, 19–26.

[7] Monopoly agency in charge of salt and tea in Sichuan Province.

distribution in Guizhou were removed to ensure a smooth process of salt transportation, distribution, and consumption.

While Ding Baozhen's salt tax reform realized the unified collection of salt taxes, he abolished all *likin* checkpoints in Guizhou province and no longer collected salt *likin* in Guizhou. However, this would undoubtedly lead to a decrease in salt tax revenue in Guizhou. In order to make up for this, Ding's reform required that the Salt and Tea Committee in Sichuan Province return a part of the salt tax uniformly collected from the production and sales links to the Chief Secretary of Guizhou. Specifically, the annual salt *likins* were paid to the Chief Secretary of Guizhou as a one-time payment from the salt tax revenue collected[8] and were fixed as a stable assistant payment (协济款 xiejikuan)[9] according to the total amount of salt *likins* due from Guizhou. Since Guizhou needed to gradually grasp and clarify the tax situation of the Likin Bureau, the administrators of Guizhou and Sichuan went through several negotiations. From 1880, in response to the abolition of the salt *likins* and the continued existence of other miscellaneous salt taxes, the governor of Sichuan, Ding Baozhen, and the governor of Guizhou, Cen Yuying 岑毓英,[10] negotiated several times and finally, in 1882, set aside 490,000 silver taels from the salt taxes collected from the production and distribution in Sichuan as a fixed assistant payment of salt taxes and transferred it to the provincial government of Guizhou to make up for the loss of the abolished *likins*. Moreover, they negotiated an annual increase of 80,000 taels in this fixed revenue, the total of which accounted for about 40%

[8] Ding Baozhen丁宝桢 et al. eds., Zen Fanying 曾凡英, Li Shumin 李树民 & Sun Xiangwei 孙祥伟 reedited and annotated, *Sichuan yanfa zhi zhengli jiaozhu* 四川盐法志整理校注 [Collation and Annotation of the Chronicles of Salt Administration in Sichuan] (Chongqing: Southwest Jiaotong University Press, 2019), vol. 13, "Transport8", "official transport", "Subscribe Guizhou likin", 343–346.

[9] See Ding Baozhen, *Ding wenchenggong zougao* 丁文诚公奏稿 [Memorial Drafts of Ding Baozhen], vol. 13–16 (Block printed, 1907); Ding Baozhen et al. eds., Zen Fanying Li Shumin & Sun Xiangwei 曾凡英, 李树民, 孙祥伟 reedited annotated, *Sichuan yanfa zhi zhengli jiaozhu*.

[10] Cen Yuying (1829–1889), courtesy name Yanqing and nickname Kuanguo, was born in Xilin, Guangxi. Acted successively in Yiliang County and Chengjiang Prefecture. Later moved to Yunnan Chief Envoy, Governor of Yunnan, Governor of Guizhou, and Governor of Yunnan and Guizhou. Posthumous Title "Xiangqin (襄勤)".

of Guizhou's revenue and about one-third of its expenditure.[11] At this point, the Sichuan assistant payment from salt taxes was established as a relatively stable main source of Guizhou's fiscal revenue.

The purpose of Ding Baozhen's salt law reform was to organize Sichuan's financial and salt administration and to solve the problem of uneven sales. To achieve this purpose, the Guizhou provincial government's implementation of salt tax collection was not so different from the aid payment method formulated by the Ministry of Revenue in the Qing dynasty before the Taiping Rebellion.[12] However, in essence, there was no unified arrangement by the Ministry of Revenue 户部, only partly operationalized in the Sichuan salt sales area. Therefore, it is better to regard Ding Baozhen's salt tax assistant payment to Guizhou as an elaborate institutional arrangement, and as a necessary political transaction to rectify the salt administration. If the basis of these political transactions was shaken, the transfer payment of the salt tax would inevitably be affected. This is the background of the period of warlord melee at the beginning of the period of the Republic of China.

2.2 *The Emergence of Salt Distribution and the Opium Business: An Alternative and Its Unsustainability (1918–1935)*

The attack on Sichuan by the Protectorate Army (护国军 *huguojun*) in the fourth year of the Republic of China led to a bad relationship between the Guizhou military government and the Sichuan authorities, which was followed by a long period of mutual attacks between the Guizhou warlord Liu Xianshi and his successors and the Sichuan authorities.[13] One of the consequences of this was that the Sichuan authorities stopped assisting Guizhou with salt tax payments in 1918.[14] The military government of

[11] See Zhou Tianshou 周恭寿 eds., *Minguo Xu zunyifu zhi* 民国续遵义府志 [the Continuation Gazetteer of Zunyi Prefecture, the Republic of China] (Chengdu: Bashu Press, 2000), vol. 9, "Tax" 2.

[12] See Ren Keccheng et al. eds., *Minguo guizhou tongzhi*, "Qianshi zhi", vol. 29, 3.

[13] Wang Boqun 王伯群, "Guizhou dui guomin geming zhi gongxian" 贵州对国民革命之贡献 [Guizhou's Contribution to the National Revolution], in *Guizhou zhengxie wenshi ziliao cungao xuanbian* 贵州政协文史资料存稿选编 [Selected Manuscripts of Cultural and Historical Materials] (Guiyang: Guizhou People's Press), ed. Wang Hengfu 王恒富 et al., vol. 1, 5–13.

[14] Zhang Xiaomei 张肖梅, *Guizhou jingji* 贵州经济 [Guizhou Economy] (Chongqing: National Economic Research Institute), N1.

Guizhou had to find a way to fill this financial gap. The direct alternative to the salt tax was to liberate salt transportation and marketing and to set up a customs office called the Bureau of Expense Contributions from Each County (各县饷捐征收局 *gexian xiangjuan zhengshouju*) to restore the salt *likin*[15]; on this basis, the Guizhou military government also passed a resolution in 1918 to encourage the cultivation and production of opium and to levy a provincial tax on opium[16] to make up for the shortfall of revenue.

The quasi-*linkin* levied by the Bureau of Expense and Contributions were collected by the Bureau from each county at a rate of 10 *yuan* per packet of salt. In essence, an independent salt tax collection system was formed to ensure that the salt tax could feed provincial finance.[17] Because there was not enough tax revenue left for the county governments, the counties levied their own various contributions on top of the rates for the so-called local financial expenses.[18] These salt contributions were mainly divided into two categories: one was levied in accordance with the volume of salt passing through the salt ports, mostly at 5 yuan per packet[19] of salt and this is calculated in *likin*; the other category was Salt Merchants' Entry Contributions (盐商入境捐 *yanshang rujingjuan*), set up by the *likin* bureaus in border counties such as Yanhe, Tongzi, Chishui, Dading, Weining, Jinping, Tongren, and Rongjiang, which were levied at a ratio (从量征收 *congliang zhengshou*)[20] of 3 yuan per packet of salt. In fact, it was the first time that salt merchants paid salt tax on their

[15] Ibid.

[16] Zhang Xiaomei, *Guizhou jingji*, N62.

[17] Financial Investigation Division of the Ministry of Finance ed. *Ge shengqu linian caizheng zhuangkuang huilan* 各省区历年财政状况汇览 [Summary of financial status of provinces and regions over the years], 1925, 13–25.

[18] Zhang Xiaomei, *Guizhou jingji*, N62.

[19] The unit of measurement for Sichuan salt is 12 Yin per Zai, 50 packs per Yin, 108,000 Chinese jin per Zai, and 180 Chinese jin per pack. See Deng Qingtang 邓庆棠, "Yanhangjie yu Guizhou yanwu" 盐行街与贵州盐务 (Yanhang (Salt Firm) Street and the Salt Administration in Guizhou), in *Guizhou gongshang shiliao huibian* 贵州工商史料汇编 [Compilation of Historical Materials of Industry and Commerce in Guizhou], ed. Guizhou Provincial Committee of the Democratic National Construction Association & Guizhou Provincial Federation of Industry and Commerce, no. 3 (1985): 47–61.

[20] Financial Investigation Division of the Ministry of Finance ed., *Ge shengqu linian caizheng zhuangkuang huilan*, 199–207.

own behalf.[21] The increase and abolition of miscellaneous taxes were more arbitrary, and it was impossible to estimate the scale accurately, which in turn made the scale of salt taxation more volatile.

The total revenue collected from salt taxes, including the *likins* and the salt merchants' contributions, increased and then decreased. In 1917, when the Bureau of Expense Contributions was not yet established, the salt assistant payment was 659,300 yuan,[22] but in 1918, when the salt expense contributions were levied, only 399,300 yuan was collected, a reduction of nearly half.[23] Because of this, opium was unbanned that year with the intention of filling the gap in revenue.[24] Thereafter, the rates gradually increased. In 1924, the tax revenue gradually increased to 2,041,200 yuan. However, after 1925, the opium tax gradually fell until 1928. Under Zhou Xicheng's 周西成 administration, he had to adopt a new strategy: "recruit merchants and give them charter in assigned salt ports" (招商认岸 *zhaoshang ren'an*). If the government could establish a fixed group of salt merchants to trade salt and contribute specific amounts (total = 1.5 million yuan/year) at the end of the year, the shortage of the total taxes levied would be compensated for by these merchant groups.[25] In terms of *likins*, the scale of salt *likins* collected at the beginning of the seventh year of the Republic of China reached 841,400 yuan,[26] then declined year by year to only 222,100 yuan[27] in 1924, and shrank to 120,000 yuan in 1928.[28] The size of the salt merchants' contributions collected by the Likin Bureaus from each port was even more volatile: from 1,182,900 yuan in 1918 to 220,600 yuan in 1924. By 1931, the salt merchant contributions in Yanhe County could

[21] Financial Investigation Division of the Ministry of Finance ed., *Ge shengqu linian caizheng zhuangkuang huilan*, 213–216.

[22] The statistical unit of the Ministry of Finance of the Beiyang Government is used here. One silver dollar is equal to about 0.72 taels of silver.

[23] Financial Investigation Division of the Ministry of Finance ed., *Ge shengqu linian caizheng zhuangkuang huilan*, 73–84.

[24] Zhang Xiaomei, *Guizhou jingji*, N62.

[25] Zhang Xiaomei, *Guizhou jingji*, N1.

[26] Financial Investigation Division of the Ministry of Finance ed., *Ge shengqu linian caizheng zhuangkuang huilan*, 33–37.

[27] Financial Investigation Division of the Ministry of Finance ed., *Ge shengqu linian caizheng zhuangkuang huilan*, 113–118.

[28] Zhang Xiaomei, *Guizhou jingji*, N62.

not continue to be collected and had to be stopped.[29] At the same time, the collection of salt *likins* also faced an important external pressure: the national government's campaign to cut *likins* and raise taxes in 1931.[30]

Likins were a kind of notorious tax that hindered the development of industry and commerce.[31] Since the Mackay Treaty signed by the governments of Great Britain and the Chinese Qing Dynasty in 1902, many authorities had already suggested to abolish *likins*.[32] By 1931, the official abolition of *likins* and the introduction of a separate sales tax had become an irreversible trend and an important tax reform measure of the national government.[33] The abolition of *likins* had led to the abolition of the salt merchants' contributions in Guizhou by 1931; on the other hand, the collection of a series of salt *likins* had reduced the legal salt entry in Guizhou from about 106,459,740 pounds in 1918 to about 27,000,000 pounds[34] in 1935. Considering that the population and demand for salt in Guizhou should not have changed significantly, this indicated that nearly three-quarters of the salt was lost to smuggling channels. Therefore, the collection of salt *likins* was under two major pressures after 1931: namely administrative abolition and loss of legal salt. By 1935, all the *likins* and contributions were abolished and replaced by a unified sales tax levied by the Ministry of Finance, and only 80,000 yuan of salt sales tax was collected that year.[35] So far, the channel to support Guizhou's

[29] "Yanhe xian zhengfu guanyu chengfu tingshou yanjuan shiyi de zhiling" 沿河县政府关于呈复停收盐捐事宜的指令 [Instructions of the Yanhe County Government on Suspension of Salt Donations1932040], 0037-19-1-1-3-35, in *Zhongguo wujiang liuyu minguo dang'an congkan yanhe juan* 中国乌江流域民国档案丛刊·沿河卷 [The Yanhe County Volumes of the Archive Series of the Republic of China in the Wujiang River Basin], ed. Wang Wenxue 汪文学 et al. (Guiyang: Guizhou People's Press), "Yanhe County Government", vol. 1, book 2, 44.

[30] Ma Yinchu 马寅初, *Caizhengxue yu zhongguo caizheng—lilun yu xianshi* 财政学与中国财政—理论与现实 [Public Finance and Chinese Finance—Theory and Reality] (Beijing: The Commercial Press, 2006), 351–374.

[31] Ibid.

[32] Ibid.

[33] Lin Meili林美莉, *Xiyang shuizhi zai jindai zhongguo de fazhan* 西洋税制在近代中国的发展 [The Development of Western Tax System in Modern China] (Shanghai: Shanghai Academy of Social Sciences Press, 2020), 67–138.

[34] Calculated according to Financial Investigation Division of the Ministry of Finance, 1925, 199–207, Zhang Xiaomei, *Guizhou jingji*, N62.

[35] Zhang Xiaomei, *Guizhou jingji*, N59.

finances through the salt tax was completely blocked, and if no solution was found, the shortfall from lost salt taxes alone would reach 820,000 yuan.

Unlike the salt tax, the local opium tax had been maintaining a high growth rate and only faced pressure from the national government's periodical anti-smoking campaigns. After the Guizhou provincial government started encouraging opium cultivation in 1918, opium tax revenues rose from 590,000 yuan in that year to a peak of 3.41 million yuan in 1934, making it the main source of revenue for the Guizhou military government.[36] The provincial tax on opium was levied in accordance with the special commodity likin (tehuo lijin 特货厘金). It was set at 1250 yuan per 1000 taels shipped out of the country, while cultivators were exempt from field taxation as a production incentive. This led to Guizhou becoming the most serious opium growing and exporting region of the time. After the national government took control of the Guizhou provincial government and reorganized it in November 1935, Guizhou was designated the opium prohibition zone, and the provincial tax on opium was abolished and replaced by a subsidy on specialties compensated by the Ministry of Finance of the National Government, initially set at 2.2 million *yuan* per year but paying out only 1.75 million yuan in 1936.[37] Thus, the path of replacing salt tax with opium tax was effectively blocked.

In 1935, before the opium tax was abolished, Guizhou's annual revenue was 4,936,135 yuan, of which 3.41 million yuan was from opium taxes, accounting for 69.1%, over half of the total; the actual fiscal expenditure was 660,320 yuan, with opium taxes accounting for 51.6%, making it the absolute main force supporting fiscal expenditure. Looking at the salt tax, at this time there was no longer an annual revenue of 1.62 million yuan from salt *likins*, and salt tax revenue only consisted of central subsidies and sales tax, 800,000 yuan in total, accounting for only 16.2% of the fiscal revenue of the year. However, the salt tax was still the second largest tax source after the opium tax. Considering the special nature of the opium tax, the salt tax accounted for 52.4% of the general fiscal tax revenue excluding for opium tax; in terms of fiscal expenditure, the salt tax occupied 12.1% of Guizhou's fiscal expenditure in 1935. It remained one of the most important components of Guizhou's finances.

[36] Zhang Xiaomei, *Guizhou jingji*, N62.

[37] Ibid.

Considering the unsustainability of opium taxes and their compensation payments, the fiscal deficit of Guizhou after 1935 must have been much higher than 1,666,885 yuan.[38] Apart from opium taxes, a new, stable source of fiscal revenue had to be found.

2.3 The Manifestation of the Salt Tax Dilemma: The Re-establishment of Government Supervision and Merchant Sales and the Re-emergence of the Salt Assistant Payment (1936–1941)

After the opium tax ceased to exist, Guizhou's fiscal revenue was still dominated by the salt tax; it was necessary to stabilize and increase Guizhou's salt tax revenue in order to expand and secure the province's fiscal system. In early 1936, Miao Qiujie 缪秋杰, who was then the Sichuan Salt Transport Ambassador, went to Guizhou several times to negotiate, and, in May 1936, he reached an agreement with the Guizhou government on a plan to reorganize the transportation of salt from Sichuan to Guizhou and to resume the assistant payment of salt taxes from Sichuan to Guizhou.[39] The proposal to resume the payment of salt taxes to Guizhou was filed by the Ministry of Finance and was in essence a transfer payment approved by the central government. The proposal was divided into three parts. First, the plan was to resume the "official supervision and merchants sales" model of moving Sichuan salt into Guizhou and to specify the sales area in Guizhou. Second, the plan was to negotiate the establishment of management branches of the Guizhou Salt Administration in Yong An, Ren An, Qi An, and Fu An salt ports to collect a unified salt transportation and distribution tax on salt entering Guizhou. Salt merchants paid this tax in advance, and they were able to reimburse this amount from subsequent sales. When salt entered Guizhou, it was no longer subject to a commodity export tax. Third, and finally, the salt transportation and distribution tax in Guizhou was to be paid to the Ministry of Finance by the Guizhou salt administration. The Ministry of Finance then returned a 1.5 million yuan co-payment and and additional 120,000 yuan in education funds to the Guizhou provincial government.[40] In this

[38] Zhang Xiaomei, *Guizhou jingji*, N7.

[39] Zhang Xiaomei, *Guizhou jingji*, N1.

[40] Ibid.

way, Guizhou received financial compensation of 1.62 million yuan in total, while the original central government subsidy for the abolition of the *likins* remained unchanged, based on the premise of restoring the "government supervision and merchant sales" model.

All these tax policy initiatives were officially launched on January 1, 1937. Until 1941, when the salt tax collection method was changed and the salt monopoly began, Guizhou experienced relatively rapid development in salt transportation and distribution.[41] Since the salt tax was paid by the salt merchants at the ports and they were given the right to make up for it in subsequent sales,[42] the Guizhou Salt Administration Bureau implemented relatively strict management of these merchants, specifying a reasonable range for what they could defer.[43]

The salt tax levied on the transportation and sale of Sichuan salt that Miao Qiujie agreed upon was characterized by a uniform levy and then a uniform, fixed refund amount,[44] so the total refund amount was unchanged regardless of changes in the quantity of salt sold. Nearly 1.62 million yuan was initially agreed upon by Miao Qiujie and the Guizhou provincial government[45]; after that, in 1938, an additional 240,000 yuan per year was added to the Guangdong Salt Association, mainly for the salt merchants of twelve counties in South Guizhou to purchase and sell Guangdong salt in Guangxi, in an arrangement similar to the one for Sichuan salt.[46] Thus, by 1938, the total amount of all salt-related payments reached 2.66 million yuan, accounting for 51.5%[47] of Guizhou's fiscal revenue in that year and again becoming Guizhou's number one source of revenue. Later in 1939, Guizhou completed the

[41] See Zhang Xiaomei, *Guizhou jingji*, Ch. 4 .

[42] Zhang Xiaomei, *Guizhou jingji*, N1.

[43] General situation of salt affairs in this province, M41-1-8 General Situation of Guizhou Salt Affairs, M41-1-8, 13, Guizhou Provincial Archives.

[44] Zhang Xiaomei, *Guizhou jingji*, N45.

[45] At this time, it is legal currency, and it is calculated according to the rules of the legal currency reform. Before 1939, the legal currency and silver dollar were equivalent.

[46] *Guizhou caijing ziliao huibian* 贵州财经资料汇编 [Guizhou financial data compilation], Guizhou Provincial Finance and Economics Commission, internal information, 1950, "Fiscal", 374.

[47] Ibid.

land declaration and had a revenue of 775,000 yuan from field assignments,[48] further increasing the diversity of the provinces financial sources. In the same year, the central government increased the monthly subsidy of the production of nitrate to the Guizhou provincial government by 20,000 *yuan*. This accounted for the potential fiscal loss that would result from the transfer of nitrate production from the General Salt Administration to the central government. Therefore, a salt tax assistant payment of 2.9 million yuan was finally agreed upon. These financial and taxation arrangements made Guizhou's provincial revenue relatively abundant before 1941.

In this period, salt taxes were still paid in advance by salt merchants at the salt ports in accordance with the customary practice, and the salt merchants were allowed to reimburse the payment for what they made in sales. The salt tax levied on the salt sold at the ports was called "port tax" (岸税 *anshui*), and the tax rate was not uniform but was set according to the cost of the salt produced at the ports. The port tax rate was lower for salt produced in places with high salt production costs. The port tax rate was higher, where the cost of salt production was low.[49] Among the four salt ports in Sichuan, the Ren An, Qi An, and Fu An were the main distribution ports of the Furong Saltern (富荣盐场 *furong yanchang*), and the port tax was 4.7 yuan per 100 *jin*[50]; Yong An was a distribution port of the Qianle Saltern (犍乐盐场 *qianle yanchang*), and the production cost of the Qianle Saltern was higher, so the shore tax was 3.5 yuan per 100 *jin*.[51]

In terms of salt demand, the population of Guizhou increased nearly threefold due to the influx of state employees and migrants from other provinces after the outbreak of the war, which meant nearly three times

[48] *Guizhou caijing ziliao huibian*, 387.

[49] Yang Gongshu 杨公庶 and Wang Shunxu 王舜绪, "Chuannan yanchang gaikuang yu guangxi gongye zuijin zhi zhanwang" 川南盐场概况与关系工业最近之展望 [General Situation of South Sichuan Saltworks and Recent Prospects of Related Industries], in *Zhongguo kangri zhanzheng shiliao congkan: jingji ji gongye* 中国抗日战争史料丛刊: 经济·工业 [Chinese Anti-Japanese War Historical Materials Series: Economy and Industry], Yu Heping ed. (Beijing: Elephant Press, 2016), vol. 372, 36, 1937.

[50] Ibid.

[51] Yang Gongshu and Wang Shunxu, "Chuannan yanchang gaikuang yu guanxi gongye zuijin zhi zhanwang", 80, 1937.

the amount of salt needed to be transported in Guizhou.[52] The more salt was shipped, the more tax was levied, and, in theory, Guizhou's salt tax revenue was guaranteed. However, the actual situation was that the growth of revenue from the salt tax was not satisfactory. From 1939 to 1941, the total amount of salt taxes in Guizhou decreased year by year, and the lowest amount was only 105.1 million yuan in 1940, which was only 75%[53] of the total in 1938. The total amount of salt taxes in Sichuan was reduced and the amount of money returned to Guizhou was fixed, so pressure was gradually created. The direct reason for the weak growth of salt taxes and even the decline of the total amount was inflation in the district ruled by *Kuomintang*. From 1938 to 1941, the price of salt in Guiyang city soared to more than eleven times[54] what it had been, and the tax rate per unit did not increase. The increase in the price of salt reduced the effective tax rate per unit,[55] and this rate dropped by 12% between 1940 and 1939. The port tax rate in Guizhou dropped to 3.08 yuan per 100 *jin*. It dropped to 4.14 yuan per 100 *jin* in Yong An and 4.14 yuan per 100 *jin* in the other salt ports. This led to a decrease in the salt tax levied at the salt ports of Sichuan, which inevitably put pressure on the fixed assistant payment based on the actual price of salt after inflation.

2.4 Direct Financial Intervention of the Central Government (1942–1946)

To solve the problem of salt tax collection, the national government's Ministry of Finance, on the one hand, revised the salt tax collection method in September 1941 and changed it from a unit tax to an ad valorem tax.[56] On the other hand, at the end of 1941, the Ministry of Finance converted land taxes (田赋 *tianfu*) into in-kind taxes to ease food supply problems in district ruled by *Kuomintang*.[57] First, let us review

[52] Guizhou Provincial Finance and Economics Commission ed. *Ge shengqu linian caizheng zhuangkuang huilan*, 11–28.

[53] Ding Changqing 丁长清 et al., *Minguo yanwu shigao* 民国盐务史稿 [Draft of History of Salt Affairs in the Republic of China] (Beijing: People's Press, 1990), 407.

[54] Ding Changqing 丁长清 et al. eds., *Minguo yanwu shigao*, 399.

[55] Ding Changqing 丁长清 et al. eds., *Minguo yanwu shigao*, 409.

[56] Ding Changqing 丁长清 et al. eds., *Minguo yanwu shigao*, 402–410.

[57] Guizhou Provincial Finance and Economics Commission, 1950, 392.

this change from land taxes to in-kind taxes. Since land taxation was made a matter of provincial finance in 1937, the change to in-kind taxation reduced Guizhou's provincial revenue by about 775,000 yuan, but the impact was minimal because provincial finance was already integrated into central finance. The change of the salt tax from a unit tax to an ad valorem tax in September 1941 changed the old port tax to a 30% sales tax,[58] which was directly reflected in the price of salt; this tied the collection of salt taxes to each salt transaction. This change in regulation meant merchants were unable to make compensation/reimbursement of advance payments from their total income. This, coupled with the fact that salt merchants, who were effectively distribution agents under the monopoly system, experienced a decline of autonomy in the sale of salt.[59] From a salt merchant's point of view, they were still responsible for the collection of the sales tax according to the customary practice, but they were not in control of the specific compensation, which undoubtedly made things more difficult for them: it was not up to a salt merchant to determine the smoothness of the graded transportation and distribution of salt. Specifically, the valorem tax rate of 30% almost eliminated inflationary erosion of real tax revenue and thus amounted to a tax increase. After September 1941, if the valorem tax levy was converted into a quantitative levy, it was 13.25 times the 1939 valorem tax rate.[60] For the Guizhou government, this was an uneven fact that in 1949 (in terms of the monetary standards in 1939) the payment increased to 46.37 yuan per 100 *jin* in Yong An and 62.27 yuan per 100 *jin* in the other three salt ports. The increase in salt taxes alone nullified the merchants' net profit of 20 cents per 100 *jin* approved in 1939.[61]

Thus, although the salt tax reform abolished most of the local surcharges on salt taxes, it still put a very heavy burden on salt merchants.[62] Since authority over provincial finance had been transferred to the central government, the goal of the Guizhou Salt Administration

[58] Ding Changqing 丁长清 et al. eds., *Minguo yanwu shigao*, 402–410.

[59] See Chapter 3 for details on the behavior of salt merchants under the monopoly system.

[60] Ding Changqing 丁长清 et al. eds., *Minguo yanwu shigao*, 409.

[61] General situation of salt affairs in this province, M41-1-8 General Situation of Guizhou Salt Affairs, 13, in Guizhou Provincial Archives.

[62] Ding Changqing 丁长清 et al. eds., *Minguo yanwu shigao*, 402–410.

Bureau was no longer to collect transfer payments (from the four main salt ports in Sichuan), submit them to the central government, and receive the distributive revenue (2.6 to 2.9 million yuan). The Bureau's daily work was now (after 1942) to collect the domestic salt taxes for Guizhou. In other words, Guizhou only needed to focus on how much tax could actually be collected from the salt merchants in Sichuan. During this period, the Nationalist government claimed to be focused on people's livelihoods to ensure the supply of salt during the war,[63] and this claim has been echoed in previous scholarship.[64] However, the focus of the Guizhou Salt Administration Bureau during this period was on whether salt merchants paid the full amount of taxes. To take just one example, since the Ministry of Finance had not explicitly stipulated whether the insurance compensation needs to be completed to cover the tax payment, the Guizhou Salt Administration Bureau repeatedly requested Yong An merchants for land transport should not be insured and that the other three ports should still pay the tax on the salt loss that is damaged in the transportation and should not declare the insurance cost as a discount in the salt price.[65] This shows that the Guizhou Salt Administration Bureau was as concerned about the adequacy of salt tax collection as it was about the protection of people's livelihoods.

In parallel with these tax reforms, there was also an important reform of the fiscal system: namely, the Ministry of Finance replaced provincial tax administration with a dispatched agency responsible for provincial taxation. At the same time, all strategic materials during the war, such as tobacco, alcohol, tea, sugar, and salt, were turned into state monopoly commodities.[66] This reform meant two major changes to Guizhou's fiscal system: first, the central government directly intervened in and controlled the province's taxation; second, a series of reforms in tax collection methods changed Guizhou's revenue structure. The purpose of the

[63] State Administration of Taxation ed., *Zhonghua minguo gongshang shuishou shi: yanshuijuan* 中华民国工商税收史：盐税卷 [History of Industrial and Commercial Taxation in the Republic of China: Salt Tax] (Beijing: China Financial and Economic Press, 1999), Chapter 3.

[64] Lin Meili 林美莉, *Xinyang shuizhi zai jindai zhongguo de fazhan*, 63–138.

[65] State Administration of Salt Affairs Lu Yun (32) No. 2399 on behalf of insurance premium related matters, Guizhou Salt Administration Insurance Premium, M41-1-4757, Guizhou Provincial Archives.

[66] Ma Yinchu 马寅初, *Caizhengxue yu zhongguo caizheng—lilun yu xianshi*, 186–188.

central government's consolidation of Guizhou's provincial finances was to make the finances of counties independent.[67] Taxes that used to belong to provincial finance could be transferred to county-level finance to ensure county governments' adequate expenditures. The central government also allocated 50% of Guizhou's business tax revenue to county-level finance to make up for the shortfalls of the county governments.[68] Because the central government and the local government split business taxes, the provincial government, which was dominated by the central government, was more concerned about the smooth collection of taxes. Since the provincial financial system was in fact under the management of an agency dispatched from the central government, it was in a better position to coordinate the provincial tax bureaus, the Salt Administration Affairs Bureau, and the trade and financial agencies of the central government in Guizhou, including the Ministry of Finance's Fuxing Company (复兴公司 *Fuxing gongsi*), to achieve better control of tax collection.

For salt merchants, since the advance payment of salt taxes could only be recovered through distribution, there was no option but to transfer the salt tax to the next level of traders. However, the salt tax increased rapidly from 1944 to 1946, before the monopoly system was abolished, to more than 990 times[69] the ad valorem tax on the value of the *fabi* 法币 in 1939. Such a high tax was reflected in the price, and with the already high inflation, the price of salt in Guiyang rose to more than 1,914 times[70] the 1939 price in 1946. Such high salt prices made it difficult to reach fractional transactions at the end of salt consumption,[71] so that the salt tax, which was passed on from one level to another, could not be recovered from sales and eventually accumulated in the distribution channels of the salt merchants. The difficulty of collecting salt taxes in Guizhou had evolved from a difficulty of the wartime situation to a difficulty of actual collection.

67 Ibid.

68 Ibid.

69 Ding Changqing 丁长清 et al. eds., *Minguo yanwu shigao*, 409.

70 Ding Changqing 丁长清 et al. eds., *Minguo yanwu shigao*, 399.

71 "Summary of Difficulties in Underwriting Salt for Cooperatives in This Province", Salt distribution underwriting rules, 52, M41-1-3042, Guizhou Provincial Archives.

2.5 *The Dilemma of Salt Taxation and the Decline of Salt Merchants: Transformation and Struggle (1947–1949)*

Along with the abolition of the salt monopoly in 1946, volume basis salt taxation resumed[72] and the autonomy of provincial finance was partially restored.[73] However, neither the reform of salt taxation nor the partial restoration of provincial finance could change the increasingly difficult situation of salt tax collection in Guizhou.

The quantity-based taxation method (pay ad valorem tax) was restored and unified nationwide at 110 yuan per 100 *jin*.[74] In 1946, when commodities' prices had soared to more than 1914 times the prices of 1939, the reduction of the regular tax did not reduce the pressure on salt merchants, because the provincial finance was only partially restored; with the central government only transferring 50% of business taxes and 20% of income taxes originally allocated to county-level government to the provincial finance, funds were even more stretched at the provincial and county-levels.[75] As a result, a variety of surcharges were again levied. These surcharges reached a level of 7340 yuan per 100 *jin* by the end of 1946.[76] In 1947, during the hyperinflationary period under the National Government, the surtaxes were increased tenfold.[77] After 1948, with the reform of the gold yuan voucher (金圆券 *jinyuanquan*), the unofficial increase of the salt tax was so much that it could not be calculated.

Paying such a high tax was an impossible mission for salt merchants, so from 1947 onward, even though they were gradually moving toward free shipping and distribution, the traditional salt merchant groups took on more varied business strategies or simply withdrew from the salt business to cut their losses. Most of those who persisted in the salt business were in advantageous business situations or were already engaged in a variety of activities, such as the Yong An merchants led by Liu Xiyi and the Anshun salt merchants represented by Wu Xiaogao, who formed separate nation-wide salt companies and participated in the organization of tobacco,

[72] Ding Changqing 丁长清 et al. eds., *Minguo yanwu shigao*, 402–410.

[73] Ma Yinchu 马寅初, *Caizhengxue yu zhongguo caizheng—lilun yu xianshi*, 186–188.

[74] Ding Changqing 丁长清 et al. eds., *Minguo yanwu shigao*, 402–410.

[75] Ma Yinchu 马寅初, *Caizhengxue yu zhongguo caizheng—lilun yu xianshi*, 186–188.

[76] Ibid.

[77] Ding Changqing 丁长清 et al. eds., *Minguo yanwu shigao*, 409.

brewing, and manufacturing industries to diversify and respond to the dilemma presented by the salt transportation and marketing industry.[78]

The merchants who could not afford to switch to other industries or who were new to the market had to give up their salt businesses. In January 1948, two salt companies, Shu Tong 蜀通 Company and Datong 大通 Company, which operated in Fu An, declared bankruptcy and publicly auctioned off their salt transportation and distribution licenses to offset the salt taxes they had to pay.[79] By the time the Communist Party's newly established Military Takeover Committee (军事接管委员 *junshi jieguan weiguanhui*) took Guizhou over in 1949, salt merchants and retail stores that were bankrupt or owed tax accounted for 90% of the salt retail market in Guiyang city.[80] Salt distribution in Guizhou province was paralyzed until the Communists gained power in 1949.

2.6 The Role of Currency and Finance: Were Monetary and Financial Policies Sufficient to Solve the Salt Tax Fiscal Crisis?

In this section, we focus on the role of currency and finance in the distribution of salt and the collection of salt taxes in modern Guizhou. In fact, salt taxes in Guizhou were closely related to the situation of currency market, because salt taxes were levied and paid in the form of money, and the tax burden resulting from their collection ended up in salt transactions at all levels. Furthermore, salt was a necessity with a low or even near-zero elasticity of demand[81]; its production depended mainly

[78] See Chapter 7.

[79] Jiang Fuhu 蒋傅笏, director of Daye Salt Firm office in Chongqing, sent a letter to Zhang Fuzhong 张辅仲, manager of Daye Salt Firm Guizhou branch, regarding the Chongqing liquidation day salt merchant's bankruptcy request for assistance, Private Correspondence among Salt Merchants, M41-1-4328, Guizhou Provincial Archives.

[80] Guizhou Provincial Finance and Economics Commission, *Guizhou caijing ziliao huibian*, 638–645.

[81] This refers to the price elasticity of demand, which is generally used in economics to measure the degree to which the quantity demanded changes with changes in commodity prices. Generally speaking, when the absolute value of the price elasticity of demand is less than 1, the commodity can be called inelastic; that is, when the commodity price changes, the impact on demand is small. Salt is a necessity of life, lack of salt will lead to low sodium content in the body, loss of appetite, weakness of limbs, dizziness, and other symptoms. Therefore, the demand for table salt is often rigid, and its price elasticity

on production techniques and quantities at different times. For Guizhou, Sichuan was the main source of salt and more than sufficient in terms of quantity and production, so the supply of salt was flexible,[82] and the price elasticity of that supply was relatively high.[83] Generally speaking, the less elastic party bears more of the tax burden of a transaction, so the bulk of the salt tax burden fell on the salt consumer. In other words, consumers' spending on salt had a greater impact on the completion of the salt tax.[84] With this in mind, all factors that affect consumer spending on salt would have an impact on the final completion of the tax. Among them, the first one to consider is currency.

If we look at the basic market transactions in Guizhou's economic life since 1882, we will find an important problem that has been plaguing the province: a lack of small denomination of currency for basic market transactions. The problem of small currency in Guizhou has been long-standing, and, since the Qing Dynasty, it has manifested in the shortage of coins minted: from the late Ming Dynasty to 1729, when the official minting of coins by the Bureau of Guizhou Mint (宝黔局 *Baoqianju*) was set up in the eighth year of Yongzheng,[85] Guizhou "had no copper coins to trade", so private minting was rampant, and even merchants "carried copper coins from Yunnan to Guizhou in exchange for silver".[86] Market transactions were made with either silver or barter. The shortage of small

of demand is close to zero. See Andreu Mas-Colell, Michael D. Whinston and Jerry R. Green, *Microeconomic Theory* (Oxford University Press, 1995), 45–64 (Oxford University Press, 1995).

[82] In the middle of the Qing Dynasty, the annual output of Furong saltern alone could reach 4.32 million dan, or 432 million jin, while the annual salt demand in Guizhou did not exceed 200 million Chinese catties. See Yang Gongshu and Wang Shunxu 杨公庶, 王舜绪, 1937, 36.

[83] Similar to the price elasticity of demand, it is generally used in economics to measure the degree to which the quantity supplied changes with changes in the price of a commodity.

[84] Andreu Mas-Colell, Michael D. Whinston and Jerry R. Green, 1995, 45–64.

[85] Zhang Tingyu 张廷玉 et al., *Qingchao wenxian tongkao* 清朝文献通考 [Comprehensive Examination of Literature in Qing Dynasty] (Shanghai: The Commercial Press, 1936), vol. 13, "Currency".

[86] E'ertai(Ortai) 鄂尔泰 et al., *Yongzheng zhupi yuzhi* 雍正朱批谕旨 [Collection of Yongzheng Emperor's Vermillion Edicts] (Beijing: Beijing Library, 2008), Book 7, "E'ertai qingkai qiansheng guzhu zhu" 鄂尔泰请开黔省鼓铸疏 [E'ertai's Petition of Opening Minting of Money in Guizhou Province].

denominations of money made it difficult to conclude small transactions in Guizhou, and it was necessary to "lose its price"[87] in order to complete them: i.e., one of the parties in the transaction suffered a loss. Even after the official minting of coins in 1729, the shortage did not improve, as private minting was still prohibited.[88] This situation did not change even after Ding Baozhen's reform in 1882. In fact, since the first year of Guangxu in the late Qing Dynasty, 1875, the shortage of coins led to the prevalence of all kinds of privately issued small bills in the eastern region of Guizhou.[89] These small bills of five, ten, or even a hundred *wen* made up for the shortage of copper coins.

Let us return to the issue of salt tax collection. Despite the shortage of small denominations of currency, the collection of the salt tax was not significantly affected in this period. The reason for this is twofold: first, the Silver-Copper dual track system (银钱并行 *yinqian bingxing*) of the Qing Dynasty did not strictly determine the ration of silver to copper coins, which was conducive to the use of silver when the supply of copper was low; second, the low cost of private casting and the private issuance of money stamps meant people relied on small local trusts creating local currency to supplement the shortage of small currency.[90] These regional currencies allowed the basic consumption of salt to be paid for without difficulty. In fact, even after the Republic of China, warlord politics led to the free issuance of local currencies in Guizhou, and this issuance served to compensate for the shortage of small denomination, thus keeping the collection of salt taxes intact, even though the creditworthiness of such currencies were low and they were often liquidated due to lack of reserves.[91] The situation changed after the Nationalist government officially took control of Guizhou in November 1935. The unified fiat currency (法币 *fabi*) entered Guizhou with the National Government's

[87] Ibid.

[88] Mo Youzhi 莫友芝 and ZhengZhen 郑珍 eds. *Daoguang zunyi fuzhi* 道光遵义府志 [Gazetteer of Zunyi Prefecture Edited During Daoguang Reign] (Chengdu: Bashu Press, 2013) (vol. 41, Memorabilia 3, 23–26 (Chengdu: Bashu Press, 2013).

[89] Zhang Xiaomei 张肖梅, *Guizhou jingji*, N1-2.

[90] A more detailed study of the invention of local currencies can see Akinobu Kuroda 黑田明伸, trans. Heping 何平, *Huobi zhidu de shijieshi—jiedu "fei duichengxing"* 货币制度的世界史—解读"非对称性" [The World History of Monetary System—Interpretation of "Asymmetry"] (Beijing: China Renmin University Press, 2007), 96–99.

[91] Zhang Xiaomei 张肖梅, *Guizhou jingji*, N1-2.

political control and replaced the various local currencies in circulation as the only legal tender in just one year.[92] Accordingly, the power to freely create local currencies in Guizhou was withdrawn, the instability of the bills was resolved, and the issue of keeping enough money in circulation to meet demand became a problem for the national government to consider and solve. The shortage of small denominations of money became part of the demand for money, a problem of fiat coinage, or what Thomas J. Sargent and François R. Velde called the big problem of small change.[93] In theory, since paper money could be exchanged for coins without restriction, the problem of change was not as intractable as it had been in the past minting era and was relatively easy to solve.[94] Thus, the currency needed for the salt exchange was not a problem, and it was not reflected in the collection of salt taxes. In fact, as mentioned in Section 2.3, until 1941, when the measurement of the salt tax was changed, there was no problem in collecting the full amount of the tax because the effective tax rate was still slightly reduced. After 1941, two changes made the tax collection difficult in salt trade once again: firstly, the change from a volume-based commodity tax collection to ad valorem tax collection. As mentioned above, the new collection model involved a substantial tax increase. Compared to volume-based tax collection, the ad valorem tax collection is directly linked to price, which is equivalent to placing the tax burden on both parties of the transaction. Secondly, there was the intensification of inflation after 1941. The inflation, together with the ad valorem salt tax, greatly increased the price of salt, turning what had previously been a commodity that could be purchased with small change into a product that required large amounts of cash. As salt is an indispensable commodity, this greatly increased the proportion of household income spent on it, making it increasingly difficult for consumers to purchase it and making transactions difficult to conclude.

From the salt merchant's perspective, although less burdened by tax increases, but the need to pay taxes in advance and seek to compensate in the transaction, consumers can hardly afford the high price of salt. The result naturally makes it more difficult to recoup funds, the first to bear

[92] Zhang Xiaomei 张肖梅, *Guizhou jingji*, N13.

[93] Thomas J. Sargent and François R. Velde, *The Big Problem of Small Change* (Princeton: Princeton University Press), 4–5.

[94] Thomas J. Sargent, François R. Velde, *The Big Problem of Small Change*, 317.

the brunt of the grassroots public stores (公卖店 *gongmaidian*) and cooperatives, these grassroots salt sales organizations directly to the retail salt, so generally experienced the difficulty of sales.[95] The situation resulted in the difficulty of recouping funds and merchants cannot make up for the capital turnover. In the end, the pressure of capital shortage[96] was eventually transferred to the salt distributors, which resulted in an increasingly strong demand for capital for these salt distributors.[97]

Thus, inflation was transmitted through the ad valorem salt tax and the special characteristics of the salt trade, which was reflected in the difficulty of meeting the demand for salt. How to solve the problem of unsatisfied demand? The economists of the national government, represented by Zhang Jia'ao 张嘉璈, agreed that the supply should be expanded by increasing the quantity of salt shipped and sold by salt merchants.[98] The direct result of this analysis was to increase investment in salt merchants,[99] aiming to increase the supply of salt, calm the commodity's soaring price, and meet the daily demand of consumers. Thus, the credit granted to salt merchants started with a deposit and was expanded to a discount or even a credit overdraft after 1947.[100] However, this credit expansion contributed to further inflation, so that salt prices continued to rise, and consumers were unable to complete salt transactions due to the sharp devaluation of their cash holdings. Consumer demand was still not met, thus creating a vicious circle.

Therefore, financial intervention, especially credit support from various banks, had not only failed to solve the problem of financial recovery faced

[95] Summary of difficulties in underwriting salt for cooperatives in this province, M41-1-3042 Salt distribution underwriting rules, Guizhou Provincial Archives, 52.

[96] The government of Zhenfeng County reported the management measures of salt distribution stores in Zhenfeng County, M41-1-3041 About the price of salt transportation and sales and the constitution of the salt store, Guizhou Provincial Archives.

[97] Correspondence between Fu'an salt merchant Zhang Xienan and Zhang Fuzhong on financing matters in June 1948, M41-1-4328 Private Correspondence among Salt Merchants, Guizhou Provincial Archives.

[98] Kia-Ngau Chang, *The Inflationary Spiral: The Experience in China 1939–1950* (Cambridge: The MIT Press, 1958), 400.

[99] Kia-Ngau Chang, *The Inflationary Spiral: The Experience in China 1939–1950*, 192–227.

[100] In July 1947, the Guizhou Salt Administration Sub-bureau reported on the border salt discount case, 43-1-400 Water and land transportation and fire insurance letter for salt water storage in Guizhou District Salt Transport Office, in Guiyang Municipal Archives.

by salt merchants but had also made it more difficult for salt transactions, which were characteristically cash transactions, to be completed because of inflation. In turn, this meant it was more difficult for the salt tax to be realized in these transactions. Thus, both the changing pattern and status of salt taxation in Guizhou's finances and the counterproductive effects of trying to solve the salt tax problem implied that using this tax as the main source of Guizhou's revenue was risky for the province's financial stability. Something had to change.

3 The Rise of the Fiscal Revenue Pattern Dominated by the Tobacco Industry and Commerce Tax

After the outbreak of the war, Guizhou became an important transportation hub and industrial base in the rear, and a large number of inwardly relocated and newly built enterprises contributed to the development of industry and commerce in the province.[101] While the rapid development of industry and commerce changed the socio-economic landscape of Guizhou, it also brought an opportunity to change the province's fiscal pattern: the sales tax revenue generated by industry and commerce was relatively stable and sustainable. Many new industries and businesses emerged in Guizhou. Most notably, however, the cigarette industry, which started with the promotion of American tobacco,[102] relied on Guizhou's industrial and financial support and drove the province to become the largest tobacco cultivator in the country in the first half of the twentieth century, while generating high sales tax revenues. Unlike the bumpy process of generating tax revenue from the shipping and trading of salt, the process of generating tax revenue from cigarettes and other tobacco products was sustainable and stable, and the trading of cigarettes and tobacco was characterized by its ability to effectively combat inflation.

101 *Kangzhanshiqi neiqian xinan de gongshang qiye* 抗战时期内迁西南的工商企业 [Industrial and Commercial Enterprises Moving to the Southwest During the Anti-Japanese War], ed. Chinese People's Political Consultative Conference Southwest Cultural and Historical Data Collaboration Conference (Kunming: Yunnan People's Press, 1989).

102 See Chapter 5 for details.

3.1 The Rise of the Tobacco Industry and Stable Tobacco Taxes: The Role of Credit

In 1939, the Guizhou Agricultural Improvement Institute began trial plantings of American tobacco in Guiding County.[103] Subsequently, the cultivation of American tobacco and the tobacco industry in Guizhou rose rapidly. By 1943, Guizhou ranked first in the country in terms of tobacco cultivation, production, and sales.[104] This also brought the province significant tax revenue. The reform of Guizhou's fiscal system beginning in 1942 determined that 50% of locally collected sales tax and 20% of income tax were to be returned to the county by the central government.[105] In the tobacco industry, however, the sales tax rate for the cigarette industry alone was as high as 60%, and the excise tax rate for the export of other raw materials, such as tobacco, was also 50%; the local tax rate allowed for tobacco transactions was 14%, and the tax rate for specialty products was 10%. The total of these taxes grew year by year from 1/4 to 40% after 1943,[106] eventually becoming the first pillar of Guizhou's local fiscal revenue.

The steady increase in sales and commodity taxes paid by the tobacco industry and related industries resulted from the development of tobacco and cigarette industries,[107] but was also related to a series of measures and institutions that supported the development of the tobacco industry at the time. In short, the Guizhou provincial government supported the development of tobacco cultivation and the cigarette industry with a series of industrial and financial policies: i.e., credit-based promotion of industrial development while achieving credit settlement of transactions and

[103] Yang Runan and Hu Rengtong 杨汝南,胡礽同, "Guizhousheng nongzuowu zhi gaijin" 贵州省农作物之改进 [Improvement of Crops in Guizhou Province], in *Guizhou nongye gaijinsuo* 贵州省农业改进所 [Guizhou Agricultural Improvement Institute], M62-2-158, ed. Jiang Guosheng 蒋国生 et al. (Guiyang: Guizhou People's Press, 2006), 539–557.

[104] Chinese People's Political Consultative Conference Southwest Cultural and Historical Data Collaboration Conference, *Kangzhanshiqi neiqian xinan de gongshang qiye*, 304.

[105] Ma Yinchu 马寅初, *Caizhengxue yu zhongguo caizheng—lilun yu xianshi*, 186–188.

[106] Guizhou Provincial Finance and Economics Commission, *Guizhou caijing ziliao huibian*, 373.

[107] See Chapter 6.

taxes, thus freeing the market for cigarettes and their products from the influence of cash transactions.

Thanks to Wu Dingchang's financial support for industry and commerce in Guizhou after 1937,[108] direct and indirect investments were also made by the central bank of the national government, the Bank of China, the Bank of Communications, and the China Farmers Bank.[109] This direct investment accounted for more than 60% of the tobacco introduction[110] and promotion, and 90% of the shares of Guizhou Tobacco Company, which was owned by Guizhou Enterprise Company.[111] The indirect investment, i.e., the various credits granted, covered the entire process of tobacco cultivation, primary processing, and marketing, conducted in Guiding.[112] In 1942, Guizhou Bank, after realizing the joint bank settlement of other local banks nationwide, launched a foreign exchange deposit and bill settlement business for tobacco and its products (i.e., cigarettes), which increased the convenience of tobacco export transactions.[113] After 1945, local financial institutions, including Guizhou Bank, also participated in supporting Guizhou's tobacco enterprises to settle liquidity and purchase and sale payments.

The deep involvement of finance in tobacco and its products has formed the Guizhou tobacco financial system based on credit settlement. Specifically, the production and exchange of tobacco and its products in Guizhou depend on bank credit, which is essentially a bookkeeping

[108] Wu Dingchang 吴鼎昌, *Huaixisuibi* 花溪随笔 [Huaxi Essay ·Volume 1] (Guiyang: Guizhou Provincial Printing Office, 1943).

[109] "Guizhou yancao gongsi zhangcheng" 贵州烟草公司章程 [Articles of Association of Guizhou Tobacco Company], in *Guizhousheng qiye gongsi* 贵州省企业公司 [Guizhou Provincial Enterprise Company], Book 2, 1200, Guizhousheng danganguan 贵州省档案馆 et al. ed. (Guiyang: Guizhou People's Press, 2003).

[110] Zhang Xiaomei 张肖梅, *Guizhou jingji*, G25-31.

[111] Guizhousheng danganguan 贵州省档案馆 et al. ed., *Guizhousheng qiye gongsi*, 1200.

[112] Liu Daokui 刘道揆, "Guiding de meiyan shichang" 贵定的美菸市场 [Guiding American Tobacco Market], in *Guiding wenshi ziliao xuanji* 贵定文史资料选辑 [Selected Collection of Guiding Literature and History Materials], Series 4, ed. Guiding County Committee of the Chinese People's Political Consultative Conference Cultural and Historical Data Research Committee, 1987, 169–173.

[113] Guizhousheng danganguan 贵州省档案馆 et al. ed., *Guizhousheng qiye gongsi*, 1373–1394.

and settlement system that relies on credit exchange.[114] Let us take the purchase and sale of tobacco raw materials as an example to illustrate the role of this settlement system: usually, before the purchase and sale of these materials, cigarette manufacturers apply in advance to the Guizhou office of the Ministry of Finance's Bureau of Tobacco Monopoly, and after approval by the Bureau of Tobacco Monopoly, checks are issued from banks. Subsequently, the cigarette manufacturer makes a unified purchase of tobacco leaves through tobacco factories (烟庄 *yanzhuang*) and production cooperatives. This purchase is accomplished through large transactions in which the purchaser, after grading and pricing the tobacco, draws the purchase price from the bank based on the check issued by the tobacco factory, prepares a form to register the purchase, and prepares a shipping order to accompany the purchased commercial tobacco to the tobacco factory responsible for the purchase and reconciliation by the clerk of the Bureau of Tobacco Monopoly of the Ministry of Finance. After the tobacco monopoly office compares the bank statement with the bill of lending, it collects the excise tax from the tobacco buyer, and the tobacco factory collects the sales tax after the production of the finished product, so all reconciliation and tax collection occurs under the bank account.[115] Similarly, the wholesale and sale of cigarettes are done by bank transfer or check payment under the supervision of the monopoly authorities. The whole process is carried out through the bank to ensure the safety of funds and to give statements and purchase vouchers from both financial and physical lines respectively. Thus, the transactions involving capital flows stemming from tobacco and its products are separated, and all taxes generated in the process are collected through the banks. In this way, as long as the commercial chain of tobacco production, distribution, processing, and even final sale was complete and could continue to operate, the tax authorities could obtain a steady stream of tax revenue through these separate financial flows.

114 Mark Manning, Erlend Nier, and Jochen Schanz ed., *The Economics of Large-value Payments and Settlement* (Oxford: Oxford University Press, 2009), 24–38.

115 Measures for the Control of Smoked Tobacco Leaves of the Guiding Tobacco Monopoly Office of the Ministry of Finance, M60-1-8096, Guiding County Tobacco Transportation and Marketing Case, Guizhou Provincial Archives, 13.

3.2 Tobacco and Its Products and Inflation: Consumption Diversification and the Quasi-Monetary Properties of Tobacco

Undoubtedly, commodity production and consumption in China were subject to the extremes of inflation in the late 1940s, as were tobacco products in Guizhou. Unlike salt, however, although cigarettes were a hobby and addictive, the degree of choice in the cigarettes themselves was very large; in short, the types and brands of cigarettes were extremely varied. Sometimes the same tobacco factory even produced dozens of cigarette products with varying prices and qualities but highly similar tastes, and according to a 1944 statistic, in only Guiyang, Zunyi, Duyun, and Zhenyuan,[116] which belonged to the Guiding Monopoly Control Area By the end of 1948, there were still 58 major brands of cigarettes on sale.[117] Such a large number of choices made the demand elasticity of cigarette consumers large: i.e., when faced with price changes these consumers could easily downgrade their consumption by buying cigarettes of lower quality but with the same taste, or by buying low-end cigarettes in quantity instead of quality to maintain the level of consumption satisfaction without increasing the proportion of expenditure. This eliminated the effects of inflation to the greatest extent possible. For producers, producing as many cigarettes as possible at different price points also maximized consumers' reliance on their products, thus ensuring sales revenue. Once the sales revenue was guaranteed, it meant that the commercial chain of tobacco production, transportation, processing, and even final sale was stable and tax revenue was naturally guaranteed.

On the other hand, tobacco also had special attributes that performed certain quasi-monetary functions, such as portability, ease of preservation without spoilage,[118] ease of identification without quality problems,[119] ease of division and calculation, and relative stability of value; in addition,

[116] Statistical Table of Cost and Profit of Tobacco Manufacturers in Guiding District in 1944, 0-7-12 Guiding Office of the Tobacco Monopoly Bureau of the Ministry of Finance, Guiding County Archives.

[117] Industry association membership survey statistics, 43-1-926, in Guiyang Municipal Archives.

[118] Compared to table salt.

[119] Compared to precious metals.

tobacco was accepted as a valuable commodity not only in private transactions but also in the public sector[120] and banks.[121] This gave tobacco the properties of a local currency of sorts, replacing the national government currency, which had been devalued to the point of no credit.[122] In this sense, it can be argued that the local production and sale of tobacco leaf also allowed it to perform a direct fiscal payment function. Thus, Guizhou was able to establish a revenue pattern dominated by tobacco taxes after 1943 not only because of the rapid rise of the tobacco industry but also because the rise of this industry was accompanied by a relatively well-established foundation for credit payment. The diversified nature of cigarette consumption and the value-keeping properties of tobacco itself were also key. This and the use of credit circumvented the instability of cash transactions and ensured that tax revenue from tobacco and its products grew rapidly. Thus, it increased the stability of Guizhou's revenue structure.

4 Conclusion

By examining the formation process of the main structure of Guizhou's fiscal revenue from 1882–1949, the establishment to the loss of the salt tax as a primary source of revenue, and the formation of a revenue pattern dominated by tobacco and its products, we find that the stability of the province's fiscal revenue was determined by the stability and availability of tax sources. Salt consumption, based on small amounts of currency as well as cash transactions, strongly depended on the ease of transactions. Therefore, in the turbulent environment of the first half of the twentieth century, the difficulty of transactions due to the insufficient value of small currency and cash amplified by hyperinflation prevented the formation of salt consumption cash flows that provided a stable tax base, thus making it

120 Yunlong Township's school donation case centered on the township's public-produced American tobacco leaves, 0–2-87 Yunlong Township Office, 10, Longli County Archives.

121 Meng Haoqi 孟皓琪, "Zhenyuan he Zunyi de nongye baoxian" 镇远和遵义的农业保险 [Agricultural insurance in Zhenyuan and Zunyi], in *Minguo shiqi Guizhou baoxian dangan shiliao huibian* 民国时期贵州保险档案史料汇编 [A Compilation of Historical Materials of Insurance Archives in Guizhou During the Republic of China], ed. Meng Haoqi 孟皓琪 (Guiyang: Guizhou People's Press, 2021).

122 Akinobu Kuroda, trans. He Ping, *Huobi zhidu de shijieshi*, 96–99.

difficult to realize the salt tax, which gradually lost its status as the main source of fiscal revenue in Guizhou; in contrast, tobacco and its products depended on the credit payment support of the tobacco industry and banking industry to achieve stability from production to consumption, which in turn avoided the problem of insufficient small currency, achieving a stable tax base and forming a stable source of fiscal revenue. In this way, the emergence and formation of the main body of industrial and commercial fiscal revenue represented by tobacco and its products and the replacement of the fiscal structure dominated by the salt tax was a revolutionary turn for Guizhou's finances, coinciding with the move from a premodern system that relied on small denomination of currency and cash transactions to a modern credit-based fiscal system.

CHAPTER 7

Making Cooperatives on the Salt-Tobacco Road: State Organizational Embeddedness in the Distribution and Production of Salt and Tobacco (1937–1949)

Yujing Tan and Haoqi Meng

In this chapter, we focus on the influence of and changes to cooperatives along the trade of salt and tobacco. This chapter depicts and analyzes how cooperatives, which were established based on regional administrative units such as counties, towns, and villages, mobilized rural production and consumption during the Republican period and gradually spread to all corners of the rural areas during the New Deal period of Wu Dingchang in the 1930s and 1940s.

By constructing a system of organizations between the capital city and villages, cooperatives became embedded in the daily life of households and, through the control of consumption, they were able to manage the graded retailing of salt, a key commodity in daily life.[1] Controlling the sale of salt in this way further reduced the viability of salt merchants, who had to diversify their investments[2]; once they controlled the consumption of salt, the cooperatives moved to regulate the production and sale of

[1] See Chapter 3, about the salt sales and monopoly networks.

[2] See Chapter 5, the case study of diversification by salt merchants.

B. Jiang et al., *State, Market and Salt-Tobacco Road in Modern China (1935–1949)*, https://doi.org/10.1007/978-981-97-7654-2_7

another important product—tobacco. Cooperative operations gradually expanded from tobacco processing into the upstream and downstream supply chain of the tobacco industry, including cultivation and sales. This control not only ensured that tobacco taxes were more easily collected by provincial government,[3] but also entailed control of the circuits between production, distribution, exchange, and consumption, thus embedding the daily labor process and creating the conditions for the state's future monopoly on the purchase and marketing (统购统销 *tonggou tongxiao*) of daily commodities.[4] The cooperatives and grassroots economic organizations, eventually controlled the basic consumption channels of urban and rural residents in Guizhou and the production and sale of tobacco products.

This chapter is divided into three parts. The first part describes the establishment of the cooperative organizational system in Guizhou from the provincial to the township levels, and the process by which cooperatives controlled mass consumption in rural areas, including credit, agricultural products, and eventually salt. This section also summarizes the changing consumption cycles and patterns in rural areas and shows that cooperatives became an important organizational tool for mobilizing grassroots agricultural business during Wu Dingchang's reform in Guizhou.[5] As an organizational tool, cooperatives penetrated and controlled the basic needs of rural areas and changed the demand transaction patterns in these areas. The second section describes how cooperative organizations controlled the entire process of tobacco distribution, exchange, and consumption by participating in the production, acquisition, and cultivation of tobacco. This section focuses on analyzing how the cooperatives' role of controlling the distribution and consumption of daily goods (e.g., salt) overlapped with their role of controlling the production and marketing of tobacco. The third section concludes by reiterating the role of state power penetration and decentralization in the developmental history of cooperatives.

[3] See Chapter 6, tobacco finance establishment.

[4] Michael Mann, *The Sources of Social Power, Volume 1: A History of Power from the Beginning to AD 1760*, (Cambridge: Cambridge University Press), 32.

[5] Wu Dingchang 吴鼎昌, *Qianzheng wunian* 黔政五年 [Five Years of Guizhou Administration], Overview of Cooperation (Guiyang: Guizhou Enterprise Company Printing Office, 1943), 109. Collection materials of Guizhou Provincial Archives.

1 The Formation of the Cooperative Organization System and Cooperatives' Control of Consumption at County and Township Levels in Guizhou

After the outbreak of the Second Sino-Japanese War, cooperatives in Guizhou developed significantly. From 1937 to 1944, when Wu Dingchang was in power, comprehensive cooperatives engaged in production, while consumption and credit cooperatives covered all counties, cities, and towns, as well as some larger villages in the province. At the provincial level, Guizhou's government had established the Guizhou Provincial Cooperative Business Management Office (CBMO), which was responsible for the registration and management of local agribusiness cooperatives (e.g., consumption cooperatives and credit cooperatives). As an administrative agency, the provincial CBMO had to separate its functions and set up a Cooperative Business Agency to manage Cooperative Unions at the county level, as well as to deal with purchasing, marketing, and insurance.[6] At the county level, there was a general Consumer Transportation Credit Cooperative Union in each country that was responsible for the management of cooperatives in villages and townships. A county-level cooperative union for the distribution of important agri-industrial production tasks was also organized by the provincial government. At the village and township level, General Township and Village Cooperatives that dealt with production, consumption, and credit loans were established in each town. During this time, Guizhou formed a three-tier system for purchasing and marketing: the Provincial Cooperative Business Management Office (CBMO), county-level Cooperative Unions, and Township and Village Cooperatives.

During Wu Dingchang's time in power, he initiated the reform of provincial governance with the guidance of county-level governance. In other words, when Wu reformed the model of provincial governance, he emphasized that the existing county-level local governance should be taken into account.[7] During this period, the main functions of local

[6] This organization was reorganized in 1944 into the more cooperative Provincial Cooperative Association.

[7] Wu Dingchang 吴鼎昌, *Huaxixianbixubian* 花溪闲笔续编 [Huaxi Leisurely Writing Sequel] (Guiyang: Guizhou Enterprise Company Printing Office, 1940), 28. Collection materials of Guizhou Provincial Archives.

cooperatives, as a new form of organization, were (1) to arrange and distribute credit loans for agricultural production during the war and (2) to manage and lead the local purchasing, transportation, and marketing of agricultural products, agricultural tools, and seeds in rural areas.[8] By participating in the basic consumption and supply of rural areas, cooperatives in turn controlled the rural consumer market. After 1942, the cooperatives became the main sub-county salt supply sector in Guizhou through their participation in the formation of sub-county-level channels for the salt monopoly in the province.[9] This allowed the cooperative system in Guizhou to gradually control the hierarchical retail network of salt, thus embedding itself in the daily life of the population and becoming the central marketing organization for daily consumer goods.

In general, the organization and establishment of the three-tier cooperative system for purchasing and marketing in Guizhou went through three stages. The first stage stretched from October 1937 to October 1938. In October 1937, the provincial government established township cooperatives in accordance with the "Rules for the Organization of Provincial Cooperative Committees (各省合作委员会组织规程 *gesheng hezuo weiyuanhui zuzhi guicheng*)," and, in May 1939, Guizhou promulgated the "Measures for the Registration of Cooperative Societies of the County Governments of Guizhou Province (贵州省各县政府合作社接办登记办法 *guizhousheng gexianzhengfu hezuoshe jieban dengji banfa*)." At this point, the provincial government organized county-level Cooperative Unions to coordinate the management of cooperatives in each town and village.[10] By October 1938, the township and village cooperatives covered 1,327 townships in more than 71 counties. Township and village cooperatives nominally implemented rural mutual credit, though, in essence, the initial credit funds were provided by the Bank of China. During this period, the majority of township-level cooperatives

[8] Zhang Xiaomei 张肖梅, *Guizhou jingji* 贵州经济 [Guizhou Economy] (Chongqing: National Economic Research Institute, 1939), N1–30.

[9] "The Cooperative Business Administration Bureau of the Ministry of Social Affairs, Guiding Pilot Zone Cooperatives, please promote the presentation of cooperatives underwriting salt," in Guizhou Provincial Cooperative Business Management Office, M71-1-79, Guizhou Provincial Archives, 55.

[10] Wu Dingchang 吴鼎昌, *Qianzheng wunian* 黔政五年 [Five Years of Guizhou Administration] (Guiyang: Guizhou Enterprise Company Printing Office, 1943), 109–111. Collection Materials of Guizhou Provincial Archives.

credit cooperatives, followed by production cooperatives and transportation cooperatives. There were only two consumption cooperatives for agri-products marketing.[11] According to the Model Charter of Rural Cooperatives (农村合作社模范章程 *nongcun hezuosh mofan zhangcheng*), the main function of credit cooperatives was to grant rural credit loans.[12] Due to the large number of borrowing households lacking the necessary collateral and the extreme hardship of the farmers, it was difficult for farmers to repay these loans on time. By January 1939, the recovery rate of credit loans to farmers had dropped to less than 60%.[13] Overall, the development of these initial township-level cooperatives, with their goal of facilitating mutual credit for farmers, was limited and slow to expand.

The second stage of establishing the three-tier cooperative system took place between May 1939, when township-level cooperatives were reorganized, and 1941, when the unified Provincial Cooperative Business Management Office was formed. This is when county-level Cooperative Unions were established. In May 1939, the Guizhou provincial government issued a new method for organizing cooperatives, the Measure for the Registration of Cooperative by the County Governments of Guizhou (贵州省各县政府合作社接办登记办法 *guizhousheng gexianzhengfu hezuoshe jieban dengji banfa*), on the grounds that "the counties are far away and it is inconvenient to travel to and from them." According to this measure, the provincial government's goal was to optimize the organization of cooperatives in townships, reduce the number of cooperatives at the township level,[14] and promote the integrated operation of cooperatives. Thus, in terms of organization, the provincial government set up county-level Cooperative Unions to unify the management of township cooperatives and "in principle, cease to handle single-function cooperatives."[15] The provincial government of Guizhou also pushed county-level

[11] Zhang Xiaomei 张肖梅, *Guizhou jingji*, 17.

[12] Zhang Xiaomei 张肖梅, *Guizhou jingji*, 1–30.

[13] Wu Dingchang 吴鼎昌, *Qianzheng wunian*, 109.

[14] Tian Jinfeng 田锦凤, "Guizhou jiefangqian de hezuoshiye" 贵州解放前的合作事业 [Cooperative Undertakings Before the Liberation of Guizhou, in *Guizhou jinrong huobishi luncong* 贵州金融货币史论丛 [Guizhou Finance and Currency History Collection], ed. Guizhou Provincial Institute of Finance, (Guiyang: People's Bank of China Guizhou Branch, 1986), 172–185.

[15] Wu Dingchang 吴鼎昌, *Qianzheng wunian*, 112–114.

Cooperative Unions to construct agricultural warehouses for the collection, storage, and, sale of basic living materials in accordance with the Measure for Cooperatives Run Agricultural Warehouse (合作社兼营农仓办法 *hezuoshe jiaying nongcang banfa*) promulgated in October 1937 and the Measure for Simplified Agricultural Warehouse (简易农仓办法 *jianyi nongcang banfa*) promulgated in January 1938. Moreover, on the basis of their storage business, these agricultural warehouses could also handle mortgage loans and insurance business.[16] In this way, the function of these cooperatives expanded from handling credit loans to handling mortgage loans. In accordance with the practice of the time, mortgage loans required simultaneous storage of collateral, so it became a necessity for cooperatives to also operate agricultural warehouses. Furthermore, the county-level cooperatives, and their affiliated township and village cooperatives, began to get involved in storage and transportation in addition to offering credit loans, and therefore carried out the purchase of agricultural products in accordance with the relevant measures of agricultural warehouse management.[17] They began to sell certain production materials, such as agricultural instruments and seeds,[18] as well as textiles, such as bolts of cloth and cotton yarn.[19] Township and village cooperatives gradually became the only trade organizations below the county-level.

As depicted in Chapter 2, before the establishment of cooperatives-run warehouses in rural Guizhou, all sales of textiles, production materials, and agricultural products depended on bazaars. The traders in these markets were all itinerant merchants who only appeared at fixed times.[20] This way of trading left the initiative in the hands of merchants and did not allow farmers to meet their basic needs in real time. The emergence of permanent institutions such as cooperatives, which also operated agricultural warehouses, changed this situation: cooperatives ran permanent stores at the township level, with permanent staff, so that residents of a

[16] Meng Haoqi 孟皓琪 ed., *Minguo shiqi Guizhou baoxian dangan shiliao huibian* 民国时期贵州保险档案史料汇编 [A Compilation of Historical Materials of Insurance Archives in Guizhou During the Republic of China], volume 1, (Guiyang: Guizhou People's Press, 2021), 70–73.

[17] Wu Dingchang 吴鼎昌, *Qianzheng wunian*, 112–114.

[18] Wu Dingchang 吴鼎昌, *Qianzheng wunian*, 115.

[19] Wu Dingchang 吴鼎昌, *Qianzheng wunian*, 113.

[20] Zhang Xiaomei 张肖梅, *Guizhou jingji*, 1–25.

township and nearby rural areas could trade at any time.[21] This greatly increased the basic production of rural populations and changed the patterns of basic consumption in rural areas. Periodic centralized trading persisted but was supplemented by daily trading.

The third period of the formation of the cooperative organization system in Guizhou began with the establishment of the Cooperative Business Administration in 1941 and ended with the establishment of a basic pattern of cooperative salt distribution in 1943. During this period, the provincial, county, and township cooperative organizations were formed through the reorganization of the provincial cooperative management structure by the provincial government and the establishment of the Cooperative Business Agency, which was responsible for supervising, registering, organizing, and directing county-level cooperatives. At the same time, through a series of cooperation between the Cooperative Business Agency and the Guizhou Salt Administration Bureau, the cooperative system in Guizhou intervened in the consumption of salt at the township and village levels, thus forming a unified marketing of basic consumer goods. It was also responsible for accepting production orders and allocating them to the county-level cooperatives for completing ordering,[22] and the orders during this period mainly included materials such as grain and cotton cloth for military needs from all level governments.[23]

In addition to receiving production orders and purchasing essential household goods on behalf of the cooperatives and distributing them to county associations, the newly established agency actively collaborated with the Guizhou Provincial Salt Administration Bureau. They participated in the reform of the salt monopoly and salt distribution system in 1941, underwriting salt for the cooperatives and eventually forming a network of power relations at the township level, squeezing out old-style salt retailers.[24] In 1942, the Guizhou Provincial Cooperative Business Agency and the Guizhou Provincial Salt Administration Bureau reached

[21] "Survey on Salt Sales by Machang Township Credit Cooperative in Huangping County," in Guizhou Provincial Salt Administration Bureau, M41-1-3042, Guizhou Provincial Archives.

[22] Wu Dingchang 吴鼎昌, *Qianzheng wunian*, 109–111.

[23] "The purchase and sale contract between the Cooperative Business Agency and Guiding County Cooperative Association," in Guizhou Provincial Cooperative Business Management Office, M71-1-75, Guizhou Provincial Archives, 30.

[24] See Chapter 3, about the salt sales and monopoly networks.

an agreement to operate a cooperative salt distribution system in Guiding county on a trial basis. The agreement stipulated that the Guizhou Cooperative Business Agency would purchase salt quotas from the Guizhou Salt Administration Bureau at the same price as salt distributors and distribute them to the Guiding county-level Cooperatives Union according to the population and quantity of salt sold in the area. At the same time, the Guiding County Cooperatives Union established an inventory for inspection by the Guiding Salt Administration Bureau. This was no different from the traditional salt distribution system under which salt distribution stores and public stores in counties and cities below the provincial level were operated and supervised.[25] By December 1942, seven counties, including Zhijin, Zhenfeng, Zunyi, Tongren, Huangping, Dingfan, and Bijie, had applied to the Guizhou Provincial Salt Administration Bureau through the Provincial Cooperative Business Agency. These requests were all approved, and these counties successively increased their capital by organizing their township cooperatives to distribute salt.[26]

The above developments ended the part of Guizhou's history where there were no salt underwriting points below the county level and where the province relied on merchants to purchase salt from county salt distribution stores and retail it freely. This change established the organizational basis for the Salt Administration Bureau to implement a strict salt monopoly based on the principle of "granting salt according to the population,"[27] and it impacted the authority of the old-style salt merchants who operated county salt stores. This reduced the market share of the salt merchants in the county salt stores and create, creating competition and reducing their market shares. This public stores (公卖店 *gongmaidian*) further pushed the salt merchants out of the salt distribution system.

[25] "Rules of Salt Department of Cooperatives in Guiding County," in Guizhou Provincial Cooperative Business Management Office, M71-1-79, Guizhou Provincial Archives, 71.

[26] "Salt sales situation of cooperatives in each county," in Guizhou Provincial Cooperative Business Management Office, M71-1-135, Guizhou Provincial Archives.

[27] "Report by Li Qinggao from the Guizhou Salt Management Office at the Guizhou Senate Inaugural Meeting," in Guizhou Provincial Salt Administration Bureau, M41-1-99, Guizhou Provincial Archives, 42.

By 1945, just before the end of the War, all cooperative salt sales-points in Guizhou below the county level were taken over by township cooperatives.[28] By this time, the three-tier organizational system consisting of the cooperative business agency,[29] the county cooperatives, and the township cooperatives had been formed, which included the purchase and sale of agricultural products and materials, and on this basis, the distribution of salt for basic consumer goods was controlled, thus achieving control over the consumption of residents at the county level and below.

2 From Consumption to Production: Cooperatives' Control of the Tobacco Industry

For the cooperatives to control consumption they had to gain further control of the exchange, distribution, and production of local commodities. For this reason, the cooperative system set up workshops one after another to gradually penetrate and control daily production. Here, the penetration of the cooperative system into the tobacco industry was most typical and important, and was based on two purposes: one was to increase the cooperatives' own capital through organizational embeddedness, and the other was to conduct tobacco tax audits more easily. In this context, becoming organizationally embedded meant that the state used bureaucratic out-posting and created new governing organizations in order to gradually enter the manufacturing sector and further influence and regulate the sale of goods. Compared to market-driven enterprises and free traders, organized and affiliated factories could provide relatively stable tax revenue.

This change was reflected around the time of the establishment of the Guiding Tobacco Factory.[30] In November 1939, the Cooperative Business Administration Bureau of the Ministry of Economic Affairs, in cooperation with the Guizhou provincial government, established the Guiding

[28] Details of cooperative sales of salt, M41-1-3042, Salt distribution underwriting rules, etc. Archives of Guizhou Provincial Salt Administration Bureau, Guizhou Provincial Archives.

[29] After 1944, it was reorganized into a provincial association. See Guizhou shehui zuzhi gailan: 1911–1949 贵州社会组织概览: 1911–1949 [An Overview of Social Organizations in Guizhou: 1911–1949] (Guiyang: Guizhou People's Press, 1996), 124–125.

[30] See Chapter 3, The Rise of the Cigarette Industry in Guiding.

Cooperative Experimental Zone.[31] The administrative office of the zone was responsible for managing cooperative business in Guiding County and investigating the economic situation in the countryside, as well as assisting rural cooperatives at all levels in production, operation, and the retail of agricultural tools and consumer goods. In 1943, the Guiding Cooperative Experimental Zone set up the East Guizhou Cooperative for Commodity Supply and Marketing Agency, which was responsible for shipping and processing the products of the cooperatives in the area and, subsequently, purchasing the materials needed by the cooperatives wholesale.[32] The operation of the Guiding Cooperative Experimental Zone initially formed a cooperative supply and marketing system that included eleven counties in East Guizhou: Guiding, Longli, Pingyue, Duyun, Dushan, Majiang, Weng'an, Huangping, Lushan, Shibing, and Zhenyuan.[33] By 1944, on the basis of the supply and marketing agency, Guiding Cooperative Experimental Zone and the Guiding branch of the Bank of Guizhou collaborated to set up the Guiding Tobacco House (贵定烟庄 *guiding yanzhuang*),[34] which the Guiding Cooperative Experimental Zone sent administrative personnel to operate. The Tobacco House unified the purchase of the American tobacco produced by the Guiding cooperatives and handled transportation and distribution services, so that the cooperative organizations in Guiding further controlled the purchase and sale of tobacco. The capital of Guiding Tobacco House was 1.5 million *yuan*, and the acquisition was financed by the Bank of Guizhou, mainly as a pledge loan secured by the tobacco leaves to be acquired by the Guiding Tobacco House. The Guiding branch of the Bank of Guizhou provided short-term pledged loans on

[31] *Guizhou shehui zuzhi gailan: 1911–1949* 贵州社会组织概览: 1911–1949 [Overview of Social Organizations in Guizhou] (1996, Guiyang: Guizhou People's Press), 125.

[32] Hu Duanzheng 胡端正, "Woren guidingxian lianshe jingli de qianqianhouhou" 我任贵定县联社经理的前前后后 [The Story Behind My Appointment As Manager of the Guiding County Association], in *Guiding wenshi ziliao xuanji* 贵定文史资料选辑 [Selections of Guiding Cultural and Historical Materials], Series2, ed. Cultural and Historical Materials Research Committee of Guiding County Committee of Chinese People's Political Consultative Conference, 1983, 24–34.

[33] *Guizhou shehui zuzhi gailan: 1911-1949* 贵州社会组织概览: 1911–1949 [Overview of Social Organizations in Guizhou] (Guiyang: Guizhou People's Press, 1996), 125.

[34] "Report on the request for instructions from the Guiding County Branch of the Bank of Guizhou regarding the establishment of *Guiding Salt Factory*," in Guiding Branch of the Bank of Guizhou, 0-14-9, Guiding County Archives, 66–67.

a monthly basis in accordance with the capital contribution agreement to support the Guiding Tobacco House's acquisition of tobacco leaves produced by the cooperatives and their shredding and processing.[35] The primary task of the Guiding Tobacco House was to meet the needs of Guizhou Tobacco Company, and, after its establishment, it took over the company's tobacco purchasing, which was undertaken by the Tobacco Purchasing Committee, jointly run by the Bank of Guizhou Bank and Guizhou Tobacco Company.[36] This purchasing accounted for nearly 40% of Guiding's tobacco market. On this basis, the Guiding Tobacco House also ventured into the transportation of tobacco purchased by other tobacco factories, and the amount of tobacco involved reached 1.7 million pounds, accounting for 60% of Guiding's total annual tobacco volume.[37] Pricing power and control over the transportation and sale of Guiding tobacco was realized. In 1945, the busiest year of Guiding's tobacco business, the company purchased and shipped 3,000 pounds of tobacco a month.[38]

We return to the political and economic context of the development of Guizhou's interwar tobacco industry to further understand the process and results of cooperative involvement in tobacco production.[39] The most important industry in Guizhou during the interwar period was the tobacco processing industry that emerged in the 1940s, which not only created and expanded the tobacco consumer market but also provided a steady stream of tax revenue.[40] In order to increase the capital of cooperatives to operate effectively under inflationary developments, the Guizhou Provincial Cooperative Business Agency and the Guiding

[35] "Report on the purchase and sale of smoked tobacco leaves by the Guiding County Branch of the Bank of Guizhou," in Guiding Branch of the Bank of Guizhou, 0-14-9, Guiding County Archives, 96–97.

[36] "Report on the request for instructions from the Guiding County Branch of the Bank of Guizhou regarding the establishment of guiding Yanzhuang," in Guiding Branch of the Bank of Guizhou, 0-14-9, Guiding County Archives, 66–67.

[37] "Explanation on Guiding Bank of Guizhou Branch's investment in Guiding Yanzhuang transportation and sales business," in Guiding Branch of the Bank of Guizhou, 0-14-9, Guiding County Archives, 61–62.

[38] "Guiding Yanzhuang Overdraft Application," in Guiding Branch of the Bank of Guizhou, 0-14-9, Guiding County Archives, 87–88.

[39] See Chapter 4, The Rise of the Cigarette Industry in Guiding.

[40] Guizhou Provincial Finance and Economics Commission eds., *Guizhou caijing ziliao huibian*, 60–82.

Office of the Tobacco Monopoly Bureau of the Ministry of Finance, in consensus, promoted cooperative participation in cigarette production at the two largest production centers, Guiyang and Guiding.[41] The cooperatives started with hand- and semi-machine-rolled cigarettes.[42] The Guiding Office of the Tobacco Monopoly Bureau of the Ministry of Finance negotiated with the Guizhou Provincial Cooperative Business Agency, stipulating that the cigarettes made by the cooperatives were to be uniformly approved by the Bureau at a uniform cost and profit, and were to be uniformly acquired and offered for sale, with the monopoly interest tax levied by the Guiding Branch of the Yunnan-Guizhou District Commodity Tax Bureau at a rate of 50% before the cigarettes left the factory.[43] After 1945, the cooperatives gradually transitioned to machine-made cigarettes. The number of tobacco factories participating in the cooperatives decreased significantly, but they all achieved large-scale production.[44]

As cooperatives became involved in the tobacco processing industry, tobacco raw materials became increasingly important, and Guizhou tobacco became increasingly important in the national market, with prices rising year by year. The market boom brought about a wave of post-war tobacco cultivation fever in the core areas of tobacco production, including Guiding, Longli, Pingyue, Zhenyuan, and Zunyi.[45] This boom in tobacco cultivation brought about changes in the organization of tobacco cultivation. By this stage, the tobacco industry had experienced a large-scale movement toward cooperatives. It is important to note that the specialty-production cooperatives that emerged during this period differed from the township cooperatives that had been involved in tobacco farming during the war.

[41] Guizhou Provincial Finance and Economics Commission eds., *Guizhou caijing ziliao huibian*, 143–146.

[42] Ibid.

[43] "Able of Approved Profit and Ex-factory Patent Tax Rates of Cigarette Cooperatives," in Guiding County Chamber of Commerce, 0-12-13, Guiding County Archives, 6.

[44] Guizhou Provincial Finance and Economics Commission eds., *Guizhou caijing ziliao huibian*, 143–146.

[45] Guizhou Provincial Finance and Economics Commission eds., *Guizhou caijing ziliao huibian*, 310.

First, American Tobacco Growers Cooperatives were no longer registered on the basis of geographical divisions[46]; i.e., they were no longer registered under the name of "such-and-such village" or "such-and-such township's first cooperative," but rather under the more formal names of "farm" or "production center." Accordingly, their scope was no longer limited to the formation of the territory, but the actual land purchased or leased for production, so that these were essentially production farms formed under the name of "cooperative." The advantage of these production cooperatives established beyond administrative divisions was that there were no limitations on scale, allowing for a larger association of land and capital. At the same time, these cooperatives were able to obtain more favorable loan terms than companies, thus facilitating the financing rapid expansion of tobacco farming.[47]

Secondly, in terms of business content and methods, unlike in the past, the new tobacco production cooperatives combined the functions of growing American tobacco, harvesting and processing roasted tobacco, and selling the processed rough tobacco to tobacco factories or overseas buyers. Because of the larger scale of production and financing, these cooperatives were able to build smoke houses and warehouses for the storage and fermentation of roasted tobacco, which cooperatives could not undertake in the past, thus incorporating the functions of the middlemen (i.e., tobacco farms) that used to collect and store rough tobacco into the new cooperatives' scopes of daily operation.[48] This de facto completed the transformation from simple tobacco growers to tobacconists that integrated tobacco growing and primary processing. In this way, the cooperatives not only realized a new scale of tobacco cultivation, but also eliminated the processing and storage links in the

[46] "The cooperatives engaged in growing American tobacco during the war were township cooperatives," in Guizhou Provincial Department of Construction, M60-1-9257, Guizhou Provincial Archives, 7.

[47] Meng Haoqi ed. 孟皓琪, *Minguo shiqi Guizhou baoxian dang'an shiliao huibian*, 174.

[48] In the past, tobacco leaves were produced by tobacco farmers and cooperatives and then sold to tobacco farms for rough processing and smoking, because tobacco farmers did not have a smokehouse. See Liu Daokui 刘道揆, "Guiding de meiyan shichang" 贵定的美烟市场 [Guiding American Tobacco Market], in *Guiding wenshi ziliao xuanji* 贵定文史资料选辑 [Selected Collection of Guiding Literature and History Materials], Series 4, ed. Guiding County Committee of the Chinese People's Political Consultative Conference Cultural and Historical Data Research Committee, 1987, 169–173.

production process, saving costs and increasing bargaining power. At the same time, their management was different from the semi-compulsory participation of the township cooperatives in the past. The new cooperatives were formed on a voluntary basis and managed internally according to a corporate system, which improved operational efficiency and reduced administrative oversight.[49]

Finally, in terms of organizational structure, since the registration of cooperatives had been decentralized to county-level Cooperatives Union during this period, and for the purpose of enhancing the economic self-sufficiency of county-level Cooperatives Union, the American Tobacco Growers Cooperative was incorporated into the management of county-level Cooperatives Union in 1946 and became a type of institution managed by the American Tobacco Production and Marketing Department under the county cooperative societies.[50] It was then divided into two parts, the acquisition and sales departments, as required by the Guizhou Provincial Department of Finance. This organizational change rationalized the collection and storage of American tobacco and downstream sales separately, monitoring the two categories of unified purchase and unified sale, and put the unified sale and the unified sale of salt under one category of management, thus realizing the unified sale of two types of monopoly commodities.[51]

Up to this point, the local government-led cooperative movement was far from fully penetrating the tobacco industry and had not yet fully penetrated the tobacco trading market. In 1947, the provincial tax bureau conducted a tax reform to the county tax bureau regarding the tobacco industry, and this further stimulated the enthusiasm of county-level governments to control the tobacco trade.[52] This tax-sharing reform was led by the provincial tax bureau with the primary purpose of increasing county's revenues and supplementing provincial fiscal shortfalls. The Guizhou Provincial Department of Finance established a new

[49] "Guiding County American Tobacco Production and Marketing Cooperative Proposed," in Guizhou Provincial Department of Finance, the Republic of China, M39-1-65, Guizhou Provincial Archives, 9.

[50] Ibid.

[51] Hu Duanzheng 胡端正, "Wo ren guidingxian lianshe jingli de qianqianhouhou," 24–34.

[52] Guizhou Provincial Finance and Economics Commission eds., *Guizhou caijing ziliao huibian*, p423.

local tax: the "Tobacco Transaction Tax." The tax rate was set at 15%, and the tax was levied on traded cigarettes. Traders were required to pay the tax on transactions of more than 50 *shijin* (500gram = 1 shijin). It was collected on behalf of the county government by the Yunnan-Guizhou District Commodity Tax Bureau staff at each county branch or management office, and "half of the tax goes to the local government and half to the respective province."[53]

Because the county Cooperatives Union participated in and controlled the processing, storage, and production of tobacco at the county level, it made sense as the main body for establishing market management transactions. In September 1947, the Longli County Government and the Guiding Branch of the Yunnan-Guizhou District Commodity Tax Bureau jointly agreed to set up the American Tobacco Exchange, which was managed by the Longli County Cooperatives Union. It was to establish a market based on a fixed site selected by the Longli county government.[54] The county government used the Cooperatives Union's existing office and warehouse as the Cooperative Union's office and baking tobacco baking warehouse, and the County Cooperative Union assigned staff to be responsible for the storage and grading of American tobacco. The Guiding Branch of the Yunnan-Guizhou District Commodity Tax Bureau sent commissioners to be responsible for the collection of transaction taxes, and the county government sent employees to be responsible for day-to-day work and coordination of the exchange site. The American Tobacco Exchange established special bylaws that defined the composition of personnel, business content, daily management, profit distribution, and accounting systems. At the same time, the American Tobacco Exchange also established rules for trading American tobacco. It was responsible for grading and purchasing not only the American tobacco leaves produced by the cooperatives but also the American tobacco leaves grown by tobacco farmers outside the cooperatives. It was also responsible for the unified sales of the flue-cured tobacco collected and stored to downstream tobacco factories and overseas tobacco buyers approved by the Tobacco Monopoly Bureau of the Ministry of Finance. This set of institutional arrangements formed a new tobacco distribution and trading

[53] Ibid.

[54] Consultation on the establishment of the American Tobacco Exchange, 0-5-24 Longli Chamber of Commerce, 44. Archives of the Longli Chamber of Commerce during the Republic of China in the Longli County Archives.

system with county-level Cooperative Union as the mainstays of tobacco acquisition and trading.[55] By the end of 1948, Guizhou's provincial government had established a unified market for tobacco leaf purchase and trading operations in thirty-nine major tobacco-producing counties, including Guiding, Guizhu, Longli, Pingba, Pingyue, Zhenyuan, and Zunyi, with county-level Cooperative Union as the mainstay.[56]

In the end, the cooperative organization system was able to control the last link of exchange in the tobacco industry. This meant that the cooperative system at the provincial, county, and township levels, with county-level cooperatives as its mainstay, had mastered the entire industrial chain of Guizhou's tobacco industry, thus completing its control over the production of this important commodity.

3 Conclusion

From the sale of salt to control of the entire production, distribution, exchange, and consumption chain of the tobacco industry, the three-level cooperative organization system in Guizhou province, completed its penetration and control of key sectors and key nodes in the daily life and production of Guizhou's residents. This laid the foundation for the furthering formation of a unified purchasing and marketing system; at the same time, it also realized an overlap between the salt consumption network and the tobacco production and consumption network at the micro level.

In 1951, the CCP-controlled Guizhou provincial government established the new People's Cooperative Business Management Office (人民合作事业管理处 *renmin hezuo shiye guanlichu*) on the basis of the former Guizhou Provincial Cooperative Business Administration Bureau of the national government. This new office's first task was to establish supply and marketing cooperatives at all levels, based on the original cooperative societies in each county. It was also tasked with expanding the scope of supply and marketing cooperatives to include tobacco, wine, tea, sugar, fabric, cotton yarn, matches, salt, grain, and other key commodities and industrial products to form a comprehensive pattern of unified purchasing

55 "Articles of Association of American Tobacco Exchange," in Longli Chamber of Commerce, 0-5-24, Longli County Archives, 45–52.

56 Guizhou Provincial Finance and Economics Commission eds., *Guizhou caijing ziliao huibian*, 503–512.

and marketing.[57] A series of key developments outlined in this chapter lead to one outcome. The founding of cooperatives in 1937 witnessed the formation of county-level cooperative societies and the gradual control of the sale of production and living materials in rural areas and even the sale of salt and the formation of a three-level cooperative unified purchasing and marketing mechanism at the provincial, county, and township levels. Cooperatives played a crucial role in this process: by transforming the forms and cycles of production and consumption in the mountainous villages of southwestern China, they became a permanent part of peasant life, replacing the market trade represented by bazaars and becoming a tool and network of state control over daily rural life. The emergence of the cooperative system at the county and township levels in Guizhou was a precursor to the intensification and culmination of the CCP state power that followed.

[57] *Guizhou Provincial Chronicle Compilation Committee ed., Guizhousheng gongxiao hezuoshe zhi* 贵州省供销合作志 [Chronicle of Guizhou Province Supply and Marketing Cooperation] (Guiyang: Guizhou People's Press, 2003), 21–23.

CHAPTER 8

Conclusion: A Salt-Tobacco Road with Institutional Risks and Business Opportunities

Yujing Tan and Zhao Zhou

In this book, the authors explore the historical records of salt and tobacco merchants, as well as local officials in Guizhou during the Republican period (1912–1949). The research focuses on how salt merchants strategically interacted with central and local governments to maintain their business advantages and influence in local affairs. Additionally, the book examines how these merchants reshaped their socio-economic networks through investment in the tobacco trade and the construction of the salt-tobacco road from the late 1930s to the end of the 1940s.

The chapters respond in turn to the questions we asked at the beginning of this book: how Guizhou salt merchants develop their business and seek financial initiatives amidst the tensions of central-local government relations (Chapters 2 and 4), how they faced escalating government control over economic activity in wartime (Chapters 4 and 5), and, how the government (and local governments in particular) mobilize the merchants in moments of crisis through new industrial policies and financial instruments (Chapters 3 and 6).

The importance of Guizhou to the study of commodity trade and economic history lies in its relationship to the state. Previous studies have

B. Jiang et al., *State, Market and Salt-Tobacco Road in Modern China (1935–1949)*, https://doi.org/10.1007/978-981-97-7654-2_8

revealed that, though it seems that Guizhou has been generally recognized as an "isolated island", with the effort from the central government and the development of long-distance trade, Guizhou gradually became a hinterland for a broader market, rather than an isolated island in Qing Dynasty. Based on historical sources and established academic works, articles in this book discuss the significance of salt and tobacco as essential commodities, and also outline the changes in political and business relations in war, political changes, and technological development in modern Guizhou. The author of Chapter 2, Meng, analyzes the process of formation of commodity trade routes in Guizhou and indicates that the closer central cities are to the main transportation routes or distribution centers of materials, the more integrated the market becomes into the commercial network. Nonetheless, small regional local markets below the county level remain independent. These characteristics of Guizhou's trade routes still existed when the KMT government tried to implement effective control of Guizhou and influenced how the two commodities discussed in this book distributed.

The state's shift of the revenue generator from salt to tobacco witnessed an industrial transformation of the salt merchants, as well as a reformation and expansion of the local business networks established by traditional salt transportation. These local networks were primarily informal alliances between merchants and local bureaucrats. In Chapter 3, Jiang explores how salt merchants in Guizhou adapted to the salt reforms during the late Qing dynasty and then coordinated salt monopoly during the wartime in the Republic of China. They formed new relationships with local officials and established business organizations to safeguard their interests and regain political and social capital. The growing influence of these local business organizations expanded local government control over salt administration, which in turn led to increased corruption. This situation raised concerns at the central state level about the emerging connection between new local commercial organizations and local power. The dynamic between merchants and the government, as well as the state and the market, experienced significant shifts during the reforms from the late Qing to the Republican period. Merchants faced risks not only from market forces but also from a series of institutional changes.

However, these systemic upheavals did not impede Guizhou salt merchants' risk-fighting strategy and innovation. They utilized all the resources of formal and informal networks to diversify risks and negotiate their rights and interests with the state. They had a new understanding of the role of industrial and tax policies and reconceptualized the state amid institutional transitions. Among them, establishing financial institutions and social organizations was an important way for them to secure their rights. This explains why local salt merchants still developed their businesses during the significant socio-economic transition in Guizhou from the late Qing to the Republic of China. As described and analyzed by Zhou and Meng in Chapter 4, when the central government tried to expand the tobacco industry as a means of expanding the source of tax revenue, the local merchants, such as salt merchants, and the local government conspired to marginalize small producers of local tobacco strategically and expanded the local salt merchants' authority in the salt trade. By imposing a tobacco transaction tax, local governments facilitated the transformation of tobacco into a circulating good in its own right (which could be used as a tax deduction), and merchants financialized the process of tobacco production through to sale, using bills to transact business, thus giving tobacco and its products a monetary character. In Chapter 5, Jiang explicitly uses the case of merchant Liu Xiyi to illustrate how merchants understood and practiced the financial innovations that the state made to mobilize and integrate local tax resources. In the state's attempt to launch new regulations on salt transportation, the power of the traditional salt merchants (sitting merchants at salt ports) was weakened. Liu Xiyi, a traditional salt merchant, set up a bank with his business partners and fought against the large financial institutions endorsed by the central government. In asserting and reinforcing their local influence, local merchants gained the support of officials from the central government and local authorities with local backgrounds, and Liu's financial business expanded to include investments in the tobacco industry, where he purchased local tobacco factories amid a policy crackdown and used modern financial instruments to launch a successful tobacco business.

The salt merchants' attempts to invest in tobacco were mainly influenced by the reforms of the state's industrial, trade, and tax policies at the time. The state itself, from the late Qing to the Republican period, responded to crises at home and abroad and underwent fragmentation and reconstruction. The role of the state underwent essential changes. This edited book also argues that the shift from salt to a tobacco-based fiscal system meant not only the government's reidentification of tax resources but also its governance of the local economic and social communities on the frontier. The institutional response to the political and economic chaos and the state's attempt to govern the frontier was the main reason for the state's reform and modernization of its fiscal system. At the same time, we agree with Rosenthal and Wong's claim that the state governance during the period of political and economic chaos was never just to conduct good governance and gain legitimacy but had to further view the tax reform as a tool to extract benefits from the merchant community.[1] Based on these findings, we further argue that the reform of the tax system in different periods has, in turn, led to changes in the central-local relationship, and local business interests (formed by local businessmen and local bureaucrats in a tension-filled and interdependent nexus) have continuously adjusted their cooperation and business strategies, utilized industrial policies and tax reforms to diversify their business risks, and even contributed to the transformation of industry and society.

Chapter 6 pointed out that in constructing a new tax source and centralized financial pattern in Guizhou, the local government has constructed a fiscal system centered on tobacco with the help of the speculative behavior of merchants. In this way, the local financial dilemma was freed from the dependence on the amount of real money in circulation, and a new financial pattern based on credit was constructed. It should be noted here that this great transition was rooted in the tension between central government and local government. In Chapter 7, Tan and Meng demonstrated that during the Anti-Japanese War period, local governments supported salt merchant groups to actively construct grassroots salt purchase and sale networks with the aim of embedding cooperatives, a new mobilized organization for the purchase and sale of everyday consumer goods, into the network of transportation and sale of consumer goods (mainly tobacco) below the county level, in order to consolidate the tobacco market in Guizhou. In 1947, the central government-controlled provincial tax bureau conducted a tax reform to the county tax bureau regarding the tobacco industry, further stimulating the enthusiasm of county-level governments to control the tobacco trade. The cooperatives were instrumentalized and formalized as an organization to achieve the provincial government's taxation goal. The local government nationalized tobacco production units and increased its ability to tax tobacco. After 1947, the national government further reformed the tobacco-focused cooperative organizations, allowing them to expand

[1] Rosenthal, Jean-Laurent, and R. Bin Wong. *Before and Beyond Divergence: The Politics of Economic Change in China and Europe* (Harvard University Press, 2011), 183–207.

in townships. Power entered people's daily lives further through the expansion of tobacco cooperatives.

1 Implications

The relationship between the modern state and the market is an essential topic in empirical and theoretical studies about how trade and economic activity expanded.[2] Complex political-economic arrangements underlie trade, and the state is a vital force that dominates these political-economic arrangements (which often manifest themselves in policies of taxation, industry, money, and social management). Much of the discussion of trade in economic history has been about the institutional arrangements for long-distance trade, i.e., the policy environment in which trade is realized. The dominant answer to this question is that trade and market economies are formed where the hand of the state is least involved. These studies have, in turn, contributed to economic theory and analyzed the role of the state. Although recent research has noted the role of the state in facilitating free trade, the state-market dichotomy continues to dominate the study of economic history. In this context, the relationship between the state and the merchant is central to the discussion.

This European economic history thinking has also shaped the study of modern Chinese economic history. Business networks and merchant groups have become a topic of great interest in the study of modern economic history.[3] The formation of merchant groups, the relationship between business organizations and the state, the social networks formed

[2] Erikson, Emily, *Between Monopoly and Free Trade: The English East India Company* (NH: Princeton University Press, 2014).

Cox, Howard, The Global Cigarette: Origins and Evolution of British American Tobacco, 1880–1945 (New York: Oxford University Press, 2000).

[3] Mann, Susan, *Local Merchants and the Chinese Bureaucracy, 1750–1950* (Stanford: Stanford University Press, 1987).

O'Brien, Patrick K., "Afterword: Reflections on Fiscal Foundations and Contexts for the Formation of Economically Effective Eurasian States from the Rise of Venice to the Opium War". In Bartolomé Yun-Casalilla and Patrick K. O'Brien with Francisco Comín Comín, eds., *The Rise of Fiscal States: A Global History, 1500–1914* (Cambridge and New York Cambridge University Press, 2012): 442–441; Metzger, Thomas. "The Organizational Capabilities of the Ch'ing State in the Field of Commerce: The Liang-huai Salt Monopoly, 1740–1840". In W.E. Willmott, ed., *Economic Organization in Chinese Society. 1972*; rpt. (Taipei: SMC Publishing Inc, 1994), 21–24.

by merchants through business activities, the flow of important commodities, and other major topics have also received increasing attention from researchers.[4] Existing studies of business networks and merchant groups reveal the socio-economic landscape of China since the late imperial period, especially the place and role of trade and economic organizations in the construction of modern society.[5]

We further argue that the merchant community's strategic response to the state's policy reforms and their negotiation of this transition is a testament to their agency and influence on the state-market relationship. On one hand, focusing on the merchants' initiatives of network building, this edited book contributes to this research concern and shows how the merchant community reshaped and mobilized new networks by reconfiguring and exploiting existing local government-business relations. On the other hand, based on Michael Mann's theoretical concern of the despotic and infrastructural power of state, this edited book empirically indicates that business network (social) capital, as an informal institution, and the formal regulatory institutions of the state are mutually constructive and that business associations and merchants can reshape social capital in the midst of institutional change and in the tension of the centralized state, to achieve more significant economic and political interests.

In addition, this book contributes a more dynamic study of the relationship between the state and the merchant (and merchants' agency). This study emphasizes not only the significance of Guizhou in the study

[4] Ho, Ping-ti. "The Salt Merchants of Yang-Chou: A Study of Commercial Capitalism in Eighteenth-century China," *Harvard Journal of Asiatic Studies* 17, no. 1/2 (June 1954): 130–168; Kwan, M. B., *The Salt Merchants of Tianjin: State-Making and Civil Society in Late Imperial China* (Honolulu: University of Hawaii Press, 2001); Adshead, Samuel A.M., *The Modernization of the Chinese Salt Administration, 1900–1920* (Cambridge: Harvard University Press, 1970); Benedict, Carol. *Golden-Silk smoke: A History of Tobacco in China, 1550–2010* (LA: University of California Press, 2011); Brook, Timothy., "Smoking in Imperial China," in Sander L. Gilmand and Zhou Xun, eds. *Smoke: A Global History of Smoking* (London: Reaktion Books, 2004), 84–91; Cochran, Sherman, *Big Business in China: Sino-foreign Rivalry in the Cigarette Industry, 1890–1930*, vol. 33 (Harvard University Press, 1980).

[5] Zelin, Madeleine. "Managing Multiple Ownership at the Zigong Salt Yard". In Madeleine Zelin, Jonathan K. Ocko, and Robert Gardella, eds., *Contract and Property in Early Modern China* (Stanford: Stanford University Press, 2004), 230–268; Zelin, Madeleine. *The Merchants of Zigong: Industrial Entrepreneurship in Early Modern China* (New York: Columbia University Press, 2005); Bian, Morris L. *The Making of the State Enterprise System in Modern China: The Dynamics of Institutional Change* (Harvard University Press, 2005).

of Chinese socio-economic history but also a perspective that consistently brings local-central tensions to bear on cross-regional business networks and highlights the role of local authorities and merchants. Their relationship is antagonistic when the state acts as a tax collector. When the state tries to free itself from burdensome fiscal responsibilities, its relationship with merchants becomes delicate. It should be noted here that the state is an assemblage of multiple layers of power and function. The interests of central and local governments do not often coincide. In particular, local bureaucrats, as agents of local authority, always have their own interpretations of central policies and practices that align with local interests. As local merchants responded to reforms in industrial and tax policies, local authorities unleashed the interpretive space of policies to local business associations. Local governments constructed their infrastructural power while negotiating with those merchants in Guizhou. More importantly, this research indicates the significance of locality in understanding specific political-economic transformations and turmoil and in the creation of new state-market relations in the modern economic history of China.

Glossary

四川盐茶道 Sichuan Salt and Tea Committee
厘金 Likin: a kind of local business tax in late Qing dynasty
法币 fiat currency
坐商 tradesman
游商 itinerant merchant
盐号 salt firm
盐业公司 salt company
盐场 salterns
盐引 salt certificates
布政司 provincial administration commissioner
盐务总局 General Salt Administration Bureau
贵州盐务管理局 Guizhou Salt Administration Bureau
官督商销 official supervision and merchant sale
捆商制度 the system of bundling merchants together
代运 transport tenders
代销/承销 distribution tenders
分级运销 graded transportation and distribution
银元 silver dollar
贵州合作事业管理处 Guizhou Provincial Cooperative Business Management Office
合作事业管理局 Cooperative Business Administration Bureau
云贵区货物税局 Yunnan-Guizhou Commodity Tax Bureau
合作社联社 Cooperatives Union

B. Jiang et al., *State, Market and Salt-Tobacco Road in Modern China (1935–1949)*, https://doi.org/10.1007/978-981-97-7654-2

消费运输信贷合作联社 Consumer Transportation Credit Cooperative Union
综合类乡镇合作社 General Township and Village Cooperative
合作业务代营局 Cooperative Business Agency
贵州农业改进所 Guizhou Agricultural Improvement Institute
贵州企业公司 Guizhou Enterprise Company
烟草洽购委员会 Tobacco Purchasing Committee
统购统销 State monopoly for purchase and sale
贵州省档案馆 Guizhou Provincial Archives (GPA)
贵阳市档案馆 Guiyang Municipal Archives (GMA)
贵定县档案馆 Guiding County Municipal Archives (GCMA)
龙里县档案馆 Longli County Municipal Archives (LCMA)
三穗县档案馆 Sansui County Municipal Archives (SCMA)
贵州财政厅 Guizhou Provincial Department of Finance
贵州建设厅 Guizhou Provincial Department of Construction
贵州民政厅 Guizhou Provincial Departmeng of Civil Affairs
合作事业管理局 The Cooperative Business Administration Bureau
合作社物品供销社 Cooperative for Commodity Supply and Marketing Agency
烟草洽购委员会 The Tobacco Purchasing Committee
烟类专卖局贵定办事处 The Guiding Office of the Tobacco Monopoly Bureau
美烟种植合作社 American Tobacco Growers Cooperatives

Bibliography

Archives

Guizhou Provincial Archives

M8, Guizhou Provincial Department of Civil Affairs, the Republic of China: M8-1-4009.

M39, Guizhou Provincial Department of Finance, the Republic of China: M39-1-65.

M41, Guizhou Provincial Salt Administration Bureau: M41-1-8, M41-1-99, M41-1-3041, M41-1-3042, M41-1-3492, M41-1-4328, M41-1-4757.

M43, Yunnan-Guizhou District Goods Tax Bureau: M43-1-10.

M58, Guizhou Postal Bureau: M58-1-4445.

M60, Guizhou Provincial Department of Construction: M60-1-7333, M60-1-7350, M60-1-8016, M60-1-8096, M60-1-9254, M60-1-9257.

M66, Southwest Veterinary Disease Control Office: M66-1-65.

M71, Guizhou Provincial Cooperative Business Management Office: M71-1-75, M71-1-79, M71-1-135.

MG12, *Guizhou Nongcun shenghuo teji* 贵州农村生活特辑 [Guizhou Rural Life Special Issue], 1944.

Guiyang Municipal Archives

43, the Chamber of Commerce: 43-1-319, 43-1-400, 43-1-869, 43-1-926.

B. Jiang et al., *State, Market and Salt-Tobacco Road in Modern China (1935–1949)*, https://doi.org/10.1007/978-981-97-7654-2

Guiding County Archives

0-7, Guiding County Tobacco Monopoly Office: 0-7-1, 0-7-3, 0-7-9, 0-7-12, 0-7-13, 0-7-13, 0-7-36, 0-7-58,

0-10, Guiding Branch of the Hunan-Guangxi-Guizhou District Direct Taxation Bureau of the Ministry of Finance: 0-10-42, 0-10-47, 0-10-66,

0-11, Guiding Branch of the Yunnan-Guizhou District Goods Taxation Bureau: 0-11-26.

0-12, Guiding County Chamber of Commerce: 0-12-8, 0-12-12, 0-12-13,

0-14, Guiding Branch of the Bank of Guizhou: 0-14-4, 0-14-9, 0-14-38, 0-14-46

0-17, Guiding County Branch of the Yunnan-Guizhou District Direct Taxation Bureau: 0-17-138.

Longli County Archives

0-2, Yunlong Township Office: 0-2-87.

0-5, Longli Chamber of Commerce: 0-5-24.

Pengshui County Archives

J-1-136-11, *Wujiang shangxia wuchan yunsong* 乌江上下物产运送 [Cargo Transportation, Uptream and Downtream of Wujiang River].

Sansui County Archives

M-1, County Government:M-1-5843.

Compilation or Selection of Literary and History Materials

The *Selection of Literature and History Materials* is a kind of reference work for modern and contemporary history of China, normally edited by a research committee conducted by the Chinese People's Political Consultative Conference (the CPPCC).

Bijie wenshi ziliao xuanji 毕节文史资料选辑 [Selected Bijie Literature and History Materials]

Dafang wenshi ziliao xuanji 大方文史资料选辑 [Selection of Dafang Literature and History Materials]

Nanming wenshi ziliao xuanji 南明文史资料选辑 [Selected Materials of Nanming District Literature and History]

Guiding wenshi ziliao xuanji 贵定文史资料选辑 [Selected Collection of Guiding Literature and History Materials]

Guiyang wenshi ziliao xuancui 贵阳文史资料选粹 [Selected Materials of Guiyang Literature and History]
Guizhou wenshi ziliao xuanji 贵州文史资料选辑 [Selected Materials of Guizhou Literature and History]

Journals

Lixing yuekan 励行月刊 [Lixing Monthly]
Guizhou qiye jikan 贵州企业季刊 [Guizhou Enterprise Quarterly]
Jingji daobao 经济导报 [Economic Herald]
Yanwu gongbao 盐务公报 [Salt Bulletin]
Yanwu yuebao 盐务月报 [Salt Monthly]
Faling zhoukan 法令周刊 [Law Weekly]
Shangbiao gongbao 商标公报 [Trademark Gazette]

Veritable Records of the Ming Dynasty

Yingzong shilu zhi jintai fulu 英宗实录之景泰附录 [The Records of Jingtai Emperor in the Appendix of the Veritable Records of Yingzong Emperor]
Xianzong Shilu 宪宗实录 [Veritable Records of Xianzong Emperor]
Xiaozong Shilu 孝宗实录 [Veritable Records of Xiaozong Emperor]

Other Works Cited

Adshead, Samuel A.M. *The Modernization of the Chinese Salt Administration, 1900–1920*. Cambridge: Harvard University Press, 1970.

Benedict, Carol. *Golden-Silk smoke: A History of Tobacco in China, 1550–2010*. LA: University of California Press, 2011.

Bian, Morris L. "Xifang xuejie zuijin sishinian dui Zhongguo qiyeshi yanjiu de pingshu" 西方学界最近四十年对中国企业史研究的评述 [A Critical Examination of Western Studies of Chinese Business and Economic History]. *Economic and Social History Review*, 4(2018) :104-124.

———. "Redefining the Chinese Revolution: The Transformation and Evolution of Guizhou's Regional State Enterprises, 1937–1957." *Modern China* 41, no. 3 (2015): 313–350.

———. *The Making of the State Enterprise System in Modern China: the Dynamics of Institutional Change*. Harvard University Press, 2005.

Brook, Timothy. "Smoking in Imperial China." In *Smoke: A Global History of Smoking*, edited by Sander L. Gilmand and Zhou Xun, 84–91. London: Reaktion Books, 2004.

Caizhengbu faling zhangze huibian 财政部法令章则汇编 [Compilation of Ministry of Finance Acts and Regulations], ca. 1940s.

Cao, Shuji 曹树基. *Zhongguo yimin shi* 中国移民史 [The History of Immigration]. Fuzhou:Fujian Education Press, 1997.

Chang, Kia-Ngau, *The Inflation Spiral: the Experience in China 1939–1950*. Cambridge: The MIT Press, 1958.

Chen, Fende 陈棻德. "Cong xiaoshanfan dao dashangjia——dui Liuxiyi facai zhi mi de pojie" 从小商贩到大商家——对刘熙乙发财之"谜"的破解 [From Small Peddler to Big Merchant——the Decipherment to the "Mystery" of Liu Xiyi's Fortune]. In *Guiyang wenshi congkan* 贵州文史丛刊 (Guizhou Literature and History Series), 2005(4): 22–24.

Chen, Hongyou 陈洪友. *Minguo shiqi Henan shougongjuanyan yanjiu (1912-1949)* 民国时期河南手工卷烟研究 (1912-1949) [Study on Hand-rolled Cigarettes in Henan During the Period of Republic of China (1912-1949)]. PhD dissertation, Nanjing University, 2012.

Chinese People's Political Consultative Conference Southwest Cultural and Historical Data Collaboration Conference ed. *Kangzhanshiqi neiqian xinan de gongshang qiye* 抗战时期内迁西南的工商企业 [Industrial and Commercial Enterprises Moving to the Southwest During the Anti-Japanese War]. Kunming: Yunnan People's Press, 1989.

Cochran, Sherman. Encountering Chinese Networks: Western, Japanese, and Chinese Corporations in China, 1880–1937. Berkeley: University of California Press, 2000.

———. *Big business in China: Sino-foreign Rivalry in the Cigarette Industry, 1890-1930*. Cambridge, Mass: Harvard University Press, 1980.

Cox, Howard. The Global Cigarette: Origins and Evolution of British American Tobacco, 1880–1945. New York: Oxford University Press, 2000.

De Loecker, Jan, Jan Eeckhout and Gabriel Unger. "The Rise of Market Power and the Macroeconomic Implications." *The Quarterly Journal of Economics* 135, no.2(2020): 561–644.

Deng, Qingtang 邓庆棠. "Yanhang jie yu Guizhou yanwu" 盐行街与贵州盐务 [Yanhang(Salt Firm) Street and the Salt Administration in Guizhou]. In *Guizhou gongshang shiliao huibian* 贵州工商史料汇编 [Compilation of Historial Materials of Industry and Commerce in Guizhou], edited by Guizhou Committee of China National Democratic Construction Association, no.3(1985): 47–61.

Deng, Xiaoke 邓效可, "Dengxiaoke lici Sichuan yanzhengbu zhi shu" 邓效可力辞四川盐政部职书 [Deng Xiaoke's Resignation Statement Toward Sichuan Ministry of Salt Affairs]. In Jing Taobai 景本白, *Yanzheng gemingshi* 盐政革命史 [History of the Salt Revolution], Appendix, 11–23. Beijing: Salt Administration Magazine, 1929.

Ding, Baozhen 丁宝桢, *Ding wenchenggong zougao* 丁文诚公奏 稿 [Memorial Drafts of Ding Baozhen]. Block printed, 1907.

Ding, Baozhen et al eds. *Sichuan yanfa zhi zhengli jiaozhu* 四川盐法志整理校注 [Collation and Annotation of the Chronicles of Salt Administration in Sichuan]. Reedited and annotated by Zen Fanying 曾凡英, Li Shumin 李树民 and Sun Xiangwei 孙祥伟. Chongqing: Southwest Jiaotong University Press, 2019.

Ding, Changqing 丁长清 et al. eds. *Minguo yanwu shigao* 民国盐务史稿 [Draft of History of Salt Affairs in the Republic of China]. Beijing: People's Press, 1990.

Ding, Wenjian 丁文江. *Manyou sanji* 漫游散记 [Selected Travelogues]. Kunming: Yunnan People's Press, 2008.

Duan Zhao'ao 段兆鳌. *Guiding xian zhi gao* 贵定县志稿 [Draft of Gazetteer of Guiding County]. Reprint, Guiyang: Guizhou Provincial Library, 1964, and Guiyang: Guizhou People's Press, 2018.

E'ertai(Ortai) 鄂尔泰 et al. eds. Yongzheng zhupi yuzhi 雍正朱批谕旨 [Collection of Yongzheng Emperor's Vermillion Edicts]. Beijing: Beijing Library, 2008.

Erikson, Emily. *Between Monopoly and Free Trade: The English East India Company*. NH: Princeton University Press, 2014.

Fang, Xianting 方显廷. *Fangxianting huiyilu* 方显廷回忆录 [Memoir of Fang Xianting]. Beijing: the Commercial Press, 2006.

Financial Investigation Division of the Ministry of Finance ed. *Ge shengqu linian caizheng zhuangkuang huilan* 各省区历年财政状况会览 [Summary of Financial Status of Provinces and Regions Over the Years]. Financial Investigation Division of the Ministry of Finance, 1925.

Giddens, Anthony. "State, Society and Modern History." In *Contemporary Sociological Theory*. 3rd edition, 277–285. Chichester: Wiley-Blackwell, 2012.

Gerschenkron, Alexander. "Economic Backwardness in Historical Perspective." In *The Globalization and Development Reader: Perspectives on Development and Global Change (Second Edition)*, edited by J. Timmons Roberts, Amy Bellone Hite and Nitsan Chorev, 62–78. Chichester, West Sussex, UK: Wiley Blackwell, 2014.

Guizhou caijing ziliao huibian 贵州财经资料汇编 [Guizhou Financial Data Compilation]. Compiled by Guizhou Provincial Finance and Economics Commission. Internal Information, 1950.

Guizhousheng fuquan yancaokexue yanjiusuo 贵州省福泉烟草科学研究所. *Guizhou kaoyan zaipei* 贵州烤烟栽培 [Guizhou Flue-cured Tobacco Cultivation]. Guiyang: Guizhou People's Press, 1979.

Guizhou Provincial Chronicles Compilation Committee. *Guizhousheng gongxiao hezuoshe zhi* 贵州省供销合作志 [Chronicle of Guizhou Province Supply and Marketing Cooperation]. Guiyang: Guizhou People's Press, 2003.

———. *Guizhou sheng zhi yancao zhi* 贵州省志·烟草志 [Chronicles of Guizhou Province: Tobacco]. Guiyang: Guizhou People's Press, 2002.

Guizhou Provincial Archives ed. *Guizhousheng qiye gongsi* 贵州省企业公司 [Guizhou Provincial Enterprise Company]. Guiyang: Guizhou People's Press, 2003.

———. *Guizhou shehuizuzhi gailan: 1911–1949* 贵州社会组织概览: 1911—1949 [An Overview of Social Organizations in Guizhou: 1911—1949]. Guiyang: Guizhou People's Press, 1996.

Guizhousheng shizhiban 贵州省史志办 ed. *Guizhou dili zhi* 贵州地理志 [Gazetteer of Guizhou Geography]. Guiyang: Guizhou People's Press, 1994.

Guo, Zijian, 郭子健. "Jindai zhongguo maotaijiu pinpai de yanjin" 近代中国"茅台酒"品牌的演进 [Evolution of the "Maotai" Liqour Brand in Modern China], *Modern Chinese History Studies*, 1(2022): 82–94.

Guo, Zizhang 郭子章. *Qiancao* 黔草 [Works in Guizhou], ca.1601.

Gu, Yanwu 顾炎武, *Tianxia junguo libing shu* 天下郡国利病书 [On Benefit and Faults of the Empire's Local Administration]. Reprint, Shanghai: Shanghai Ancient Books Press, 2012.

Hayami, Yujiro, and Godo Yoshihisa. *Development Economics: From the Poverty to the Wealth of Nations (Third Edition)*. NY: Oxford University Press, 2005.

Hayami, Yujiro, and V.M. Ruttan. "Factor Prices and Technical Change in Agricultural Development: The United States and Japan, 1880-1960." *Journal of Political Economy* 78, no.5(1970): 1115–1141.

Hintze, Otto., "The State in Historical Perspective." In *State and Society: A Reader in Comparative Political Sociology*, edited by Reinhard Benix et al., 154–169. Boston: Little, Brown & Co., 1968.

Hintze, Otto and Felix Gilbert. *The Historical Essays of Otto Hintze*. NY: Oxford University Press, 1975.

Ho, Ping-ti. "The Salt Merchants of Yang-Chou: A Study of Commercial Capitalism in Eighteenth-Century China." Harvard Journal of Asiatic Studies, vol. 17, no. 1/2 (June 1954): 130–168.

Hosie, Alexander. *Three Years in Western China:A Narrative of Three Journeys in Szechwan, Kweichow and Yunnan*. Reprint, Bangkok: White Lotus, 2001.

Huangfu, Qiushi 皇甫秋实. *Weiji zhong de xuanze: zhanqian shinian de Zhongguo juanyan shichang* 危机中的选择:战前十年的中国卷烟市场 [Choice in the Crisis: Cigarette Market in Pre-war China]. Shanghai: Orient Press Company, 2015.

Huang, Guoxin 黄国信. *Guojia yu shichang: Mingqing shiyan maoyi yanjiu* 国家与市场: 明清食盐贸易研究 (State and Market: Salt Trade of Ming-Qing Period). Beijing: Zhonghua Book Company, 2019.

———. *Qu yu jie: Qingdai Xiang Yue Gan jielin diqu shiyan zhuanmai yanjiu* 区与界: 清代湘粤赣界邻地区食盐专卖研究 [Regions and Boundaries: An Analysis of Qing Salt Monopoly at the Provincial Border of Hunan, Guangdong and Jiangxi]. Beijing: SDX Joint Publishing Company, 2006.

Hunan Provincial Chronicles Compilation Committee ed. *Hunansheng zhi dijiujuan gongye kuangchan zhi yancaoye* 湖南省志第九卷·工业矿产志·烟草业 [Hunan Provincial Chronicles Volume 9, Industrial Minerals, Tobacco Industry]. Changsha: Hunan People's Press, 1997.

Jian, Zhen 鉴真, "Guizhou jindai jiechu de qiyejia Hua Zhihong" 贵州近代杰出的企业家华之鸿 [Hua Zhihong, An Outstanding Modern Entrepreneur in Guizhou]. *Guizhou dang'an* 贵州档案 [Guizhou Archives], Issue 2(1996): 34–35.

Kuroda, Akinobu 黑田明伸. *Huobi zhidu de shijieshi* 货币制度的世界史 [The History of the Monetary System]. Translated by He Ping 何平, Beijing: China Renmin University Press, 2007.

Kwan, Man Bun. "Salt Wars". In *Living and Working in Wartime China*, edited by Brett Sheehan and Wen-hsin Yeh, 195–235. Honolulu: University of Hawaii Press, 2022.

———. *The Salt Merchants of Tianjin: State-making and Civil Society in Late Imperial China*. Honolulu: University of Hawai'i Press, 2001.

Lee, James Z. *The Political Economy of a Frontier: Southwest China*, 1250-1850. Cambridge: Harvard University Press, 2002.

Liao, Junfei 廖珺霏. "Wang Yuzhao kongan yu Qingmo chuanyan guanyun zhong de duo chong boyi" 王余照控案与清末川盐官运中的多重博弈 [Multiple Games in Wang Yuzhao's Accusation and the Official Transportation of Sichuan Salt in the Late Qing Dynasty]. *Salt Industry History Research*, Issue 1(2020): 50–61.

Li, Bozhong 李伯重. *Jiangnan de zaoqi gongyehua* 江南的早期工业化 [Early industrialization of Jiangnan Region]. Beijing: Social Sciences Academic Press, 2000.

Li, Han 李还 et al. *Miao Qiujie yu minguo yanwu* 缪秋杰与民国盐务 [Miao Qiujie and the Salt Affairs of the Republic of China]. Beijing: China Science and Technology Press, 1990.

Lin, Xin 林辛. *Guizhou jindai jiaotong shilve* [贵州近代交通史略] A Brief History of Modern Traffic in Guizhou]. Guiyang: Guizhou People's Press, 1985.

Lin, Meili 林美莉. *Xiyang shuizhi zai jindai Zhongguo de fazhan* 西洋税制在近代中国的发展 [The Development of Western Tax System in Modern China]. Shanghai: Shanghai Academy of Social Sciences Press, 2020.

Ling, Ti'an 凌惕安. *Xiantong junshi shi* 咸同军事史 [Military History of Guizhou in Xianfeng and Tongzhi Period], 1931.

Liu, Shifan 刘时范. *Qiandong shibian jiyao* 黔东事变纪要 [Record of Riots in Eastern Guizhou], 1943.

Liu, Yuyuan 刘裕远. "Liu Xiyi de fajia yu shuaibai" 刘熙乙的发家与衰败 [The Rise and Fall of Liu Xiyi]. In *Guizhou gongshang shiliao huibian* 贵州工商史料汇编 [Compilation of Historical Materials of Industry and Commerce in Guizhou], edited by Guizhou Committee of China National Democratic Construction Association, no.1(1985): 23–36.

Li, Xiaolong 李晓龙. "Jindai yanwu jiuchang zhengshui gaige yu guanshang boyi" 近代盐务就场征税制改革与官商博弈 [The Reform of Taxation at Production Place in Salt Industry and The Game Between Officials and Businessmen in Modern China]. *Journal of Historical Science*, 12(2020): 41–52.

Lu, Liangzheng 卢征良 and Zhu Yingui 朱荫贵. "Kangzhan shiqi shengying qiye gongsi xingzhi yanjiu" 抗战时期省营企业性质研究 [The Character of the Provincial Enterprises in Modern History], Social Science, 9(2020): 150–163.

Mann, Michael. *The Sources of Social Power, Volume 1: A History of Power from the Beginning to AD 1760*. Cambridge: Cambridge University Press, 2012.

———. *The Sources of Social Power: Volume 2, The Rise of Classes and Nation-states, 1760–1914. Vol. 2*. Cambridge: Cambridge University Press, 2012.

Mann, Susan. *Local Merchants and the Chinese Bureaucracy, 1750–1950*. Stanford: Stanford University Press, 1987.

Ma, Qi 马琦. *Ghuojia ziyuan: qingdai diantong he qianqian kaifa yanjiu* 国家资源:清代滇铜和黔铅开发研究 [National Resources: Research on the Development of Lead Ore in Guizhou and Yunnan Copper Mine in Qing Dynasty]. Beijing: People's Press, 2013.

Ma, Yinchu 马寅初. *Caizhengxue yu zhongguo caizheng—lilun yu xianshi* 财政学与中国财政—理论与现实 [Public Finance and Chinese Finance: Theory and Reality]. Reprint, Beijing: The Commercial Press, 2006.

Ma, Zhenkun 马震崑 et al eds. *Minguo sinanxian zhi gao* 民国思南县志稿 [Draft of the Gazetteer of Sinan County, the Republic of China]. Reprint, Guiyang: Guizhou People's Press, 2019.

Mas-Colell, Andreu, Michael D. Whinston and Jerry R. Green. *Microeconomic Theory*. Oxford University Press, 1995.

Meng, Haoqi 孟皓琪 ed. *Minguo shiqi Guizhou baoxian dang'an shiliao huibian* 民国时期贵州保险档案史料汇编 [A Compilation of Historical Materials of Insurance Archives in Guizhou During the Republic of China]. Guiyang: Guizhou People's Press, 2021.

Metzger, Thomas. "The Organizational Capabilities of the Ch'ing State in the Field of Commerce: The Liang-huai Salt Monopoly, 1740–1840". In *Economic Organization in Chinese Society*, edited by W.E. Willmott, 21–24. Reprint, Taipei: SMC Publishing Inc, 1994.

Mo Youzhi 莫友枝 and Zheng zhen 郑珍 eds. Daoguang Zunyifu zhi 道光遵义府志 [Gazetteer of Zunyi Prefecture Edited During Daoguang Reign]. Reprint, Chengdu: Bashu Press, 2013.

Ren, Kecheng 任可澄 et al eds. *Minguo Guizhou tongzhi* 民国贵州通志 [A General History of Guizhou, Republic of China]. Guiyang: Wentong Shuju, 1948.

Ministry of Transportation of National Government in Beijing ed. *Xiangdian xian Guizhou duan yanxian gexian shehijingji diaocha* 湘滇线贵州段沿线各县社会经济调查 [The Socio-economic Survey of the Counties Along Guizhou section of Xiang-Dian Line], 1922.

Ni Yuping 倪玉平, *Boyi yu junheng:qingdai lianghuai yanzheng gaige* 博弈与均衡:清代两淮盐政改革 [Game and Equilibrium: Reform of the Lianghuai Salt Administration in the Qing Dynasty]. Fuzhou: Fujian People's Press, 2011.

Kirby, William C. "Continuity and Change in Modern China: Economic Planning on the Mainland and on Taiwan, 1943-58." *The Australian journal of Chinese affairs*, 24 (1990): 121–141.

O'Brien, Patrick K. "Afterword: Reflections on Fiscal Foundations and Contexts for the Formation of Economically Effective Eurasian States from the Rise of Venice to the Opium War". In *The Rise of Fiscal States: A Global History, 1500–1914*. Bartolomé Yun-Casalilla, edited by Patrick K. O'Brien and Francisco Comín Comín, 442–451. Cambridge and New York: Cambridge University Press, 2012.

Peng, Kaixiang 彭凯翔, *Qingdai yilai de liangjia* 清代以来的粮价 [The Price of Grain Since the Qing Dynasty]. Shanghai: Shanghai People's Press, 2006.

Puk, Wing Kin. *The Rise and Fall of a Public Debt Market in 16th-century China: The Story of the Ming Salt Certificate*. Boston: Brill, 2016.

Qin, Heping 秦和平. "Yuoguan sanshi niandai zhonghouqi Guizhou jinyan yundong de youlai ji qi renshi" 有关30年代中后期贵州禁烟运动的由来及其认识 [The Origin and Understanding of the Anti-opium Movement in Guizhou in the Middle and Late 1930s]. *Guiyang wenshi congkan* 贵州文史丛刊 [Guizhou Literature and History Series], 3(2001): 51–61.

Reference Room of the General Salt Administration Bureau of Ministry of Finance ed. *Zhongguo yanzheng shilu* 中国盐政实录 [Records of China's Salt Administration], 1948.

Sargent, Thomas J. and François R. Velde. *The Big Problems of Small Change*. Princeton: Princeton University Press, 2014.

Shanghai Institute of Economics, Chinese Academy of Sciences, and Institute of Economics, Shanghai Academy of Social Sciences eds. *Nanyang xiongdi yancao gongsi shiliao* 南洋兄弟烟草公司史料 [Historical Materials of Nanyang Brothers Tobacco Company]. Shanghai: Shanghai People's Press, 1960.

Skinner, William G. "Marketing and Social Structure in Rural China, Part I." The Journal of Asian studies 24, no. 1 (1964): 3–43.

Skocpol, Theda. *Social Revolutions in the Modern World*. Cambridge: Cambridge University Press, 1994.

———. *States and social revolutions: A Comparative Analysis of France, Russia and China*. Cambridge: Cambridge University Press, 1979.

Song, Shu 宋树 et al eds. *Xuyongxian zhi* 叙永县志 [Gazetteer of Xuyong County]. Reprint, Taipei: Taiwan Student Book Company, 1962.

State Taxation Administration ed. *Zhonghuaminguo gongshang shuishou shi:yanshuijuan* 中华民国工商税收史:盐税卷 [History of Industrial and Commercial Taxation in the Republic of China: Salt Tax]. Beijing: China Financial and Economic Press, 1999.

Tang, Benhong 唐本洪. *Daoguang Lipingfu zhi* 道光黎平府志 [Gazetteer of Liping Prefecture edited during Daoguang Reign]. Reprint, Guiyang: Guizhou People's Press, 2010.

Tang, Mingsheng 唐明胜, *Na yan gui cang: 1800-1960 nianjian zhejiang de yanzheng bianqian yu yanchang shehui* 纳盐归仓: 1800-1960 年间浙江的盐政变迁与盐场社会 [Collecting Salt into Granary: the Changes of Salt Administration and Saltern Society in Zhejiang, 1800–1960]. PhD dissertation, Shanghai: East China Normal University, 2022.

Tang, Yuanju 唐远驹 ed. *Guizhou shailiangyan* 贵州晒晾烟 [Guizhou Sun-dried Tobacco]. Guiyang: Guizhou Science and Technology Press, 2017.

Tian, Wen 田雯. *Qian Shu* 黔书 [the Book of Qian], 1808.

Tian, Jinfeng 田锦凤, "Guizhou jiefangqian de hezuo shiye" 贵州解放前的合作事业 [Cooperative Undertakings before the Liberation of Guizhou]. In Guizhou jinrong huobishi luncong 贵州金融货币史论丛 [Guizhou Finance and Currency History Collection], edited by Guizhou Provincial Institute of Finance, 172-185. Guiyang: People's Bank of China Guizhou Branch, 1986.

Tilly, Charles. "*History and Sociological Imagining*." The Tocqueville Review 15.1 (1994): 57–72.

Torii, Ryuzo 鸟居龙藏. *Xinan zhongguo jixing* 西南中国纪行 [Travel Diary of Southwest China]. Translated by Yang Zhiqiang 杨志强. Beijing: the Commercial Press, 2020.

Wang, Fangjun 王方君. *Qingdai Guizhou yanshang yanjiu* 清代贵州盐商研究 [Research on Guizhou Salt Merchants in Qing Dynasty]. Master Thesis, Guizhou University, 2022.

Wang, Hengfu 王恒富 et al. eds. *Guizhou zhengxie wenshi ziliao cungao xuanbian* 贵州政协文史资料存稿选编 [Selected Manuscripts of Guizhou CPPCC Literary and Historical Materials]. Guiyang: Guizhou People's Press, 2006.

Wang, Wenxue 汪文学. *Zhongguo wujiang liuyu minguo dang'an congkan yanhejuan* 中国乌江流域民国档案丛刊沿河卷 [The Yanhe County Volumes of the Archives Series of the Republic of China in the Wujiang River Basin]. Guiyang: Guizhou People's Press, 2019.

Wang, Xiaojing 王晓静. "Wanqing chuanyan guanyun shangxiao zhidu de xingsu" 晚清川盐官运商销制度的形塑 [Shaping Sichuan's Salt Marketing System in Late Qing]. *Historical Review*, 3(2021): 107–116.

Wang, Luman 王璐曼. *Money and Trade, Hinterland and Coast, Empire and Nation-state: An Unusual History of Shanxi Piaohao, 1820-1930*. PhD dissertation, University of Southern California, 2014.

Wen, Chunlai 温春来, *Cong yiyu dao jiujiang: Song zhi Qing Guizhou xibeibu diqu de kaifa yu rentong* 从"异域"到"旧疆": 宋至清贵州西北部地区的制度、开发与认同 [From the Foreign Land to the Old Territory: Development and Identity in Northwestern Guizhou From Song to Qing Dynasty]. Beijing: Social Sciences Academic Press, 2019.

Wu, Dingchang 吴鼎昌. *Huaxi suibi chubian* 花溪随笔(初编) [Huaxi Essays· Volume 1). Guiyang: Guizhou Provincial Printing Office, 1943).

———. *Huaxisuibi xubian* 花溪随笔(续编) [Huaxi Essays· Volume 2]. Guiyang: Guizhou Provincial Printing Office), 1943.

———. *Qianzheng wunian* 黔政五年 [Five Years of Guizhou Administration), Overview of Cooperation]. Guiyang: Guizhou Enterprise Company Printing Office, 1943.

Wu, duo 吴铎. "Chuanyan guanyun zhishimo" 川盐官运之始末 [The Beginning and the End of Official Salt Transportation in Sichuan], *Zhongguo jindai jingjishi yanjiu jikan* 中国近代经济史研究集刊 [Journal of Modern Chinese Economic History Research], Volume 3, Issue 2(1935): 143–261.

Wu, Guolin 吴国霖 et al. *Guizhou miaoyi yanjiu* 贵州苗夷研究 [Study on Hmong in Guizhou], Guiyang: Wentong Shuju,1941.

Wu, Xiaogao 伍效高. "Wo fanyun "qiantu" waixiao de jingguo" 我贩运"黔土"外销的经过 [My Experience of Exporting Guizhou Opium]. In *Guizhou Gongshangye Shiliao Huibian* 贵州工商史料汇编 [Compilation of Historial Materials of Industry and Commerce in Guizhou], edited by Guizhou Committee of China National Democratic Construction Association, no. 3(1985): 1–17.

Wu Xiaoxin 邬晓辛 and Lv Yantao 吕延涛. "Dingbaozhen yu Qingmo Guizhou yanzheng" 丁宝桢与清末贵州盐政 [Ding Baozhen and Guizhou Salt Administration in Late Qing]. *Salt Industry History Research*, 2(1989): 36–40.

Xia, Heming 夏鹤鸣 et al. eds. *Guizhou hangyunshi gujindai bufen* 贵州航运史·古近代部分 [Guizhou Ancient Modern Shipping History]. Guiyang: Guizhou People's Press, 1993.

Xue, Peixuan 薛培暄 ed. *Gaige yanfa wenti huilu* 改革盐法问题汇录 [Compilation of Questions on the Reform of Salt Law]. Nanjing: General Salt Administration Bureau, 1947.

Yang, Runan 杨汝南 and Hu Rengtong 胡礽同. "Guizhou nongzuowu zhi gaijin" 贵州省农作物之改进 [Improvement of Crops in Guizhou Province]. In *Guizhousheng nongye gaijinsuo* 贵州省农业改进所 [Guizhou Agricultural Improvement Institute], edited by Jiang Guosheng 蒋国生, 539–557. Guiyang: Guizhou People's Press, 2006.

Yang, Ting 杨亭, "Shiyan gongmaidian:Kangri zhanzheng shiqi guojia tongzhi de jicing shishi" 食盐公卖店:抗日战争时期国家统制的基层实施 [The Salt Monopoly Shops:the Practice of National Monopoly at the Grass-roots Level

During the War of Resistance]. In *Guizhou wenshi congkan* 贵州文史丛刊[Guizhou Literature and History Series], 1(2021): 62–68.

Yang, Xingqin 杨兴勤. Zhongguo zhanshi yanwu wenti 中国战时盐务问题 [China's Wartime Salt Issues]. Chongqing: National Press, 1943.

Yan, Xiu 严修. *Xunxiangguan shiqian riji* 蟫香馆使黔日记 [A diary of working in Guizhou]. Guiyang: Guizhou People's Press, 2019.

Institute of Economics, Shanghai Academy of Social Sciences ed. *Yingmei yan gongsi zaihua qiye ziliao huibian* 英美烟公司在华企业资料汇编 [Compilation of Materials on British American Tobacco's Enterprises in China]. Beijing: Zhonghua Book Company, 1983.

Yu, Heping 虞和平 ed. *Zhongguo kangri zhanzheng shiliao congkan jingji gongye* 中国抗日战争史料丛刊:经济·工业 [Chinese Anti-Japanese War Historical Materials Series: Economy and Industry]. Beijing: Elephant Press, 2016.

Yu, Jie 余杰. "Yan Anlan yu Minguo chuqi Sichuan diqu de yanwu gaige" 晏安澜与民国初期四川地区的盐务改革 [Yan Anlan and Sichuan's Reform of Salt Administration in Early Period of Republic of China]. *Salt Industry History Research*, Issue 3(2016): 64-69.

Zelin, Madeleine. *The Merchants of Zigong: Industrial Entrepreneurship in Early Modern China*. New York: Columbia University Press, 2005.

———. "Managing Multiple Ownership at the Zigong Salt Yard." In *Contract and Property in Early Modern China*, edited by Madeleine Zelin, Jonathan K. Ocko, and Robert Gardella, 230–268. Stanford: Stanford University Press, 2004.

Zhai, Yuqian 翟玉前. *Mingshi Guizhou tusi liezhuan kaozheng* 明史贵州土司列传考证 [Textual Research Biographies of Native Chieftains in the Official Dynamistic History of Ming Dynasty], Guiyang: Guizhou Guizhou People's Press, 2008.

Zhang, Honglin 张洪林. *Qingdai Sichuan yanfa yanjiu* 清代四川盐法研究 [Study on Sichuan Salt Administration in Qing Dynasty]. Beijing: China University of Political Science and Law Press, 2012.

Zhang, Tingyu 张廷玉 et al. eds. *Qingchao wenxian tongkao* 清朝文献通考 [Comprehensive Examination of Literature in Qing Dynasty]. Shanghai: the Commercial Press, 1936.

Zhang, Xiaomei 张肖梅, *Guizhou jingji* 贵州经济 [Guizhou Economy]. Chongqing: National Economic Research Institute, 1939.

Zhang, Yingqing 张应强. *Mucai de liudong: Qingdai Qingshuijiang xiayou diqu de shichang quanli yu shehui* 木材的流动: 清代清水江下游地区的市场、权力与社会 [the Flow of Timber: Market, Power and Society in the Lower Qingshui River Region in the Qing Dynasty]. Beijing: Social Sciences Academic Press, 2021.

Zhang, Zhongmin 张忠民. "Luelun kangzhan shiqi neidi shengqu qiye gongsi de zhidutezheng" 略论抗战时期内地省区企业公司的制度特征 [A Brief Discussion on the Institutional Characteristics of Enterprises and Corporations in Inland Provinces and Regions During the Anti-Japanese War]. *Shanghai Journal of Economics*, 9(2004): 72–78.

Zhang, Zhongkui 张中奎. *Gaitu guiliu yu miaojiang gaizao: Qingdai Xinjiang liuting de wanghua jincheng ji qi shehui wenhua bianqian* 改土归流与苗疆改造:清代"新疆六厅"的王化进程及其社会文化变迁 [Turning Native Rule into Regular Administration and the Conversion of Hmong Territories: the Construction of "Six Ting of New Frontiers" and the Socio-cultural Transformation]. Beijing: China Social Sciences Press, 2014.

Zhao, Hengqian 赵亨钤. *Qianchai riji* 铅差日记 [The Diary of a Lead Commissioner]. Guiyang: Guizhou People's Press, 2019.

Zhong, Liangxi 钟良曦 and Zhong Changyong 钟长永. *Chuanyan shilun* 川盐史论 [History of Sichuan Salt]. Chengdu: Sichuan People's Press, 1990.

Zhonghua minguo fagui jiyao 中华民国法规辑要 [Collection of the Laws and Regulations of the Republic of China]. Compiled by Zhongyang xunliantuan 中央训练团, 1941.

Zhou, Tianshou 周恭寿 ed. *Minguo xu zunyifu zhi* 民国续遵义府志 [the Continuation Gazetteer of Zunyi Prefecture, the Republic of China]. Reprint, Chengdu: Bashu Press, 2000.

Zhou, Zuoji 周作楫 et al. eds. *Sinanfu xu zhi* 思南府续志 [the Continuation Gazetteer of Sinan Prefecture], 1841 (the 21th year of Daoguang).

Index

B. Jiang et al., *State, Market and Salt-Tobacco Road in Modern China (1935–1949)*, https://doi.org/10.1007/978-981-97-7654-2

GPSR Compliance

The European Union's (EU) General Product Safety Regulation (GPSR) is a set of rules that requires consumer products to be safe and our obligations to ensure this.

If you have any concerns about our products, you can contact us on ProductSafety@springernature.com

In case Publisher is established outside the EU, the EU authorized representative is:

Springer Nature Customer Service Center GmbH
Europaplatz 3
69115 Heidelberg, Germany